THE DEVIL'S DOZEN

12 NOTORIOUS SERIAL KILLERS CAUGHT BY CUTTING-EDGE FORENSICS

KATHERINE RAMSLAND, PH.D.

D0106799

BERKLEY BOOKS, NEW YORK

THE BERKLEY PUBLISHING GROUP
Published by the Penguin Group
Penguin Group (USA)
375 Hudson Street, New York, New York 10014, USA

USA | Canada | UK | Ireland | Australia | New Zealand | India | South Africa | China

Penguin Books Ltd., Registered Offices: 80 Strand, London WC2R 0RL, England
For more information about the Penguin Group, visit penguin.com.

THE DEVIL'S DOZEN

A Berkley Book / published by arrangement with the author

Berkley Books are published by The Berkley Publishing Group.
BERKLEY® is a registered trademark of Penguin Group (USA).
The "B" design is a trademark of Penguin Group (USA).

For information, address: The Berkley Publishing Group,
a division of Penguin Group (USA),
375 Hudson Street, New York, New York 10014.

ISBN: 978-0-425-27077-6

PUBLISHING HISTORY
Berkley trade paperback edition / April 2009
Berkley premium edition / September 2013

PRINTED IN THE UNITED STATES OF AMERICA

10 9 8 7 6 5 4 3 2 1

Cover design by Edwin Tse.
Interior text design by Kristin del Rosario.

ALWAYS LEARNING   PEARSON *continued . . .*

The Unknown Darkness:
Profiling the Predators Among Us

Coauthored with Gregg O. McCrary

"This is a must-read for true crime fans. A beautifully written expert analysis of high-profile killers." —Ann Rule

"One of the most immensely readable and gripping accounts of serial murder I have ever read."
—Colin Wilson, author of *Serial Killers: A Study in the Psychology of Violence*

The Forensic Science of C.S.I.

"Fascinating . . . [A] must for anyone who wonders how the real crime solvers do it." —Michael Palmer

"With the mind of a true investigator, Ramsland demystifies the world of forensics with authentic and vivid detail."
—John Douglas

Piercing the Darkness:
Undercover with Vampires in America Today

"A riveting read, a model of engaged journalism."
—*Publishers Weekly*

Titles by Katherine Ramsland

THE FORENSIC PSYCHOLOGY OF CRIMINAL MINDS

THE DEVIL'S DOZEN

TRUE STORIES OF C.S.I.

BEATING THE DEVIL'S GAME

THE C.S.I EFFECT

THE HUMAN PREDATOR:
A HISTORICAL CHRONICLE OF SERIAL MURDER
AND FORENSIC INVESTIGATION

INSIDE THE MINDS OF MASS MURDERERS: WHY THEY KILL

A VOICE FOR THE DEAD:
A FORENSIC INVESTIGATOR'S PURSUIT OF TRUTH IN THE GRAVE
(with James E. Starrs)

THE SCIENCE OF COLD CASE FILES

THE UNKNOWN DARKNESS:
PROFILING THE PREDATORS AMONG US
(with Gregg O. McCrary)

THE SCIENCE OF VAMPIRES

THE CRIMINAL MIND:
A WRITER'S GUIDE TO FORENSIC PSYCHOLOGY

THE FORENSIC SCIENCE OF CSI

CEMETERY STORIES:
HAUNTED GRAVEYARDS, EMBALMING SECRETS,
AND THE LIFE OF A CORPSE AFTER DEATH

GHOST: INVESTIGATING THE OTHER SIDE

BLISS: WRITING TO FIND YOUR TRUE SELF

PIERCING THE DARKNESS:
UNDERCOVER WITH VAMPIRES IN AMERICA TODAY

DEAN KOONTZ: A WRITER'S BIOGRAPHY

PRISM OF THE NIGHT: A BIOGRAPHY OF ANNE RICE

THE WITCHES' COMPANION:
THE OFFICIAL GUIDE TO
ANNE RICE'S LIVES OF THE MAYFAIR WITCHES

THE VAMPIRE COMPANION:
THE OFFICIAL GUIDE TO
ANNE RICE'S THE VAMPIRE CHRONICLES

THE ANNE RICE READER

THE ART OF LEARNING: A SELF-HELP MANUAL FOR STUDENTS

ENGAGING THE IMMEDIATE:
APPLYING KIERKEGAARD'S INDIRECT COMMUNICATION
TO THE PRACTICE OF PSYCHOTHERAPY

Novels

THE BLOOD HUNTERS

THE HEAT SEEKERS

ACKNOWLEDGMENTS
AND DEDICATION

I was pleased to discover that my agent, John Silbersack, and editor, Ginjer Buchanan, spotted the value of this book right away. Having written fuller histories of both serial murder, *The Human Predator,* and forensic investigation, *Beating the Devil's Game,* I had noticed that some of the more inventive improvements to criminal investigation had resulted from cases of serial murder. However, in those books it was difficult to fully explore them. Thus I'm deeply grateful to John and Ginjer, who have supported me through many projects, for sharing my vision and encouraging me to write this.

Along the way, I received information, photos, or enthusiastic assistance from a number of other people. I must especially thank Michelle Mrazik and Debbie Malone from the DeSales University library, and Sharon Brown from the Macon Public Library, for digging out articles that were difficult to find. Dr. Lawrence Farwell provided his full report, and John Timpane went to Philadelphia's Free Library to get documents on the Holmes case. But then John Borowski and Waterfront Productions created excellent documentaries on both the Holmes and Fish cases, with terrific footage, and that, too, was a great help. Marilyn Bardsley, my former editor at the Crime Library, encouraged me for eight years to pursue research on serial killers, and Gregg McCrary, Robert Ressler, and John Douglas opened the doors to FBI profiling. Sir Alec Jeffreys, Mike Wild, D.A. William Heisler, Detective Joe Pochron, Chief Roger Mac-Lean, and Officer Brian Lewis provided information, interviews, and/or photos to make this a better book. I'm grateful to them all.

I also wish to thank Dr. Karen Walton, the provost at DeSales University, and to acknowledge the generosity of DeSales for providing release time to work on this project.

Mostly, I'm grateful for the persistent, dedicated investigators who go the extra mile to solve cases and bring killers to justice. To them, I dedicate this book. I appreciate their work and am pleased to have the opportunity to showcase it and provide their example to future investigators.

CONTENTS

CONTENTS

INTRODUCTION

They know who he is and they're closing in. After investigating seven gruesome murders that exploited the victims' weaknesses, intrepid investigators have chased down the killer, ready to corner him . . . or shoot him. Their lives are on the line, because he's been extremely clever and they can't be certain if he'll outsmart them, but their weapons are ready and they pray for the advantage. At least, that's how it goes in fiction.

Novels and films often play up the supposed excitement of chasing a serial killer, and while such cases are actually rare, in the history of law enforcement some killers have posed such a challenge that they've inspired extraordinary efforts or forensic innovations. Thus we have factual tales that do feature suspenseful sparring between genuine villains and heroes. From the detection of arsenic to the analysis of brain patterns, serial murder has been intricately intertwined with investigative invention. Extraordinary killers command extraordinary methods, and so we present twelve tales of killers who have affected the forensic culture. Among the first was a nineteenth-century poisoner from Nuremburg, Germany.

At age forty-nine, Anna Maria Schonleben neé Zwanziger realized she might spend the rest of her life alone, in poverty. Against her will, she had married an alcoholic lawyer twice her age, but he died, leaving her in debt. She stole a valuable ring, which got her banished from her married daughter's home, and she twice tried but failed to take her own life. It was the early 1800s and a woman without means had little hope after a certain age of supporting herself. There was also evidence that she suffered from a nervous disorder and was possibly borderline psychotic. She'd had a baby out of wedlock and a miscarriage, both of which had badly affected her, as had a lover's abandonment. Facing fifty and having lost her looks, Anna decided to try to win a husband by proving her worth as a domestic servant to the head of a household.

She knew she would face hurdles on this quest, especially if the man she targeted was married. But her secret weapon—her "truest friend"—was arsenic: she could always kill the wife. Anna knew that aging men were often afraid to be alone. Dependent as they were on a woman to take care of their household, such men, she believed, could be persuaded to form a partnership of convenience.

She set her sights on a Judge Glaser in Bavaria, killing

his wife, but the new widower did not respond as she'd hoped. In a huff, she moved on, finding employment with a Judge Grohmann, a widower already. However, when he married someone else, Anna retaliated by placing poison in his food, killing him and some of his servants. The wife of a third employer, a magistrate named Gebhard, was the next target. She seemed to know she was being poisoned, but her husband dismissed her suspicions. She died and he grew ill, so he sent his glassware and several food containers for analysis at the local apothecary. He learned that the saltshaker contained arsenic, so he alerted authorities.

Anna was now associated with several suspicious deaths, but the science of arsenic analysis had, at the time, barely been used in a forensic context. Toxicologists were just learning how to detect this centuries-old "inheritance powder," but in 1806, chemist Valentine Rose devised a method for confirming its presence in human organs. He had utilized Johann Metzger's 1787 discovery: when arsenious oxide is heated with charcoal and a cold plate is held over it, the heated substance forms a dark mirrorlike deposit. This was arsenic.

To develop his theory about how to detect arsenic in the human body, Rose had cut up the stomach of a victim of suspected poisoning and dissolved the contents in water. He filtered this substance before treating it with nitric acid, potassium carbonate, and lime to evaporate it into arsenic trioxide. When he treated it with coals, he derived the telltale arsenic mirror. This confirmed that the victim had been murdered.

Able with this method to prove such poisonings, investigators who arrested Anna on October 18, 1809, found several packets of the toxic substance on her person. A chemist applied Rose's innovative procedure to the organs of Judge Glaser's wife, which revealed the presence of arsenic. Since this substance had turned up in salt containers in another household where Anna had been employed, the evidence was convincing. She admitted to the double homicide, adding other names, and said she did not think she could stop. After being convicted of murder, she was beheaded in 1811.

This is the sort of story you will read in these pages. Faced with an elusive killer who has proven to be hard to identify, investigators find ways around the hurdles, setting new standards or devising new methods. As crime detection improves, the challenges increase, so many of these cases have compelling twists and turns, but history has shown that science and logic are equal to the test.

Before describing just how serial killers do get caught, let's first clarify the meaning of serial murder. Often, it comes with enormous associations based in stereotypes and misinformation.

Serial Murder

While any type of incident that involved a number of murders was once called "multiple murder" or "mass murder," investigators eventually decided that distinctions were needed. The term *serial killer* was first used in *The Complete Detective* in 1950, but it's generally agreed that during the 1976 Son of Sam case in New York, FBI special agent Robert Ressler limited the term to cases on which he and his colleagues in the Behavioral Science Unit were consulting. Thus it became the standard term for a specific type of multiple murder incident.

According to the FBI's official manual, the term *serial murder* implies that there are at least three different murder events at three different locations, with a cooling-off period between events, but the National Institute of Justice (NIJ) and some criminologists allow for only two such events. In addition, some killers bring successive victims to a single location at different times, so there are problems with the FBI's approach. To achieve clarity, in *The Human Predator,* I defined the various terms thus:

1. *Mass murder* is a concentrated response to a single event or idea, occurring in one basic locale, even if the killer travels to several loosely related spots in that general area, and there are at least four fatalities.

2. A *spree* is a string of at least three murders arising from a key precipitating incident occurring close in time to the murders, but the spate of killings is fueled by continuing and associated stress, taking place in several locales and across a relatively short period of time; there is no psychological cooling off.

3. A serial killer murders at least two people in separate incidents, with the strong likelihood of killing again. There is a psychological cooling-off period between incidents, which might serve as a time of preparation

for a later killing. He, she, or they also choose the modus operandi and may either move around to kill or lure successive victims to a single locale. They dehumanize potential victims into objects needed for the satisfaction of their goals, which can be anything from lust to greed to anger, and their behavior manifests an addictive quality.

All the criminals described in this book are serial killers. Because "cunning" implies that they know what they're doing and are generally clever enough to evade detection, all are coldheartedly psychopathic as opposed to deranged or remorseful.

Capture

Despite the FBI's use of behavioral profiling, there is no comprehensive study across decades showing how serial killers have actually been caught. An examination of three hundred cases of serial murder from different eras and in multiple countries reveals that the largest percentage of successful resolutions involved responsible—even extraordinary—investigation. Many killers, however, were caught simply because of their own errors.

While there are many steps in any investigation, especially those that last many years, there is generally something that initiates the key break in the case. Some killers retain an item once owned by a victim or they have a victim's photo. Sometimes they're caught visiting a corpse. Helicopter surveillance over a broad swath of territory caught Rochester, New York, killer Arthur Shaw-cross having lunch over the body of his latest victim. To trap a prostitute killer, a policewoman in disguise subtly collected carpet fibers from a suspect van and assisted the capture of Steve Pennell in Delaware.

A palm print identified Bobby Joe Maxwell and a fingerprint revealed Colin Ireland, while biological evidence yielding DNA nabbed Green River Killer Gary Ridgway (after a decades-long investigation). Physical evidence, such as soil, paint chips, or fiber helped investigators in other multiple murder cases, while the remains of victims found on the killer's private property caught Larry Bright and Herb Baumeister. Oddly enough, when investigators went to question Wesley Gareth Evans, identified as a friend of the chief suspect in several murders, it turned out that Evans was actually the killer. Maury Travis sent maps to reporters of where victims could be found and investigators from the state police Cyber Crime Unit who recognized the Web site design used computer logs to get his address, while background noise on a recorded phone call eventually nailed team killers Judith and Alvin Neelly.

Among the more interesting ways that killers have been apprehended were the obvious mistakes they made (aside from leaving fingerprints) that revealed their identities. Peter Goebbels dropped his ID at a crime scene—a dead giveaway—while Neville Heath signed the hotel register for a room in which he'd left a victim bludgeoned, bitten, and murdered. Harold Shipman forged a patient's will in his favor, causing surviving relatives (one was a lawyer) to take a good hard look at the signature, but more obvious was the blood on Earle Leonard Nelson's hair when he visited a barber in a town where a murder had just occurred. Over drinks, Waltraud Wagner and her accomplices joked openly about their foul deeds in an Austrian hospital and a doctor overheard them. More gruesome, Dennis Nielsen flushed chunks of flesh from his victims down the toilet of his new upstairs flat, which clogged up the system for the entire building. Four killers in the survey left the bodies of victims in their homes, which exuded such noxious odors that people called the police, and Marcel Petiot burned a pile of corpses in his building in Paris, triggering an investigation.

Another error that five killers committed was to brag to the wrong person about their deeds; Charles Schmid and Richard Biegenwald even took friends to see the corpses. Half a dozen murderers were too open about their activities, tempting fate, while Peter Mackay's final victim was a close friend. Also revealing himself was Danny Rolling, when he left his name on a recorder found at a campsite near several crime scenes.

Some killers have been apprehended in the act, generally because they grew too bold, acted compulsively, or overestimated their concealment. In the early 1900s, Jeanne Weber was caught literally red-handed as she choked the son of an innkeeper, but she was considered mad and sent to an asylum. When Georg Grossman's landlord in Germany overheard an altercation, he brought the police in time to grab Grossman, who was about to dismember a dead girl. Carroll Edward Cole was similarly caught, but he claimed that his victim, whose apartment he was in, had "just dropped dead." He got away with this for a time, but eventually he confessed.

In addition, killers like John Wayne Gacy, Joe Ball, and Billy Glaze turned up in several investigations of missing people, which then led to evidence implicating them, while family killers such as Mary Cotton and Mary Beth Tinning stood out as survivors who were always nearby when a family member died. Interestingly, Marie Noe was simply considered the "unluckiest mother alive" when, one after another, ten of her children died young, but years later she was charged with eight murders and she finally confessed.

On rare occasions, an intended victim gets away and brings back the cops. Serial killers done in by escapees include Robert Berdella, Jeffrey Dahmer, Robert Hansen, Gary Heidnik, and Jurgen Bartsch. Harvey Glatman lost out when the police happened by while he was with a victim seeking help, while a surviving victim boldly followed Ronald Frank Cooper to his home. Thomas Rath's victim had the presence of mind to memorize his attacker's license-plate number, while a victim attacked Paul Stephani so badly he had to call for an ambulance. Andonis Daglis's victim managed to persuade him that she was not his type.

If a victim doesn't turn on a potential killer, an accomplice might. Some serial killers have depended on accomplices for assistance, but when the going got tough or the accomplice acquired a conscience, the party was over. Danny Ranes learned this when his teenage buddy took police to the bodies of their victims. Catherine

Wood, the former lover and "Murder Game" partner of Gwendolyn Graham, reported their terrible deeds against the elderly, and Karla Homolka made a deal for a short sentence in exchange for information about the involvement of her husband, Paul Bernardo, in a succession of rapes and murders in Canada. But she took part in the crimes as well, as did her kid sister.

A select few have turned themselves in. Mack Ray Edwards walked to the front desk of a police station, gave them his gun, and confessed, while Wayne Adam Ford handed over a severed breast he carried in a plastic bag in his pocket. Michael Copeland and Ed Kemper both called the police themselves, and Elmer Wayne Henley turned in three—including a man he had just killed in self-defense. He led the police to twenty-seven bodies. In one of the strangest cases, Javed Iqbal pledged to kill one hundred street children in revenge, after which he would turn himself in. He did so, then killed himself.

Sometimes the killer commits an unrelated offense and thereby gets captured. A famous example of this is Ted Bundy, whose erratic driving in a stolen Volkswagen Beetle led to his arrest, but Robert Joseph Zani went one better by crashing a car in which he was carrying his tenth victim. Joel Rifkin was stopped for driving without a license plate, and a decomposing corpse was discovered in his car. Likewise, a highway-patrol officer pulled over Randy Kraft for suspected drunk driving and noticed a dead man sitting next to him.

Other arrests that turned up serial killers were for assault, homosexual solicitation, child molesting, shoplifting, kidnapping, fraud, auto theft, loitering, rape, robbery, and burglary. David Berkowitz was done in by a parking violation and Juan Martin Cantu by marijuana. Henry Lee Lucas was arrested in Texas for an illegal weapons charge, although he was suspected in two disappearances. He proceeded to confess to hundreds of murders in two dozen states (although he recanted most of these). While Jack Owen Spillman tried to escape detection by shaving his body hair and using surgical gowns, the police caught him on suspicion of burglary in an unrelated incident.

Police always hope that publishing a photo in the newspaper will help track down a killer, and sometimes it has. Staff at a restaurant recognized Joseph Duncan III when he arrived with kidnap victim Shasta Groene in his company, but the most famous example was the capture of L.A.'s "Night Stalker" Richard Ramirez when citizens recognized him from a newspaper photo and tried to beat him up. The police had to rescue him.

Overview

In this book, I have selected a dozen cases that relied on or utilized forensic innovation, including creative police procedure. We'll see detectives who go the distance and then some, as well as how the joint efforts of cops and scientists prompted an arrest or conviction. Sometimes the investigation required the prodigious coordination of a number of forensic specialties, but other times it resulted simply from a clever deception on the part of the police. In every case, the investigators had to be experienced, persistent, inventive, and aware of how to best utilize the available tools. While a single detective might seem to stand out in a given case, each relied on a support team. That joint effort will be apparent in the stories that follow.

The subject of this book is not just serial killers but provocative and intriguing investigations. Sometimes it was a process and sometimes a charismatic person, but you can be sure that each of these cases would lend itself easily to a novelist or screenwriter.

The final chapter offers a summary for investigators, drawing from each case to provide practical suggestions and inspiration to resolve future cases. Awesome effort and satisfying solutions need not be limited to fiction.

Sources

DeNevi, D., and J. Campbell. *Into the Minds of Madmen: How the FBI Behavioral Science Unit Revolutionized Crime Investigation.* Amherst, NY: Prometheus Books, 2004.

Egger, S. A. *The Need to Kill: Inside the World of the Serial Killer.* Upper Saddle River, NJ: Prentice Hall, 2003.

Everitt, D. *Human Monsters.* Chicago: Contemporary Books, 1993.

Frasier, D. K. *Murder Cases of the Twentieth Century.* Jefferson, NC: McFarland and Company, 2006.

James, E. *Catching Serial Killers.* Lansing, MI: International Forensic Services, 1991.

Kelleher, M. D., and C. L. Kelleher. *Murder Most Rare: The Female Serial Killer.* New York: Dell, 1998.

Lane, B., and Wilfred Gregg. *The Encyclopedia of Serial Killers.* New York: Ballantine, 1995.

Ramsland, K. *The Human Predator: A Historical Chronicle of Serial Murder and Forensic Investigation.* New York: Berkley, 2005.

Schechter, H. *The Serial Killer Files*. New York: Ballantine, 2003.
Wilson, Colin. *Serial Killer Investigations*. West Sussex, England: Summersdale, 2007.
Wilson, Colin, and Damon Wilson. *The Killers Among Us: Sex, Madness and Mass Murder*. New York: Warner, 1995.

ONE

H. H. HOLMES:
Deduction, Determination, and Dogged Persistence

In 1894, Detective Frank Geyer was about to learn the power of the media to turn an obscure but talented officer of the law into an international celebrity. He would find this to be both a help and a hindrance in one of the most complex homicide investigations in the history of the United States. While Geyer had no ambition to be famous, his nose for a case and his painstaking work would become a sensation. It would also set a very high standard. Sherlock Holmes, the popular British sleuth featured in a succession of tales over the previous seven years, was about to "die" (temporarily) just as this "American Sherlock Holmes" took on the very real H. H. Holmes in a case that would yield many astonishing revelations.

The difficulty of the investigation lay not just in the cleverness of the alleged serial killer, but also in the many places he had traveled and the names he had used to accomplish his dirty deeds. Holmes exploited America's mobile milieu during the 1890s to target victims. Chaos was his calling card. In *The Holmes-Pitezel Case,* Detective Geyer would write, "It is not possible to find in the annals of criminal jurisprudence, a more deliberate and cold-blooded villain than the central figure in this story." A judge concurred, viewing the case from start to finish as "stranger than any novel I have ever read." Indeed, this true story is among the best illustrations of how an intrepid investigator runs down every lead, ponders the impact of every clue, and will not give up until he has exhausted every avenue.

Missing Children

The case began in Philadelphia. On September 3, 1894, a man looking for a patent dealer on Callowhill Street ascended the stairs to an office. A stench filled the air and

Notorious turn-of-the century
serial killer H. H. Holmes.

appeared to grow worse on the second floor. When the caller spotted a decomposing corpse with a blackened face lying on the floor, he fetched the police.

They arrived and found that the victim's head, chest, and right arm were badly burned, and a match and a broken bottle of chloroform lay nearby. It appeared that he'd accidentally struck a match near an explosive solvent.

The victim was identified as Benjamin F. Pitezel, and when his wife, Carrie, was notified, she requested the life insurance payment from Fidelity Mutual of $10,000. However, an imprisoned convict informed the company that the whole thing was a scam; someone else's body had been substituted for that of the alleged victim. His warning came too late. A man named H. H. Holmes had already brought Pitezel's oldest daughter, Alice, to identify the body and settle the claim.

Given these details, an officer for the insurance company tried unsuccessfully to track down Holmes, so officials hired agents from the Pinkerton National Detective Agency to go after the scoundrel. These more experienced investigators followed Holmes's trail from state to state, gathering information about his numerous frauds, thefts, and seductions. They learned about insurance scams years earlier in Chicago that had provided him with sufficient funds to build a three-story hotel. As they built their case, they realized that Holmes, whose real name was Herman Mudgett, was among the most successful and versatile swindlers they had ever come across. If he hadn't gotten greedy and brought his schemes too close to home, he'd have still been in business. But this time, they believed they could get him.

The agents followed his trail through Chicago, Detroit, Ontario, New York, and New England. Finally, they caught up to Holmes near his childhood haunts in Vermont. They put him under surveillance and gave the information of his whereabouts, along with that of Carrie Pitezel, to police. On the afternoon of November 16, H. H. Holmes was apprehended in Boston as he prepared to board a steamship. The arresting officers told him he was being charged with the theft of a horse in Texas, so he surrendered easily, probably amused, because he knew he'd committed much more serious crimes. So did they, but they did not let on that he'd soon be extradited for murder charges to the commonwealth of Pennsylvania.

Philadelphia Detective Thomas Crawford arrived with an arrest warrant for both Holmes and Carrie Pitezel, but she alerted them to her missing children. The travelers had split into small groups to evade detectives and Holmes had taken three of the Pitezel children with him. Yet they

Detective Frank Geyer, who became famous for tracking Holmes's victims down.

were not with him now. Holmes claimed they were in the care of a woman, Minnie Williams, who had already sailed for England. He admitted to fraud, saying Benjamin Pitezel was in South America, and agreed to return to Philadelphia.

Further investigation over the next few months revealed that even the scammers had been duped: Pitezel, a supposed scammer, was indeed the victim. Holmes said that Pitezel had decided to commit suicide, but it seemed more likely that he'd been duped. Investigators surmised that Holmes had persuaded Pitezel to get insured and use his family to collect the money after his "death," but then Holmes had killed him in order to take the funds for himself. That he had committed murder raised the possibility that he might have done away with the Pitezel children as well, especially since "Minnie Williams" was nowhere to be found. Carrie Pitezel, against whom all charges had been dropped, was frantic, so Holmes was taken to the private office of District Attorney George S. Graham for further questioning.

This is where, in June 1895, Detective Frank Geyer came face-to-face with his nemesis for the first time. He had already seen Holmes that morning in the courtroom, where he'd pleaded guilty to conspiracy to defraud the insurance company. Now Geyer would have a chance to watch the fiend under pressure.

Balding and stocky, Geyer sported a thick mustache that matched his dark eyebrows and made him an imposing and memorable figure. He arrived at the D.A.'s office with the captain of police, pushing through a crowd of reporters in the hallway outside before closing the door in their faces. Although the reporters did not yet have the details they craved, they seemed to sense the buildup of a media-worthy case.

Inside, Graham told Holmes that authorities suspected that he had murdered not only Pitezel but also the missing children. "Tell us where the children are," he demanded. Their mother was anxious to be reunited with them. If they were still alive, it would be in Holmes's best interest to produce them.

Geyer wrote that Holmes played games and adjusted his strategy to whatever seemed necessary to defend himself. He watched as the trickster demonstrated a hallmark behavior of a smart psychopath: quick recovery once caught in a lie, so as to offer another that seemed more plausible. Holmes even professed delight in the opportunity to assist in finding the children. His voice failed slightly, as if he genuinely cared about these kids, and he asked the men around the table to consider what reason he might have for killing innocent babes. He was deeply offended, he said, by the accusation.

Geyer, savvy about criminals, knew better than to accept anything Holmes said at face value, despite the surprising degree of detail he provided. But he also knew that within the story Holmes told were kernels of truth, so he made a mental note of the cities that Holmes mentioned while describing his final journey. Holmes admitted to having had Alice Pitezel, fifteen, in his custody; it was she who had helped him to identify her father's corpse for the insurance payout. He had also picked up Howard, eight, and Nellie, eleven, telling Carrie where to meet him at a later date. Alice and Nellie had written letters to her, documenting their daily journey, but Holmes had never mailed them. These letters had been found on his person, giving Geyer good clues about where the children had been before they disappeared. Holmes tried to direct him to England, but Geyer knew there was no Minnie Williams and that the street in London that Holmes gave as her address was bogus. Only God knew whether Williams was even alive. From the children's letters, Geyer focused his efforts on the Midwest and certain areas in Canada.

A Desperate Game

It seemed likely that Holmes had been careful to erase every trace of what he had done. Given how widely he had traveled, the children could have been left almost anywhere—including murdered and buried—yet the D.A. was convinced that a patient investigator could uncover the necessary clues if he retraced Holmes's route.

There was no question but that Geyer was the man for the job. With twenty years of experience in the Philadelphia Bureau of Police, he had diligently achieved a reputation as the best the city had to offer. The insurance company offered funds for the trip, since they would retrieve the money from Pitezel's "accident," so Geyer agreed to make the effort, despite the fact that he was still grieving for his wife and twelve-year-old daughter, who had died only three months earlier in a tragic fire that consumed the Geyer home. While he could not get his own child back, he hoped he could spare Carrie Pitezel the agony of losing three of hers.

On June 26, 1895, the detective set out by train, carrying photos of Holmes and each of the children, along with an inventory of items and clothing associated with them. He also had photographs of the three large travel trunks they had used. He knew that a prodigious task lay before him, and, fortunately for posterity, he kept detailed notes. Much of what is known about his demanding journey derives from his own memoir.

Arriving in Cincinnati, where he joined Detective John Schnooks, he showed photographs and asked around in a few hotels for anyone who might have seen Holmes or the children. He finally found someone who remembered the small group of travelers. On September 28, they had checked into a cheap hotel under the name Alex E. Cook, one of Holmes's aliases. It was the first viable lead. The same man pointed Geyer in another direction and he soon found the next hotel at which they had stayed.

Geyer and Schnooks then talked with Realtors. Through extensive questioning, they located a woman who had seen a man resembling Holmes with a ragtag boy the age of Howard. They had come into her neighborhood to rent a house, bringing only a large stove. But Holmes had then given the stove to this woman and vacated the place. Geyer surmised that his sudden change of mind was motivated by the realization that he'd been spotted. Geyer now believed that Holmes had done away with Howard, if not all three children, and that disposing of their bodies had been on his mind.

At this point, the detective believed he "had firm hold of the end of a string which was to lead me ultimately to the consummation of my difficult mission." However, when nothing more turned up in this area, he went to Indianapolis, which, according to the letters, had been Holmes's next destination. In any event, the children were still writing letters while in this location.

Working with another local detective, Geyer located clues that gave him a better sense of where the children had been. It was an exceedingly hot day, which made the investigation burdensome, but here Holmes's perverse game became clear: like pawns, he was moving his wife (one of three) and the children around in hotels in the same city, without any party being aware of the others. He seemed to derive a thrill from the control and secrecy. Geyer could not understand why, if Holmes intended to kill the children, he would go to so much effort and expense. In those days, little was known about the motivations of dangerous psychopaths, generally referred to as people who had a mania without delirium or moral degeneracy. That Holmes might simply get a kick out of being the puppeteer who pulled the strings of his victims, while they continued to trust him, was beyond anyone's ability to hypothesize. And there was one other item of concern: one person who recalled Holmes said he'd mentioned his desire to be rid of the boy, because he'd become troublesome.

Despite his intuition that Howard had been killed in Indiana, Geyer went to Chicago and Detroit. He learned that Holmes had now added a third party to his game of rotation—Carrie Pitezel and her other two children. He had even placed her only three blocks from where he had boarded her older children, but had not allowed any of them to realize their proximity. From this location, Alice wrote something to her mother that made Geyer's blood run cold: "Howard is not with us now." If he was not with the girls and not with his mother, then where could Holmes have taken the boy? It was a solid suggestion that Holmes had killed him, especially since one of the three trunks was now missing, but since there was some slight hope that the girls could still be found, Geyer decided to concentrate on the other locations.

Holmes had said he'd left the children's trunk at a hotel in Detroit, but after questioning everyone he could find in this general area, Geyer turned up no accounts of Holmes or his companions. Another lie.

Moving on to Toronto, where the last letters from the girls had been written, Geyer found a boardinghouse where they had briefly resided. He intended to look up real estate agents to find out if a man had rented a house for only a few days. It seemed likely that if Holmes had decided to kill one or both girls, he would have tried to hide the deed in a secluded setting. Since he had arranged short-term rentals in other places, this appeared a likely modus operandi. Yet even with the help of a local detective, the task was prodigious. Geyer then enlisted a cadre of reporters. They used photos and printed the story, asking citizens for assistance. This helped inform many local Realtors of the case.

"It took considerable time to impress each agent with the importance of making a careful search for us," Geyer wrote. Publicity reduced the amount of time they spent at each office, as the checking of records had already been done. Geyer managed to locate a house that someone using the name Holmes had rented, and noticed that there was, ominously, a six-foot fence surrounding it. The family residing there was aware of some loose dirt in one place under the house. Geyer enlisted the aid of some men and led an organized dig in this area, firmly believing they would find the remains of one or more of the children.

They dug until it grew dark, and then utilized lamps for light, but finally they had to give up. Then Geyer learned that the former renter had been someone other than Holmes. All their effort had been futile. Nevertheless, the intrepid detective was certain the children had been killed somewhere in Toronto, since the letters had stopped at that city, so he persisted with his questions until he found another suspicious rental arrangement at number 16 St. Vincent Street. He went to check it out.

The Fruits of His Labor

Geyer learned from neighbors that a man had moved in with children in tow, and had asked for the loan of a spade to plant potatoes in the cellar. He had moved in with only a bed, a mattress, and a large trunk. Geyer showed photographs around and someone identified Holmes as the renter. Inside, Geyer discovered that the cellar was accessible via a trapdoor. Going down into this small, dank area with a lantern, he looked around and soon found evidence of digging in soft dirt. He bent down to look closer and was certain the digging was recent. He retrieved a spade—the same one the renter had borrowed—and pushed the blade into the dirt.

It yielded easily, so he shoved deeper, digging dirt out until he was down about a foot. This raised a stench of putrefaction that told him he was in the right spot. "Our coats were thrown off," he wrote, "and with renewed confidence, we continued our digging. The deeper we dug, the more horrible the odor became."

Getting used to it, he prepared himself for a sad discovery. He doubted this was the grave of someone's dead dog. After digging three feet, he turned up a small bone, which looked like it had been part of a child's arm, so he called the local police inspector and employed a local undertaker to take charge. After much more digging, they slowly exhumed the unclothed corpses of two girls, which Geyer believed to be Nellie and Alice Pitezel. Images of his own dead daughter must have visited him at this point. Yet further digging failed to yield another body, so it appeared that Holmes had chosen this spot for the girls only.

"Alice was found lying on her side with her hand to the west," Geyer wrote. "Nellie was found lying on her face, with her head to the south, her plaited hair hanging neatly down her back." Nellie's limbs were partly on top of Alice, so a crew of men lifted them carefully onto a sheet, carried them through the trapdoor, and transferred them to one of the pair of coffins set up in the kitchen. Her braided hair was so heavy it pulled the scalp away from her skull. Alice's remains were likewise removed and taken to the deadhouse.

"By this time," Geyer wrote, "Toronto was wild with excitement. The news had spread to every part of the city." Reporters flocked to the house to get photos and possible quotes for their stories. They had assisted and now sought their just reward. "Congratulations, mingled with expressions of horror over the discovery, were heard everywhere."

Geyer sent a telegram to Philadelphia about the day's events and later concluded in his book, "Thus it was proved that little children cannot be murdered in this day and generation, beyond the possibility of discovery."

But a definitive identification had yet to be made, and for this they needed Carrie Pitezel. She made the trip to Toronto, heavy of heart but still vaguely hopeful that the detective was wrong. Searchers had found a toy in the house that was listed in Carrie's inventory of things her children had owned, and this supported the fact that Holmes had been the renter and these bodies were the missing Pitezel children, as did pieces of partially burned clothing from the fireplace. Since the corpses were so badly decomposed, Carrie was allowed only to see the children's hair, laid on the canvas that covered them, and the teeth, seen through a hole. She recognized them at once and swooned in grief. She now knew that Holmes had lied to her and killed her children. The cause of death was found to be suffocation. It appeared that Nellie's feet had been removed and were missing, something that remained a mystery. Both girls were buried in Toronto.

But Geyer knew there was one more child to find: little Howard. Despite all that he had done this far, his trek was not over. He believed Howard was dead, but was determined to deliver the body for proper burial and mourning. He went over all the letters again, relying on logic to determine that Howard had been separated from the girls prior to their arrival in Detroit, so it was time to return to Indianapolis. Although he had struck out here initially, his instincts urged him to go over old ground and look for clues he might have missed.

He arrived on July 24. As before, he proceeded to gain the assistance of real estate agents from around the city to learn the details of short-term rentals from the previous October. By this time, Geyer's trek had attracted the attention of the nation. Newspapers reported his every move and readers followed the investigation the way they read a suspenseful piece of fiction. As a result, Geyer received many leads, which he followed, but most of them just wasted his time. "Days came and passed," he wrote, "but I continued to be as much in the dark as ever." Geyer feared that "the bold and clever criminal" might have bested him on this one. It seemed increasingly likely that little Howard would never be found.

Back in Philadelphia, Holmes read the newspapers to keep track of Geyer's journey. At first he'd felt gleefully empowered, believing that Geyer could never find the children, but with the discovery of the girls' remains, things looked grim. He had to think up a tale to exonerate himself and blame someone else. Even as he did so, a team of investigators was analyzing the children's letters and wiring more ideas to Geyer. Some items in the letters, they had found, had been overlooked or misunderstood, and with renewed care, Geyer discovered that the children had been in Indianapolis four days longer than he'd initially realized. He rechecked the house he thought Holmes had rented and narrowed the time frame during which he lost track of their movements to only two days. He believed that Howard had disappeared at some point during those two days. If only he could establish exactly where Holmes had been during this time, he was certain he would learn where Howard's body was hidden.

When Geyer heard that a child's skeleton had been discovered in Chicago, he took a train there to learn what he could, but he found that these remains were not Howard's. It was another dead end. He traveled to several more places, but instinct urged him to settle in Indianapolis and keep searching there. Despite his persistent lack of success, Geyer continued to believe he would have a breakthrough. "No less than nine hundred supposed clues were run out," he later wrote. He needed a new strategy.

He and assisting officers went to smaller towns in the area, going through them as systematically as he had done in Indianapolis. In Irvington, Geyer finally struck pay dirt. A man who had rented out a cottage in October—around the time of the two days in which Geyer had lost track of Holmes—remembered Holmes from his rude and abrupt manner. Another person recalled a boy with this irascible short-term tenant. Relieved and certain that he was at the end of the trail, Geyer proceeded to the rental property in question. With the owner's permission, he conducted a thorough search.

He found no disturbance in the floor of the cellar, which initially discouraged him, since that seemed to be Holmes's modus operandi, but he collected pieces of a trunk from a small alcove, and near it he saw disturbed dirt. Geyer dug into the area but found nothing. In a barn, he spotted a coal stove, and remembering Holmes's earlier purchase of a large stove which he'd then abandoned, Geyer suspected this was a clue. On top were stains that resembled dried blood. However, there was nothing else in the barn that indicated the boy was here. Digging in soft spots in the yard outside also failed to produce anything of interest. By nightfall, he and the owner were forced to wrap up their search, determined to renew it the following day.

Geyer went to town to send a telegram to Carrie Pitezel, asking if the missing trunk had a strip of blue calico over a seam. She wired back, identifying the trunk as belonging to her. While he was there, a newspaper editor came looking for him. Something had been found back at the property.

Geyer rushed back and learned that the owner of the cottage, along with his partner, had poked around. In a pipe hole in the chimney that led from the cellar, they discovered pieces of a charred bone—part of a skull and a femur—that had belonged to a male child. Reaching inside, they had pulled out ashes and more pieces of bone. In front of a crowd of curious people, Geyer dismantled the lower part of the chimney and found a complete set of teeth and a piece of jaw, identified by a dentist as being from a boy seven to ten years old. "At the bottom of the chimney," Geyer recorded, "was found quite a large charred mass, which upon being cut, disclosed a portion of the stomach, liver and spleen, baked quite hard. The pelvis of the body was also found."

Plenty of witnesses had seen Holmes back in October and identified him from the photograph that Geyer carried. He'd even left Howard's coat with a grocer, which was now retrieved. One young man recalled helping Holmes to install the stove, though little did he realize it had been used to incinerate a murder victim. Carrie Pitezel arrived as well, and identified various items as belonging to Howard.

Convinced he had finally, albeit tragically, found Howard Pitezel, and having his discovery confirmed by other clues, Geyer "enjoyed the best night's sleep" that he'd had in two months. The search for truth had finally reached fruition. It was now August 27, fully two months after he'd left on this journey, and five weeks since he'd found Howard's unfortunate sisters.

On September 12 in Philadelphia, Holmes was indicted by a grand jury for the murder of Benjamin Pitezel. He entered a plea of not guilty and his trial date was scheduled for October 28. Even as he donned a role for the court, people were learning much more about him from what he had left behind in Chicago. Holmes, it seemed, had quite a list of murders to his credit. Attributing four to him was only the beginning.

The Mind of a Killer

Holmes had arrived in Chicago during the 1880s, already married to two women. The city was preparing for the world's fair, or Great Exposition, which meant there was plenty of opportunity for a clever man to commit fraud and theft. Some twenty-seven million people went through the exposition during its six-month run, which overtaxed the city's resources and inspired crime, most of which the police could not investigate. Holmes was among those who took advantage, and his scheme was probably the most well planned and devious of the lot.

He had foreseen the many visitors who would be searching for lodgings as close as possible to the fair, knowing that among them would be the most vulnerable prey: single, naive women who would easily succumb to the charms of a successful and charming "doctor." He presented himself as a graduate of a prestigious medical school and a man of means. In fact, he had gained these credentials with other scams, and possibly with murder.

Holmes's first Chicago employment was as a prescription clerk at Sixty-third and South Wallace streets, but he soon took over the business from Mrs. E. S. Holton, who then "went to California" with her daughter. No one ever heard from them again, but Holmes took control of the shop. Across the road was a property that he purchased.

Soon he was gathering funds through fraud to build his three-story, hundred-room "castle," as he referred to it. When he eventually felt the need to leave, he tried to burn it down to collect insurance, but did not succeed. Before that, he clearly used the place for his favorite pastime: torture.

Given the news about Holmes's murder of the Pitezel girls, the police began an investigation of the property in July, even before Howard was found, relying on reports of missing women known to have been there with Holmes. The first floor consisted of shops and offices, but the second floor and cellar yielded something that exceeded the worst expectations. From reconstructions, it seemed that Holmes had tortured and murdered many women, disposing of their corpses in a massive furnace in the cellar or defleshing them and selling the skeletons to medical schools.

Holmes's castle included soundproof sleeping chambers with peepholes, asbestos-padded walls, gas pipes, sliding walls, and vents that Holmes controlled from another room. Many of the rooms had trapdoors, with ladders leading to smaller rooms below. One asbestos-lined room appeared to be used to incinerate its occupant alive. There were greased chutes that emptied into a two-level cellar, in which Holmes had installed a large furnace, and an asbestos-lined chamber with gas pipes and evidence of something having been burned inside. It seemed that Holmes placed chosen victims in special chambers into which he pumped lethal gas and then watched them react. Sometimes he'd ignite the gas, or perhaps even stretch a victim on the "elasticity determinator," an elongated bed with straps. When finished, he might have slid the corpses down the chutes into his cellar, where vats of acid awaited them. Searchers discovered several complete skeletons and numerous incinerated bone fragments, including the pelvis of a fourteen-year-old child. Some bone fragments, and a woman's slipper and hair, were found in the large stove he kept in his third-floor office.

Meanwhile, back in Philadelphia, Holmes insisted that he had nothing to do with any murders. Those people had either taken their own lives, he claimed, or someone else had killed them. Nevertheless, the *Chicago Tribune* announced that "The Castle is a Tomb!" and the *Philadelphia Inquirer* described many bones removed from the "charnel house." It wasn't long before true-crime pulp paperbacks were published to slake the public's thirst for sensation and turn a profit. The Chicago police estimated the number of victims to be as high as 150, although this figure was never corroborated.

To exonerate himself, Holmes, now thirty-four, penned *Holmes' Own Story, in which the Alleged Multimurderer and Arch Conspirator Tells of the Twenty-two Tragic Deaths and Disappearances in which he is Said to be Implicated.* He described Gilmanton Academy, New Hampshire, the town in which he grew up as Herman Webster Mudgett. He was born there in 1861 and claimed to have lived an ordinary life, with an ordinary set of parents and a normal schoolboy routine. He received a medical school diploma from the University of Michigan and then opened a practice. He attempted unsuccessfully to commit his first insurance fraud, helping someone to fake his own death with a purloined cadaver. From there, he did a stint as a doctor in an insane asylum. He changed his name to H. H. Holmes and posed as a pharmacist in Chicago.

"In conclusion," he wrote, "I wish to say that I am but a very ordinary man . . . and to have planned and executed the stupendous amount of wrongdoing that has been attributed to me would have been wholly beyond my power." He asked the general public to withhold their judgment until he could prove his innocence at his trial. He would also work to bring justice to those "for whose wrong doings I am today suffering." However, this publication was so transparently self-serving, not to mention boring, that readers preferred the more lurid tales provided in newspapers.

The End of the Line

Holmes's attorneys attempted to get his trial continued, but were unsuccessful. In addition, there was a struggle between Chicago and Philadelphia authorities as to who would get to try him first, but he remained in Philadelphia. Unfortunately, the judge allowed only testimony relevant to the single murder he was charged with there, that of Benjamin Pitezel, so there are no court records about other evidence, including Geyer's discovery of the murdered children.

The trial commenced as scheduled on October 28—three days before Halloween—and lasted five days. Judge Arnold allowed Holmes to defend himself, so he questioned the prospective jury members, at which point his team of attorneys left the courtroom. He demonstrated the coolness with which he handled stress and tried rejecting each person who said he had read the papers, but the judge pointed out that this was not considered a cause for challenge. "Newspapers are so numerous," he said, "that everybody now reads them, and of course, they obtain impressions from them."

The best account of what lay ahead in terms of witnesses is found in D.A. Graham's speech, reprinted in Geyer's book. He spoke for nearly two hours, describing how Pitezel had died and how chloroform had been injected into the victim's stomach after death to mimic a suicide. He also suggested that Holmes had "ruined" Alice when she was in his care in the city. Holmes appeared to be surprised by this allegation.

A reporter for the *Philadelphia Inquirer* described Holmes's performance in court as vigorous and "remarkable." He was deferential to the judge but nasty to the prosecutor. He asked for an analysis of the liquid that he was accused of using as a poison for the children (which the D.A. did not have in his possession), and he wanted reports from the most recent work done on toxicology, claiming that as a doctor, he himself could analyze them (though his credentials were false). This left the impression of a man who knew his stuff and was prepared to use science to exonerate himself.

Yet Holmes often deflected the questioning with forays into minutiae, and he frequently squabbled with the prosecutor, who was likely disturbed at having to spar in court as an equal with the defendant. Holmes made an error when, after Pitezel's corpse was described in gruesome detail, he requested a lunch break because he was hungry. He appeared to have no sense of sorrow over the supposed suicide of a longtime partner and friend, noted by the jury. For the rest of that day, while he handled his questioning in a professional manner, he failed to score any points to support his innocence. The professional witnesses all concluded that Pitezel could not, as Holmes claimed, have committed suicide.

Holmes asked that the court allow his two defense attorneys to reenter the case, and with that he relinquished his role as a criminal lawyer. While he now had competent counsel, he had probably hurt his case. Between his antics and his obvious fatigue by the end of the first day, the jury had a good look at the defendant's loss of confidence and inability to shake the strongest witnesses. He may not have admitted his guilt, but his actions indicated he'd admitted defeat. He got up only once to examine another witness—his latest paramour and third wife, who testified against him. Using a heavy dose of emotion, as if stricken by her betrayal, he nevertheless failed to move her to change her testimony about his behavior on the day that Pitezel was allegedly murdered.

The prosecution prepared to show his activities by producing thirty-five witnesses from the various places where Holmes had gone after the Pitezel murder. But the judge had ruled that the trial must be limited to the Pitezel murder, so Graham showed how he had made

Pitezel's identification, and added whatever he could about Holmes's reprehensible behavior. The prosecution proved with doctors that the chloroform that supposedly had been self-administrated had actually been forced into Pitezel postmortem.

Given Holmes's admissions about being with the victim, there was really no other choice for the fact finders who were listening. In his closing argument, which lasted over two hours, Graham called Holmes the "most dangerous man in the world" and asked the jurors not to be afraid to do their duty. They were not; they convicted Holmes of Benjamin Pitezel's murder and the judge sentenced him to death by hanging.

After his conviction, and as his attorneys prepared an appeal for a new trial (which failed), Holmes took up the pen again to make a confession, largely inspired by a $10,000 payment from the Hearst newspaper syndicate. He published it in the *Philadelphia Inquirer*. Aiming now to become the most notorious killer in the world, he claimed to have killed over one hundred people. Apparently having second thoughts, he reduced that number to twenty-seven, including Pitezel and his children. He insisted that he could not help what he'd done. "I was born with the Evil One as my sponsor beside the bed where I was ushered into the world," he lamented. "It now seems a fitting time, if ever, to make known the details of the twenty-seven murders, of which it would be useless to longer say I am not guilty."

Holmes claimed that he wanted to make the confession at this point for several reasons. He assured his readers that he was not seeking attention and that the entire enterprise was distasteful to him. As he admitted to the murders, he said he was "thus branding myself as the most detestable criminal of modern times." He thought his countenance was changing as he sat in prison, and that he looked more satanic than before. "I have become afflicted with that dread disease, rare but terrible . . . a malformation . . . My head and face are gradually assuming an elongated shape. I believe fully that I am growing to resemble the devil—that the similitude is almost completed." He self-diagnosed "acquired homicidal mania" and "degeneracy."

The criminological theories at the time were fueled by Cesare Lombroso, an Italian anthropologist and professor at the University of Turin. Lombroso had published *L'uomo delinquente,* in which he stated that certain people were born degenerates, identifiable by specific physical traits, such as bulging brows, long arms, and apelike noses. In this context, Holmes "saw" a prominence on one side of his head, a "corresponding diminution on the other side," a deficiency on his nose and ear, and similar details in the length of various limbs.

Then he turned his attention to Pitezel, indicating that from the first hour they met, he knew that he would kill the man. Everything he did for Pitezel that seemed to be a kindness was merely a way to gain his confidence. Pitezel "met his death" on September 2, 1894. Holmes showed him fake letters from Mrs. Pitezel in order to precipitate a bout of drinking. Holmes then watched and waited until he was able to come upon Pitezel in a drunken stupor in the middle of the day. He packed his bags in readiness to leave and then went to where Pitezel lay in bed, bound him, saturated his clothing and face with benzene, and lit a match. He literally burned his former accomplice alive.

Apparently Pitezel cried out and prayed for mercy, begging Holmes to end his suffering with a speedy death, "all of which had on me no effect." When Pitezel finally expired, Holmes extinguished the flames, removed the ropes, and poured chloroform into his stomach, to make the death appear to be accidentally brought about by an explosion. That way, the insurance company would quickly pay the full amount of the claim. He left the body in a position that exposed it to the sun for however long it would be before someone found him—presumably to further deform it for difficulty in identification. "I left the house," he wrote, "without the slightest feeling of remorse for my terrible acts."

As for young Howard Pitezel, Holmes also had a story to tell. He had every intention of murdering the three Pitezel children, so he ensconced them in a hotel until he could find a way that would not draw suspicion. After a week, he poisoned the boy and then cut him into pieces small enough to go through the door of a stove he had purchased. He felt no remorse about these acts, only the pleasure he had gained from killing another person. He then took the girls to Chicago, Detroit, and Toronto, where Alice and Nellie met their fate. He claimed that they were the "twenty-sixth and twenty-seventh" of his victims.

To get them ready, he told them they would soon be reunited with their mother. Then he compelled them to climb into a large trunk and closed them inside, leaving an airhole. Through it, he pumped gas, killing them. In the dirt cellar, he dug shallow graves, placing their naked bodies inside and covering them with dirt. He considered that "for eight years before their deaths I had been almost as much a father to them as though they had been my own children."

He also had a plan to end Mrs. Pitezel's life, along with those of her two remaining children, with nitroglycerine, but he was arrested in Boston before he managed to achieve this goal. He closed his confession by saying that his last public utterance would be of remorse for these vile acts. He did not expect anyone to believe him. Geyer later says in his memoir that Holmes's account, published in many papers on April 12, 1896, was so inconsistent with the facts that it was "at once discredited in police circles."

Then, according to Geyer, Holmes recanted the confession, and some of his "victims" turned up alive. When told by police that his tale was untrue, he supposedly said, "Of course it is not true, but the newspapers want a sensation and they got it."

On May 7, 1896, H. H. Holmes went to the hangman's noose, and even then, he was changing his story. Now he claimed to have killed only two people, and tried to say more, but at 10:13 the trapdoor opened and he was hanged. It took him fifteen minutes to strangle to death on the gallows.

Afraid of body snatchers who might want to steal his

corpse, Holmes had made a request: he wanted no autopsy and he instructed his attorneys to see that he was buried in a coffin filled with cement. No stone was erected to mark where it was buried. Holmes's attorneys turned down an offer of $5,000 for his body and refused to send his brain to Philadelphia's Wistar Institute, where scientists had hoped to analyze it.

So many people who'd rented rooms from Holmes during the fair had actually gone missing that estimates of his victims reached around two hundred; though the toll is unsubstantiated, it is sometimes cited even to this day. We might not know the number of his victims, but we do know that Holmes was among the cleverest serial killers of all time, and our inability to fully document his crimes attests to how well he exploited chaotic times and the lack of record keeping to cover his tracks. In light of this, Detective Geyer's painstaking detection is quite brilliant, and his work inspired many like-minded sleuths well into the next century.

While Geyer relied on logic and persistence, our next story links another fortuitous discovery in science with the investigation of a brutal serial killer who targeted children two at a time.

Sources

Boswell, Charles, and Lewis Thomas. *The Girls in the Nightmare House.* Hold Medal, 1955.

Boucher, Anthony. *The Quality of Murder.* New York: E. E. Dutton, 1962.

Franke, David. *The Torture Doctor.* New York: Hawthorn Books, 1975.

Geyer, Frank. *The Holmes-Pitezel Case: A History of the Greatest Crime of the Century.* Salem, MA: Publisher's Union, 1896.

Holmes, H. H. *Holmes' Own Story.* Burk and McFetridge, 1895.

———. Confession. *Philadelphia Inquirer,* April 12, 1896.

Larson, Erik. *The Devil in the White City.* New York: Crown, 2003.

Schechter, Harold. *Depraved: The Shocking True Story of America's First Serial Killer.* New York: Pocket, 1994.

The H. H. Holmes Case, a film by John Borowski. Waterfront Productions, 2003.

TWO

LUDWIG TESSNOW:
Secrets in Blood

It was early afternoon on September 9, 1898, in Lechtingen, Germany, near Osnabrück. Jadwiga Heidemann
was awaiting her seven-year-old daughter's return from
school. When Hannelore failed to arrive as expected,
Jadwiga went to a neighbor, Irmgard Langmeier, whose
daughter, Else, was a year older. The two girls often played
together. But Irmgard had not seen Else either, so together they contacted the school. To their horror, neither
girl had been seen that day. They alerted friends and
family, and enlisted as many people as they could to search
the surrounding woods. They were at it the rest of the
day, without result. None of the girls' friends had seen
them.

Then, as dusk settled in, one searcher came across what
looked like the dismembered limbs of a child scattered

on the ground. From clothing and personal effects on the ground nearby, Jadwiga identified the remains of her daughter. She was shocked and grief-stricken. Irmgard held out hope, since her daughter was not there in the immediate area. However, the girl had not yet returned home, so the searchers continued. An hour later, when it was nearly too dark to search any longer, they found her in an equally brutalized condition, hidden deeper in the woods within some bushes. Despite the evidence of a person committing these crimes who was aware of the need to hide them, the villagers considered other explanations, such as a roving beast. It would not be the first time that wolves had killed children, but it was early fall, not winter, when wolves were most hungry, and it was difficult to imagine them venturing this close to civilization. Even so, for the moment, it seemed the most likely explanation.

The German biologist Paul Uhlenhuth, who was first successful in distinguishing animal from human blood. His analysis of the evidence against the "werewolf" Ludwig Tessnow played an essential role in the investigation.

Bestial Degeneracy

Over several centuries, wolves have been the scapegoats for crimes that defy belief that a human could have committed them. Victims might be bitten all over, torn limb from limb, drained of blood, or disemboweled. Since these offenses seemed altogether inhuman, villagers were certain they were committed by someone possessed by a force that could only originate from supernatural evil. Some evil is so overwhelming it's nearly impossible for normal people to accept that it originated with a rational being. Such a person must have been transformed.

The belief in the possibility that humans could change shape has been traced to 600 B.C., when King Nebuchadnezzar in the Bible thought he'd suffered from a condition that made him grow out his hair and romp around as a wild beast. By the 1500s in France, lycanthropy was a diagnosable medical condition. An informative early book about the myths was *The Book of Were-Wolves* by Sabine Baring-Gould, a nineteenth-century archaeologist and historian. Shape-shifting ideas were traced from ancient times and across different cultures, with many accepting that man-beasts were the result of an encounter with the devil.

These folks were thought to dress in wolfskins at night as a way to contact Satan to gain the wolf's special powers. As the myth goes, when they managed to make "the change," they gained a period of complete abandon into blood and violence. Common tales around Europe told of hunters who had hacked off the paw of a wolf that had run away only to find that the paw in their pouch had become a woman's hand, and then they'd discover a woman in town with a mysteriously bandaged arm.

Some practitioners viewed shape-shifting as a gift, and those who possessed a strong sexual drive viewed a pact with the devil as a perfect excuse to claim that their misdeeds were beyond their control. For example, in 1521, Pierre Burgot and Michel Verdun were tried in Besançon, France. They admitted that they had pledged obedience to the "master" of three black men they'd met in exchange for money and freedom from trouble. They were then anointed in a ceremony with unguents that changed them into savage animals. Together they had torn apart a seven-year-old boy, a grown woman, and a little girl, whose flesh they consumed. They so loved lapping up the warm blood, they stated, that they could not help but continue to kill. They also claimed they had sexual relations with female wolves. The court sentenced both men to be executed for sorcery.

A pioneer in the early days of psychiatry, Richard von Krafft-Ebing's theories aided in the understanding of killers such as Tessnow.

The Psychology of Impulsivity

Lycanthropy has long been considered a form of lunacy that compels people to eat raw meat, attack others, let their hair grow, and run on all fours. By the late nineteenth century, such behavior had drawn the interest of mental health professionals, known as alienists. Richard von Krafft-Ebing, one such practitioner at the Feldhof Asylum, and a professor of psychiatry in Strasbourg, believed that without a standard diagnostic system, psychiatry could not consider itself equivalent to the field of medicine, so in 1880, he published three volumes, collectively titled *A Textbook of Insanity,* in which he outlined an elaborate system for categorizing mental diseases. By this time, insanity had already been accepted as a legal concept in England, so this medical context would cloud the waters, because it would become apparent in certain proceedings that some people who suffered from psychosis might still appreciate that what they were doing was wrong. Thus, they might be medically insane but legally sane.

Krafft-Ebing's more well-known text, published in 1886, was *Psychopathia Sexualis with Especial Reference to the Antipathic Sexual Instinct: A Medico-Forensic Study.* His approach was to identify a foundational problem, the development of degeneracy, and study it according to its manifestations in sexual deviance. He set up a theoretical framework through which to identify and interpret the various behaviors, relying on such factors as heredity, corrupting influences on the nervous system, the evolution of a motive, and a qualitative set of details about the personality. He described the details of forty-five cases that focused largely on violent criminals or extraordinarily perverse practices (in later editions, the number of cases would grow to more than two hundred). These wretches illustrated the harmful consequences of a degenerate lifestyle, which itself was often influenced by specific types of temptations. Such persons were not well equipped to resist; they might be timid, lacking in education, unable to control themselves, or of limited intelligence. Nevertheless, they were considered to be responsible for exposing themselves to situations in which their weakness of character would undermine their efforts to be good.

Krafft-Ebing found a close link between lust and the impulse to murder. By selecting cases to correspond to a simplified framework that discounted multiple motives, he offered psychiatry a "vocabulary of perversion" and a seemingly viable standard of interpretation. He was the first to try to study and categorize the varieties of perversion, especially lust murders that inspired certain types of frenzied activity closer to what a beast might do than a human being. "A great number of so-called lust murders," he wrote, "depend upon combined sexual hyperesthesia and parasthesia. As a result of this perverse coloring of the feelings, further acts of bestiality with the corpse may result." He found that the largest percentage of offenders who indulged in truly perverse acts were white males. Once they were caught, they also apparently enjoyed describing the acts.

Krafft-Ebing's work became both a professional and popular sensation, just in time to explain the bestial acts of the serial killer in Germany who had a lust for tearing apart children.

The small police force in Lechtingen began to question all the villagers to learn if anyone had seen the murdered girls that day. They failed to gain information specific to the victims, but they did hear about a suspicious man named Ludwig Tessnow, who was seen that day entering the village from the woods and whose apron was stained with some dark liquid. They went to see him, but he said he was a carpenter and the stains were from wood dye. His explanation seemed plausible enough, so they let him go.

However, one enterprising officer decided to take the investigation a step further; he went to Tessnow's workshop to see what he might find. He saw a can of wood dye, just as Tessnow had said, so he decided to try an experiment. When Tessnow was near it, he pushed it so that some spilled onto Tessnow's trousers. Since it resembled the stains seen on his clothes earlier that day, the investigator had to let the matter drop. Tessnow remained in the town, working among its inhabitants without further incident for the next four months. He then picked up and left to find work elsewhere, and the deaths of the two children went unexplained. Their mothers grieved without closure.

While Krafft-Ebing might have understood the offender who committed these crimes, his psychiatric approach could not have been used to catch him, because Tessnow had already learned an effective way to escape detection. His capture would depend on a different type of science.

Blood Work

Blood is one of the most mystifying and significant substances in life. It symbolizes so many things, from life itself to birth to kinship to death. As forensic science developed during the nineteenth century, biologists sought to better understand the activity, function, and composition of blood. One forensic interest was to distinguish human from animal blood, and another was to try to understand the activities at a crime scene that involved blood. For example, in Paris in 1869, an investigator named Gustave Macé gained fame from his quick-thinking examination of the floor of a murder/ dismemberment scene. Although the floor had been scrubbed clean, he noted that the tiles sloped toward an area under a bed. He instructed a workman to lift the tiles, presuming that blood would have pooled underneath, and he was correct. Both the analysis of blood and its patterns come under the umbrella of the discipline of serology, or the science of biological fluids.

The first method for distinguishing animal blood from human was proposed in 1841: it was heated up with a chemical and sniffed for a specific odor, but there proved to be no scientific basis to this claim. During the next decade, Ludwig Teichmann mixed blood with a solution of potassium chloride, iodide, and bromide in galactic acid, showing that hemoglobin could be changed into hemin in order to examine the shape of the resulting crystals. While useless as yet for forensic investigation, this method stood for half a century before another scientist improved upon it.

Different blood types were recognized as early as 1875, but it wasn't until 1901 that Dr. Karl Landsteiner, at the Institute of Pathology and Anatomy in Austria, named and standardized the groups. He asked colleagues for samples of their blood, and with a centrifuge he separated the clear serum from the red cells. He then placed the samples in a number of different test tubes, mixing the blood of one participant with the blood of all the others. He found that sometimes blood clumped together and sometimes the samples repelled one another. He determined from these experiments that there were three types of blood, based on differences in a substance called an antigen, which produces antibodies to fight infection. He labeled them types A (antigen A present, anti-B antibody present, but antigen B absent) and B (antigen B present, antigen A absent). A third distinct reaction was labeled C (both antigens A and B absent), but was later relabeled as O.

It took another two years, but a colleague of Landsteiner's, Dr. Adriano Sturli, discovered yet another type in which both antigens were present, so he called it type AB. It soon became clear that the blood type depended on genetic inheritance from parents, which helped with paternity tests. Types A and O are the most common in the human population, and AB the rarest.

At the same time that Landsteiner was experimenting with blood types, another young doctor was working on the distinction between animal and human blood. German biologist Paul Uhlenhuth, working at the Institute of Hygiene in Griefswald, had taken up the study of hoof-and-mouth disease, and he hoped to develop a serum to combat it. Before him, Jules Bordet, from Belgium, had shown that a vaccination elicited a specific antibody and had worked with the behavior of antigens. He was able to see a visible reaction between the antibody and antigen. Others who injected animals against infectious diseases found that foreign substances caused the production of defensive substances specific to the injected material. These "precipitins" could be utilized to distinguish different types of protein.

Uhlenhuth continued to pursue the implications of this research with other experiments, learning that if he injected protein from a chicken egg into a rabbit, and then mixed serum from the rabbit with egg white, the egg proteins separated from the liquid to form a precipitin. As he proceeded, he found that the blood of each animal had its own characteristic protein, and then, after injecting human cells into the rabbit, he realized that the test was also applicable to humans.

This was welcome news for law enforcement, because crime suspects often claimed that blood on their clothing was from animals, and as yet their stories could not be scientifically disputed. With the precipitin test, those days appeared to be over. To be certain about this result, a coroner asked Uhlenhuth to test some dried bloodstains from both animals and humans, and the results proved the test to be reliable.

Then, just four months after Uhlenhuth announced his discovery, a particularly brutal crime brought the test into the forensic spotlight.

Flashback

This incident occurred in the village of Göhren, on the resort island of Rügen. It was Germany's largest island in the Baltic and at this time no bridge connected it to the mainland. But it was nevertheless a popular tourist destination, because of its pristine beaches, white chalk cliffs, beechwood trees, and rugged but spectacular landscape. During the latter part of the nineteenth century, people went there for "rest cures," a fad at this time throughout Europe.

It was July 1, 1901, a Sunday. Six-year-old Peter Stubbe and his older brother, Hermann, eight, had gone into the woods to play. No one worried, since the pretty island was considered safe and the boys often played in the woods. But when they failed to return for supper, their parents grew concerned. They looked around the immediate area but saw no sign of their sons, so they enlisted the help of neighbors. It was growing dark and they began to fear that Peter and Hermann might be lost in the woods. By nightfall, the search party had to light torches to continue. Everyone shouted the boys' names, hoping to see them emerge or call out their location, but their voices were not heard. The search continued all night.

As the first light of day entered the woods and the weary searchers were about to give up hope, one man came across the bodies. It was the boys, both murdered. They lay together in some bushes and it was clear that their killer had crushed their skulls with a rock. More grotesque, he'd torn or cut off their arms and legs, and even removed the heart of the older boy, taking it away. The limbs were scattered about the area.

This scene resembled an incident that had occurred in the area just three weeks before. A farmer claimed he'd found seven of his sheep slaughtered, torn apart, and disemboweled. He had arrived in time to see a man running away, and while he did not recognize the person, he believed he could identify him if he saw him again. The sheep mutilation had not yet been solved.

As with the double homicide in Lechtingen, the police began interviewing everyone in the area. One villager said he had noticed the boys the day before, talking with a carpenter that he knew as Ludwig Tessnow. People tended to look askance at Tessnow, who disappeared for long stretches to travel around the country, and who lived as a recluse. No one knew him well, and one person who lived near Tessnow's home said he had seen the man on Sunday evening wearing clothing with dark stains.

Investigators went to Tessnow's home to ask some questions. He listened to their concerns about the boys, but denied any knowledge about them. Nevertheless, he

was asked to step aside while they searched his home and
carpentry shop. They found freshly laundered clothing
that bore suspicious stains. Tessnow claimed that the
stains came from wood dye, which he used daily in his
carpentry work. He told them, step-by-step, where he had
been all day on Sunday, and finally, with no evidence
against the man, the police had to withdraw. But they did
bring Tessnow in to see if the farmer whose sheep had
been slaughtered might recognize him. Indeed he did,
claiming that Tessnow was the man who had run away
from the bloody scene. Tessnow denied it, and since it
was one man's word against another's, with no witnesses,
the law enforcement officers knew that nothing much
could be done. Still, they confiscated some of the carpenter's clothing and decided to keep an eye on him.

A local magistrate, Johann-Klaus Schmidt, thought
about what had happened to the boys and recalled the
two girls who were murdered and dismembered in the
woods in a village not far away. He contacted officials
there and learned that the name of their key suspect, who
had since left the village, was Ludwig Tessnow.

The circumstances were now plain enough: Tessnow
was killing but successfully eluding arrest. Schmidt discussed the situation with a prosecutor, Ernst Hubschmann.
It turned out that he had read Paul Uhlenhuth's recently
published paper, "A Method for the Investigation of Different Types of Blood," so he went to Uhlenhuth and asked
him to examine the stains on Tessnow's clothing. Over the
course of four days, Uhlenhuth applied his method, which

involved dissolving the stains in distilled water, to more than one hundred spots that he found on the material. While some stains did test positive for the presence of wood dye, in seventeen stains Uhlenhuth also detected traces of both animal and human blood. The animal blood proved to be from a sheep. He also found human blood on the rock believed to have been the weapon used on the boys. So much for Tessnow's claim of innocence.

With this evidence, and the circumstances, Tessnow went to trial and Uhlenhuth appeared as an expert witness to explain to the judge and jury how his analysis worked. Tessnow was convicted of the murder of both Stubbe boys and sentenced to be executed. Thus a depraved killer was finally stopped.

It's assumed that, while he was not tried for the murders of the girls in Lechtingen, he was also responsible for them. He apparently suffered from the sort of bestial bloodlust that Krafft-Ebing had documented in other sex murderers and seemed nondiscriminating as to whether it was children or animals that he ripped into pieces. Although it was never determined whether his behavior was compulsive or committed during fits of psychosis, he fit the pattern of those "werewolf" killers who had been studied. Even today, what Krafft-Ebing identified is applicable to some of the most extreme cases of bloodlust and cannibalism.

Dr. Stephen Giannangelo has studied serial killers who derive a joy from their killing sprees in *The Psychopathology of Sexual Murder*. He says that they experience a "pervasive lost sense of self and intimacy, an inadequacy of identity, a feeling of no control." These things then manifest in an ultimate act of control—murder. Such killers develop deviant sexual motivations that become consuming fantasies that issue in an initial murder. When they find reward in that, they continue to look for other opportunities, refining their approach and acting out further deviance. The form it takes is influenced by whatever image or object is a sexual hot button in their fantasy. Bestial paraphilias that encourage savage attacks are obviously potentially dangerous.

We will see similar cases later in this book, including the next one. Fortunately, the killers met their match in brilliant, indefatigable investigators.

Sources

Baring-Gould, Sabine. *The Book of Were-wolves*. Blackmask Online, 2002, first published in 1865.

Douglas, Adam. *The Beast Within*. New York: Avon, 1992.

Giannangelo, Stephen. *The Psychopathology of Serial Murder*. Westport, CT: Praeger, 1996.

Guiley, Rosemary Ellen. *Vampires, Werewolves, and Other Monsters*. New York: Checkmark Books, 2005.

Lee, Henry C., and Frank Tirnady. *Blood Evidence: How DNA Revolutionized the Way We Solve Crimes*. Cambridge, MA: Perseus, 2003.

Masters, R.E.L., and Eduard Lea. *Perverse Crimes in History*. New York: The Julian Press, 1963.

Oosterhuis, Harry. *Stepchildren of Nature: Krafft-Ebing, Psychiatry, and the Making of Sexual Identity*. Chicago: University of Chicago Press, 2000.

Thorwald, J. *The Century of the Detective*. New York: Harcourt, Brace and World, 1964.

Von Krafft-Ebing, R. *Psychopathia Sexualis with Especial Reference to the Antipathic Sexual Instinct*. Revised edition. Philadelphia: Physicians and Surgeons, 1928.

Wilson, Colin, and Damon Wilson. *Written in Blood: A History of Forensic Detection*. New York: Carroll and Graf Publishers, 2003.

Wonder, A. Y. *Blood Dynamics*. San Diego, CA: Academic Press, 2001.

THREE

ALBERT FISH:
Deciphering a Deadly Document

On June 5, 1928, the *New York Times* ran an article about a missing child and a man who had taken her away two days earlier, on Sunday afternoon. New York, New Jersey, and Long Island police were notified about the incident and given a description of both. The man, in his late fifties, had called himself Frank Howard, although it was expected that this name could be an alias. He was five-foot-six, with gray hair, blue eyes, and a trimmed mustache. Of average weight, he had a bowlegged gait. When he arrived at the Budd home, he was wearing a blue suit and, by some reports, driving a small blue sedan.

This was the man's second visit to the residence of Albert and Delia Budd at 406 West Fifteenth Street. The first had been six days earlier, in response to an ad placed by their eighteen-year-old son, Edward, who sought work in the country. Howard arrived, saying he was seeking a hired hand for his chicken farm in Farmingdale, Long Island, and he offered quite a bit of information about himself, including that he took religion seriously and had six children (although he was currently separated from his wife). He seemed so open and honest that Albert and Delia believed their son would be well employed by this man, who agreed to pay fifteen dollars a week. He also agreed to hire Edward's friend, and said he would come back on Saturday to pick them up. However, he was delayed, so he sent a telegram announcing his arrival on June 3.

He came, as promised, with strawberries and a can of pot cheese. Asking for his telegram back, he slid it into his pocket. Edward was away, so the Budds sent one of their four other children to fetch him. Ten-year-old Grace came into the room, dressed in a white Communion dress and glowing with little-girl charm. Howard was delighted with her and took her on his lap. He mentioned that he was going to a birthday party for his niece at 137th Street and Columbus Avenue. He thought Grace might like to come. Delia was hesitant, but Albert observed that Grace didn't often get treats on his salary as a porter, so he granted permission. They liked the kindly, unassuming old man and believed their daughter would be safe. He promised to bring her back later, at which time he would give instructions to Edward for starting work.

However, Howard did not bring Grace back that evening, so the Budds spent an agonizing night before they sent Edward to the police. They soon learned that the address the old man had given was fictitious. Clearly, he had kidnapped their child. Little Grace Budd was described in the papers as having blue eyes and brown hair. At four feet tall, she weighed about seventy pounds and had been treated recently at New York Hospital. She wore white stockings, a white dress, a blue hat, and a gray coat.

Once again, an elusive killer would lead the police on a difficult chase, although this investigation would last so many years its solution would seem pointless to many on the team. Yet one investigator never gave up. Because of that attitude, he remained alert for news and clues.

The Search

Only a year before, the city had been rattled by another kidnapped child, Billy Gaffney, from Brooklyn. A boy who was with him at the time said the "bogeyman" had taken him. He described a thin elderly man with a mustache. Billy was never found. Something similar had happened with an eight-year-old boy named Francis McDonnell on nearby Staten Island in July 1924. He was the son of a police officer and his mother had reported a stooped elderly man in the area. His body was found, naked from the waist down, beneath a pile of branches. He had been assaulted and strangled.

Now the bogeyman had come for Grace. Police searched cellars, roofs, and hallways in the general area of the Budd home, but turned up nothing. When they checked in Farmingdale, they found no listing for a Frank Howard, and the locals there denied knowing anyone by that name. They got the same result in Farmingdale, New Jersey. But within a day, Joseph Sowley, fifty-nine, was arrested. This man liked to entice children into the hallway of his apartment building, and while there was no evidence he had visited the Budds, he was locked up for disorderly conduct.

Detectives did track down someone named Frank Howard at an address in New Jersey, but it turned out that this man, who had lived in Farmingdale at one time, had moved to Chicago, where he had died years earlier. Thus this promising lead dried up.

During those depression years, kidnapping had become a common "get rich quick" type of crime, and there were kidnapping syndicates in some of the major cities. Between 1928 and 1932, there were an estimated 2,500 kidnappings around the country. Everyone involved in looking for Grace anticipated finding a ransom note, although there was no reason for a man like Howard to expect to grow rich this way because the Budds were clearly a family of moderate means.

A postcard arrived from Station H, 173 West 102nd Street, bearing an enigmatic message: "Mr. and Mrs. Edward Budd. My dear friends, All little girl is to cellar and into water." Then a letter arrived, written in pencil, which appeared to be a death threat: "Mrs. Budd," it said. "Your child is going to a funeral. I still got her. HOWARD." It had been mailed on Wednesday from the Madison Square Station in New York.

Thereafter, the Budds were flooded with anonymous calls and letters—some kind, and some nasty—as were the police at the Twentieth Street Station. One lead sent Edward Budd with detectives to Long Island to view a man meeting the description of Frank Howard, but he was not the person they sought. Circulars containing Grace's photo were made up and sent to police departments around the city, as well as to transportation offices.

The Budds looked at photos in the police files to see if the abductor of their daughter was a known criminal, but they could not identify the elusive offender. Delia continued to believe that her daughter was being held for ransom, although no communication had arrived to that effect. A kindly woman wrote to offer Edward a job on her farm.

Four days after the kidnapping, Mrs. Budd had dramatically switched gears (as she often would) and concluded that Grace was no longer alive. The New York police sent circulars about the child to Canadian authorities in the hope that the man had crossed the border, and these were followed by packages of circulars mailed out to police departments in large cities around the country. In New York City, fifty detectives were assigned to the case.

One officer placed an ad in local newspapers aimed at telegraph agencies, asking them to look for forms that Howard might have used to send the telegram on June 2. This produced information from the Western Union office at Third Avenue and 103rd Street. They had the original. Howard might have snatched back his telegram while at the Budds, but investigators now had a sample of his handwriting. With this, they could make a comparison in the event that a suspect turned up.

On June 10, a pushcart peddler in East Harlem said he recognized an enameled can that Frank Howard had left at the Budd home as the container for the cheese he had sold to the elderly man. This peddler ran his business from 104th Street and Third Avenue, close to where the telegram was sent the day before the sale, so police fanned out to see if it might be the area where Howard resided. Detectives agreed that the abductor was more likely a city dweller than a well-to-do farmer.

Then a note arrived, postmarked at 132 Fourth Avenue, an East Harlem city postal station, which declared that the child had been spotted alive. The initials *J.F.H.* appeared to refer to Frank Howard. Mrs. Budd turned the letter over to the detectives, and they engaged the assistance of postal authorities.

The brief note stated that Grace now lived with her abductor: "I have Grace. She is safe and sound. She is happy in her new home and is not at all homesick. I will see to it that Grace has proper schooling. She has been given an Angora cat and a pet canary. She calls the canary Bill. I am a keen student of human nature. That was why I was attracted to Grace. She seemed like a girl who would appreciate nice surroundings and a real nice home." He added that he had driven with Grace past the Budds' home, but had seen too many people there, so he had declined to stop. Nevertheless, he stated that he would see to it that "some arrangements are made so Grace will be able to visit you for a short time." Detectives believed the letter was genuine and tried but failed to obtain fingerprints from it.

When police checked the area, someone affirmed that a child matching Grace's description had been seen, so all parties were buoyed with hope that she might actually be alive. They searched the neighborhood, knocking on doors to ask residents if they had seen either Grace or Howard. They heard from several people that such a child had been in the area. Delia, however, continued to believe that her daughter was dead. She knew Grace would never just go and live happily with a stranger. To her mind, the kidnapper might have written this letter but it was not a factual description.

But then, on June 18, Delia claimed she'd had a premonition that Grace would be returned to her within a few days. Now she was certain the girl was alive and well. She believed that the man who had taken her had been afraid to return her because of all the excitement. "I don't think any harm has come to her," she stated.

On July 7, the *Times* reported that detectives now had a picture of Frank Howard in their possession, identified by Grace Budd's parents. A boarder at the Budd home, John McLaughlin, confirmed the identification, as did young Edward. The picture had been obtained from a Florida prison. By early August, the district attorney's office had presented evidence to a grand jury and Assistant D.A. Harold Hastings claimed to have solved the case of who had taken the missing child. The *Times* learned he was an ex-convict already known to the police, Dr. Albert E. Corthell. An indictment was filed August 3 and a bench warrant issued for his arrest. However, at this time, they failed to locate him, as he had gone off somewhere in the Midwest. Investigators were on his trail.

In November, a fifty-year-old man and a ten-year-old girl were detained in Elmira, New York. The man had been charged with vagrancy and he fit the description the Budds had given of Grace's abductor. The girl insisted that the man was her father, and he gave his name as Thomas Davis. He admitted he had lived recently in the Bronx, but denied any involvement in the Budd kidnapping.

William F. King, a detective lieutenant at the Missing Persons Bureau, had taken over the Budd investigation, and like Detective Frank Geyer, he was the type of man who would chase down every clue, no matter how seemingly insignificant, and who would proactively devise ways to flush out more. He had worked as a fireman on locomotives, fought in World War I, and been a police officer for over a decade. While he preferred action, he had learned that patience and persistence were the most valuable traits in investigations as baffling as this one. To his mind, no unresolved case was ever closed. His job, which he took seriously, was to look into every possibility for making an arrest and to track down every lead.

King learned that the child in the company of this new person of interest did not look like Grace Budd, so he dropped any further investigation of it. Despite his unwavering efforts, there were no further leads that year or the next—just more crank letters and empty tips. King stayed busy, but he was mostly just spinning his wheels.

Grasping at Straws

The next paper chase began in late March 1930 when Mrs. Budd said she had spotted her daughter's handwriting. An envelope used to enclose a copy of the *Christian Science Monitor* was posted from Portsmouth, New Hampshire, on March 25. The envelope was addressed to Francis H. Budd, but Mrs. Budd "knew" the instant she saw it that Grace had addressed it. She looked at handwriting in Grace's old schoolbooks, then asked neighbors if they didn't agree. They did. Believing this was more than wishful thinking, she took the envelope to the police.

Detective King and another detective examined the items and found a mailing slip attached to the newspaper that bore the name Herbert J. Sherry. They found this name inside the envelope as well, along with writing in red crayon. Learning that Sherry was in a naval prison, the team went to Portsmouth, only to discover that this man had been in South Carolina at the time of the kidnapping. Handwriting experts also stated that the handwriting did not match examples they had from Grace. Although this lead fizzled out, King did not despair. A child was gone, probably dead, and the offender must be brought to justice.

In June, King arrested a man named Charles Howard, who resembled the description of Frank Howard, and set up a police lineup. Howard was a con man, arrested in Florida for fraud and theft, but Delia could not identify him and he denied any involvement in the kidnapping.

However, another woman heard about the arrest and came to the station to link the crime to her former husband, Charles Edward Pope, age sixty-seven, who sometimes used the alias Frank Howard. Mrs. Jessie Pope told police that at the time of the kidnapping, Charles had asked her to take care of a little girl he called Grace. Jessie had refused, so he'd taken the child away. She said she then fell ill for a long period and did not hear about the Budd kidnapping. When she now was shown a photograph of Grace Budd, she was positive that it was the child she had seen with her husband. Although she described different clothing than Grace had worn, the scenario seemed too good to be true. Investigators arrested Pope and searched his home.

Pope admitted he had been institutionalized in 1924, but would not say where or why. He had lived near the Budds two years earlier, but he insisted he was not guilty. Delia identified him, but since she had identified others over the past year, the detectives were dubious. With no evidence against Pope, and plenty of reason for his estranged wife to implicate him out of spite, they figured they would let him go.

But then, after a full day of methodically going through all the buildings on Pope's property in Shandaken, New York, searchers found three trunks in a garage. One contained pictures of women and "mushy" letters, but beneath all of this they found three locks of fine brown hair, like that of Grace Budd, tied together with a ribbon. The state troopers said there was no doubt the hair had come from a child. They also found a child's pair of white stockings, similar to those that Grace had worn when she disappeared, and Delia claimed she recognized the darning on them as her work. Also included among the items in this trunk was a notebook full of newspaper clippings of the unfolding kidnapping and investigation. In addition, although Pope kept pieces of correspondence dating back to the 1890s, letters from the year 1928 were missing. Neighbors said he had recently burned a pile of papers.

Two other factors seemed to seal Pope's fate. First, Grace had been part of a delegation of children who had visited an area near Pope's farm, and second, a former neighbor of the Budds testified that Pope had come to her apartment seeking the Budd residence. Not surprisingly, the grand jury bound him over for trial. (Oddly, neither Albert nor Edward Budd was asked to identify Pope as the man they had entertained in their home.)

Three months later, with Detective King on the trail, an earlier suspect, Dr. Corthell, was located in St. Louis at the Statler Hotel. Registered under an alias, he had overdosed on barbiturates and was in a hospital. King found him there, and he admitted that he had been in New York in 1928, but denied involvement in the kidnapping. The Budds were able to say only that he *might* be the man. He was transported to Manhattan.

Three days before Christmas, Pope went to trial, but his attorney had received a letter from Delia to the effect that she now believed he was not the kidnapper. In fact, three of the witnesses had decided he was not the man. Only his spiteful wife continued to stick to her story, but given their rough history, it was difficult to take her seriously. In fact, the locks of hair had come from their son. Pope was acquitted on December 24, while in February, Corthell was released as well.

It would be more than three years before the case finally came to a horrifying resolution. In the meantime, the nation was transfixed by yet another kidnapping. On the evening of March 1, 1932, Charles Lindbergh Jr., twenty months old, was taken from the second floor of the New Jersey home where his parents, Charles and Anne Morrow Lindbergh, resided. The nursemaid had discovered him missing from his bed. The Lindberghs, too, received dozens of communications, turning over bundles of money to an organization that supposedly held their child. But the baby's body was discovered not far away in the woods, killed by an apparent blow to the head. Bruno Richard Hauptmann was arrested two years later and held for trial. Even as this was going on, the Budd case was revived.

Finally, a Break

By November 1934, only the persistent Detective King was still on it. He had traveled around the country following leads and was one of the few officers who still believed the case could be solved. He had even done various things to keep it alive. Among them was to plant false information in newspapers in the hope of disturbing the kidnapper so much he would react. The point was to keep the focus on him so the tension would never let up. In fact, each time King did this, the police received a number of leads, but none had yet been helpful. Still, King did not give up, even more than six years into the case. His preferred tool was a popular gossip column in the *Daily Mirror* that Walter Winchell wrote, called "On Broadway." On November 2, King asked Winchell to write that the Bureau of Missing Persons had a new informant and expected to crack the case within the month. This time, the ruse apparently worked.

On November 11, 1934, Delia Budd received a letter, sent from the Grand Central post office. She did not read, so Edward looked over the contents, which were so disgusting and terrifying he felt certain it was from the man who had taken Grace . . . and killed her in a gruesome manner. He took the missive straight to Detective King, who read it with a sinking sense of finality.

"My dear Mrs. Budd," the writer began. He went on to state that in 1894, a friend of his had shipped as a deckhand on the steamer *Tacoma,* going to Hong Kong. They got drunk and missed getting back on the boat, so they were stranded in a country suffering from famine.

"So great was the suffering among the very poor that all children under 12 were sold for food in order to keep others from starving. A boy or girl under 14 was not safe in the street. You could go in any shop and ask for steak—chops—or stew meat. Part of the naked body of a boy or girl would be brought out and just what you wanted cut from it. A boy or girls behind which is the sweetest part of the body and sold as veal cutlet brought the highest price."

So this man reportedly acquired a taste for human flesh, and when he finally returned to New York, he kidnapped two young boys. He bound and tortured them to make their "meat" more tender. Then he killed and ate them both.

"At that time," said the letter writer, "I was living at 409 E 100 St., near—right side. He told me so often how good Human flesh was I made up my mind to taste it. On Sunday June the 3—1928 I called on you at 406 W 15 St. Brought you pot cheese—strawberries. We had lunch. Grace sat in my lap and kissed me. I made up my mind to eat her. On the pretense of taking her to a party. You said Yes she could go. I took her to an empty house in Westchester I had already picked out. When we got there, I told her to remain outside. She picked wildflowers. I went upstairs and stripped all my clothes off. I knew if I did not I would get her blood on them. When all was ready I went to the window and called her. Then I hid in a closet until she was in the room. When she saw me all naked she began to cry and tried to run down the stairs. I grabbed her and she said she would tell her mamma. First I stripped her naked. How she did kick—bite and scratch. I choked her to death, then cut her in small pieces so I could take my meat to my rooms. Cook and eat it. How sweet and tender her little ass was roasted in the oven. It took me 9 days to eat her entire body. I did not fuck her tho I could of had I wished. She died a virgin."

The letter was unsigned. Why this person would send it so suddenly was a mystery, but that he knew small details confirmed his probable role in the crime. The handwriting was identical to that on the Western Union form that King had saved from the 1928 telegram Frank Howard had sent the Budds to announce his Sunday visit.

King looked over the stationery and the envelope in which the letter had arrived. He noticed an emblem over an address that had been obscured with scribbling. It was hexagonal in shape and bore the letters NYPCBA—the New York Private Chauffeurs' Benevolent Association, located in New York City at 627 Lexington Avenue. He called the organization's president, Arthur Ennis, and asked for an emergency meeting of the members. Then he assigned other detectives to start looking at their handwriting. None matched Frank Howard's. King asked the members whether someone might have taken any of the organization's stationery.

A young man named Lee Sicowski, who worked there part-time as a janitor, admitted to taking a few sheets and envelopes, although he hadn't used them. He gave King the address of his rooming house, but when King investigated, he was crushed to find no one on the register whose handwriting matched Howard's. He questioned Sicowski again, pressuring him, and then the janitor remembered that he had stayed briefly at another rooming house, at 200 East Fifty-second Street. He recalled that he had left four envelopes with the NYPCBA insignia on a shelf over his bed there, in room 7.

King made another trip, once again filled with hope. He spoke to the landlady, Mrs. Frieda Schneider, asking about Frank Howard, but she did not know the name. The man who had taken the room after Sicowski moved out, she said, was Albert H. Fish. In case "Howard" was an alias, King described the man who had come to the Budds' residence in 1928, and that description resembled Fish: an elderly man who had boarded with the Schneiders for about two months. In fact, Mrs. Schneider said, he had left only days ago, on November 11. King asked to see the register, and using the letter to Mrs. Budd, he compared the handwriting to Fish's signature. He thought it was a match.

Detective King believed he might be near the end of his long road. The best suspect he'd ever had was nearly within his grasp, as long as he could trace where the man had gone. Although the landlady had no forwarding address, she told King that Fish's son sent him regular checks from Georgia and he had mentioned to her that one more would be coming. King alerted postal inspectors to be watching for it and set up round-the-clock surveillance at the boardinghouse. He then tracked down the address Fish had given in the letter he had written to Delia, 409 East 100th Street, and learned that an elderly man had boarded there temporarily in the summer of 1928.

Fish had also used one of the envelopes to write to a man at the Holland Hotel, but no one by that name lived there, so the letter was returned to the chauffeurs' organization. They turned it over to King.

King knew that something had to break soon. They were just steps behind this offender. Then he learned that the check from Georgia had arrived at the Grand Central postal office on December 4. It was for twenty-five dollars.

"I knew he would return for the check," King told *Times* reporters, "and I kept a constant watch on the place."

But Fish did not come right away, and King worried over whether he had sniffed out the surveillance. It was a week before the short, elderly man finally arrived on December 13 to claim his check. Mrs. Schneider called King and then detained Fish until the detective could get there to arrest him. Although Fish attempted to defend himself with a razor blade, King was much more powerful. He twisted the blade out of the shriveled old man's hand and took him to headquarters for questioning.

This "undersized wizened house painter with restless eyes and thin, nervous hands," as reporters referred to him, danced around in denial before finally confessing in lurid detail. At no point did he display any emotion. He seemed to have expected to be caught.

Fish, aka Frank Howard, stated that he had originally meant to kidnap Edward, but the boy was larger than he had expected. While at the home the second time, he had spotted Grace and decided to kidnap her instead, so using the ruse of the party, he took her away. He'd brought a parcel of tools—the "implements of hell"—with him (a saw, butcher knife, and cleaver), wrapped in a piece of four-by-six-foot canvas. He stowed this bundle near a newsstand before going to the Budds', and retrieved them with Grace in tow. Together they boarded a train, bound for Westchester County, where he once had lived. He knew of an isolated, abandoned house there, called Wisteria Cottage, that he could use.

All along, Grace had believed she was going to a party. She had even run to fetch the canvas bag when Fish left it on the train seat. But once they arrived at the dilapidated, eight-room house, he prepared to kill her. He let her play in the yard while he undressed, and then called her to come in. In an upper room, he strangled her with his bare hands, which took about five minutes. He told one person he had ejaculated twice during her struggle. Then he cut her head off, draining the blood into a can. He tried to drink some of it, but it made him ill. He sawed the body in two and left the lower torso and legs behind the door. Taking the head outside, he covered it with paper. He also removed some of the flesh, which he packaged up and took home. This is what he claimed he had mixed with carrots and potatoes to make a stew which, in a state of constant sexual arousal that lasted over a week, he consumed. Four days after the murder, he returned to the cottage to get rid of the remains. He took the torso and head into the woods and threw them over a stone wall.

"It makes my conscience feel better now that you have found her," Fish said. "I'm glad I told everything."

The Budds, father and son, had no trouble identifying Fish as the man who had come to their home. Edward lunged for him and wanted to kill him. In the *Times*, Mrs. Budd was quoted as saying, "If only I could lay my hands on that man."

Fish agreed to take police to Worthington Woods, to show them the place where he had killed Grace and tossed her remains. Her skull was visible in the dirt behind the stone wall, where a rusty cleaver, saw, and the rest of her bones were found; further searching yielded more bones in the floor of the basement of Wisteria Cottage. The police suspected more outrages and sent the bones for analysis, but failed to pin anything further on Fish: the bones were from animals. However, the media, especially the tabloid papers, had no trouble associating "the ogre" with any number of missing or dead children.

So now he had committed crimes for which he could be tried in two different jurisdictions—kidnap in Manhattan and murder in Westchester. His previous police record had been for various charges of larceny and vagrancy, although he had also been suspected in the 1927 disappearance of other children, notably four-year-old Billy Gaffney. A witness had seen them together in the vicinity of the place Fish had worked as a painter. Once he was ensconced in a prison cell, various medical people came to speak with him, even as dental records finally confirmed that Grace Budd was in fact dead. King received a well-earned promotion.

The Most Depraved Killer

Dr. Frederic Wertham, a senior psychiatrist at Bellevue Hospital, disliked the distinction between medical and legal insanity (which allowed psychotic people to be deemed guilty). Educated in Europe and England, he came to the United States in 1922 and became an outspoken and controversial figure in the psychiatric world. He founded a counseling service for the disadvantaged in Harlem and attempted to have comic books regulated.

Wertham examined Fish for over twelve hours before his trial. Fish claimed he had been married four times (two of these women denied it), and that his first wife, after having six children, ran off with another man, taking all the furniture and leaving the children for him to raise. He loved them and did a passable job, despite his poverty, seeing them to adulthood. They knew he was eccentric, but did not guess the extent of his depravity. He claimed that his wife's departure, and her faithlessness, opened up the floodgates of his sexual troubles. He figured it no longer mattered what he did, so he allowed himself to express his desires without inhibition.

It was his sex life that seemed the focus of his pathology, developing in "unparalleled perversity." Wertham counted eighteen different paraphilias, from cannibalism to vampirism to necrophilia. Fish's perverse predilections apparently had begun when he was a child, arising from episodes of severe spanking by a female teacher at an orphanage. The act aroused him, as did watching her paddle the bare bottoms of other children. Thus his developing sexual desire centered on children, especially their buttocks. "I have always had the desire to inflict pain on others and to have others inflict pain on me," Fish told the psychiatrist. Finding things with which to hurt himself was uppermost in his mind, such as inserting the stems of roses into his urethra. He even tried sticking needles in his testicles, but found the pain too intense. "If only pain were not so painful!" he stated.

To Wertham, he described his method for seducing and bribing children, often going naked under his painter's overalls so he could get himself near them and then quickly remove his clothing. He used many different aliases and chose victims from the poorest classes, especially "colored children," because they were least likely to raise a fuss or instigate an investigation. Still, he'd been forced to leave town many times when adults heard rumors about him. He also enjoyed writing obscene letters to strangers, hoping someone with a similar inclination would respond. He sought a kindred soul with whom to inflict and receive physical abuse.

Believing himself at times to be Christ or Abraham, and obsessed with sin and atonement, Fish had made a practice of beating his naked body with spiked paddles and sticking lighted cotton balls, soaked in alcohol, inside his anus. "The trouble with pain," he said, "is you get tough and always have to invent something worse." He also believed he needed to kill children ("lambs") as a human sacrifice to please God and/or save their souls. Whatever he did he justified with quotes from the Bible. (He'd once been a church caretaker and had even painted angels on its ceiling.) Among the things he did to children were binding, castration, removing parts of the penis, anal assault, and beatings. He liked to hear them cry out in pain. He would then leave them, sometimes bound, for someone else to find. In fact, he had intended to castrate the Budd boy, and had even tried to castrate himself.

Wertham did not quite believe one of the claims Fish made, but could not deny its veracity. In his drive to feel pain, Fish actually shoved needles into the area of his groin between the anus and scrotum, and according to X-ray evidence, over two dozen were still there. It seemed astounding that a man would do this, but Fish had many different religious delusions that involved being a martyr. He claimed he had performed a similar act on some of his victims. In fact, he had roamed the country and estimated he had sexually abused over one hundred children in twenty-three states.

Wertham noted that Fish admired the work of a notorious killer from Germany, Fritz Haarmann, the "Hanover Vampire," who had been convicted in 1924. Fish had a number of clippings about the man in his possession, so Wertham looked into the case. Haarmann was a butcher with a low IQ and a record of commitments to a mental institution. During the 1920s, he would find wayward young men, invite them home for a meal, force sex on them, and then murder them. He teamed up with a male prostitute, Hans Graf, who could better lure the boys. Together, over a period of five years, they trapped and killed an estimated fifty young men. They were finally stopped after someone found skeletal remains in a canal. Since Haarmann lived nearby and had been arrested before, investigators searched his home. They found clothing from several missing boys, as well as bloodstains on the walls. Under arrest, Haarmann confessed.

He referred to his victims as "game" and described how he grabbed them as they dozed after a large meal or intense sexual activity, and while sodomizing them would chew into their necks until the head was nearly severed (or so reports said). As he tasted their blood, he achieved orgasm. He would then dissect bodies and remove the organs. He'd also cut the flesh from their bodies, eat some or store it under his bed, and sell the rest as butchered meat. He claimed the obsession was too great for him to overcome. Armed with grisly evidence for twenty-seven of the murders, investigators ensured Haarmann's conviction and he was sentenced to be beheaded. Moments before the blade fell, Haarmann announced that this was his "wedding day." It sounded exactly like Fish himself— the kindred soul for whom he was searching.

To Wertham's astonishment, Fish had been committed to Bellevue twice since the kidnapping, but no one had spotted his demented fantasies as a danger to anyone. He was also picked up in New York City several times for impairing the morals of a minor, yet no one connected him to the high-profile case of Grace Budd. To sum it up, Wertham wrote, "However you define the medical and legal borders of sanity, this certainly is beyond that border." By his estimate, Fish had killed as many as five children and had intended, or tried, to kill a few more. Wertham heard figures from officials as high as fifteen, but these numbers were not corroborated.

Fish entered a plea of not guilty by reason of insanity, and was transported to Westchester for a first-degree murder trial. At this time, Bruno Richard Hauptmann was being tried for the Lindbergh kidnapping, and was convicted. Once that trial concluded, the New York media turned its attention back to the Fish proceedings. They soon had the drama they were looking for, and the *Daily News* even ran a five-part series that was supposedly Fish's depraved memoir.

Just before the trial commenced in March 1935, Fish used a sharpened fish bone from a bowl of soup to cut his chest and abdomen. However, his injuries were not serious. The guards wondered if he was trying to commit suicide, but he refused to reveal his motive. Some who had talked with him believed he was merely searching for a way to inflict pain. Alienists had already examined Fish to support or refute his plea of insanity. Fish had expressed a fear of the electric chair. He did not believe he should die.

Grace's bones were brought into the courtroom, over defense attorney James Dempsey's vigorous objections, and Fish's confession was read. Dempsey was hoping to use the fact that Fish had been a painter all his life to introduce the notion that lead poisoning had affected him mentally, but thanks largely to Detective King's testimony, he would not get very far with this idea.

King testified that Fish had admitted that he knew what he did was wrong, and had a letter Fish had written to back it up. Still, Fish had also said that "God still has work for me to do." He'd told Dr. Wertham that if the murder was not justified, an angel would have stopped him, as one had done in the Bible before Abraham nearly slew Isaac. Wertham said that Fish had practiced "every known sexual abnormality," pointing to a history of abnormal personalities in his family line. Fish's mental problems had developed over the past decade, when he became obsessed with religion. He believed he could use murder to atone for his sins, and with Grace he'd had a premonition that if she lived, some future outrage would be perpetrated on her, so he had murdered her to save her. Mixed up with all this was his insistence that God had commanded him to sacrifice a virgin. Fish, Wertham said, had no rational control over his impulses. He was dangerous but insane and should be institutionalized in a psychiatric facility. In support of this, Fish's children testified about having witnessed his self-torture and exhibitionism, and Wertham added that to be aware of right and wrong, one had to feel it—a criterion that, if followed, would surely empty the prisons.

Among the more bizarre witnesses at the trial was a woman with whom Fish had maintained a perverse correspondence in which he expressed the hope that she would whip him. She had collected his letters and admitted that for the fee he offered, she would have done what he wanted. She turned her letters over to the police, who'd contrived to set a trap, but Fish never showed up. Still, the jurors got an unpleasant taste through this witness of Fish's sexual proclivities.

For the prosecution, Dr. Charles Lambert and Dr. James Vavasour, who had seen Fish for about three hours, refuted the testimony of Wertham and another psychiatrist for the defense, finding that Fish was legally sane. Despite delusions he might experience, he knew at the time of the crime that what he had done was wrong. However, his attorney, James Dempsey, insisted that Fish was a psychiatric phenomenon, stating that "no single case history report, either in legal or medical annals, contains a record of one individual who possessed all of these sexual abnormalities."

After deliberations, the jury agreed with the prosecution, convicting Fish of murder. (Some later said they agreed that he was insane but thought he should be executed nonetheless.) As Fish awaited his sentencing, he confessed to the murder of the Gaffney boy. He said he had cut the boy into pieces and roasted his buttocks with onions and carrots, consuming the tender meat over the course of four days. The police immediately went to question him in the presence of D.A. Walter Ferris, and he confessed, confirming that what he had written was true. He also admitted to the murder of the McDonnell boy on Staten Island. If he had not been interrupted, he would have dismembered him.

On June 17, 1935, Fish went to the electric chair at Sing Sing prison. "Fish entered the death chamber with his hands clasped in prayer." In just three minutes, he was dead. He offered no last words, although supposedly he had changed his attitude, seeing the experience as a supreme thrill—"the only one I haven't tried." Some people had feared that the needles in his body might short-circuit the machine, but that did not occur. At age sixty-five, Fish was the oldest man to be executed in the electric chair. Had not an observant detective paid attention to the subtle clues and persisted despite others losing hope, Fish might have gotten away to commit yet more unspeakable crimes.

America wasn't the only country producing intrepid investigators. One of the most intriguing true-crime tales that involved outstanding detection of a serial killer was in Poland, in the case of the spider.

Sources

Albert Fish, a documentary by John Borowski. Waterfront Productions. 2007.

Extensive coverage in the *New York Times,* June 5, 1928–January 17, 1936.

Ramsland, Katherine. *The Human Predator: A Historical Chronicle of Serial Murder and Forensic Investigation.* New York: Berkley, 2005.

Schechter, Harold. *Deranged: The Shocking True Story of America's Most Fiendish Killer.* New York: Pocket, 1990.

Wertham, Frederic. *The Show of Violence.* New York: Doubleday, 1949.

FOUR

LUCIAN STANIAK:
The Art of Darkness

It was Christmas Eve in 1966, the day before a national holiday in Poland. Three sailors boarded a train in Krakow bound for Warsaw. They had looked into cheap third-class tickets for seats among the general population of riders, but decided instead to reserve seats in a semiprivate compartment. They hoped for a little peace and quiet, although they knew that others might be in the compartment as well. Nevertheless, anyone paying the extra fee was probably going to be respectful. Happy to be free for the holiday and ready to relax, they were in high spirits when they opened the door of the compartment. But the first man inside stopped short in surprise.

The odor of blood was strong, and it didn't take long to determine its source. The other men crowded in to get a better look and at first were too shocked to react. On the floor in front of them was a bleeding young woman, slumped over and seemingly unconscious. They could see that she had just been attacked, as fresh blood oozed from her bare legs and dripped to the floor, and her leather skirt had been ripped into pieces.

The young men called to her, hoping for a response, but she did not move. They thought she was probably dead. This was no way to start a holiday, especially since this woman's killer was probably still close by.

The sailors moved fast to summon a conductor. Once he ascertained that the woman was indeed dead, he went to inform the engineer, who radioed ahead to the Warsaw police. They instructed him to proceed without a single stop, straight to Warsaw. If the killer was still on the train, they wanted to prevent him from getting off. They told the engineer they would be waiting at the station to search everyone as they disembarked. They did not know then that this murder was just one of many publicity stunts

An artist's rendering of Lucian Staniak, the "Red Spider" killer who terrorized Poland in the late 1960s. *Nathan MacDicken*

performed by a killer who sought both revenge and attention.

No Sudden Moves

It was a strained trip for everyone who knew the situation. First, they had a murder victim to deal with who was bleeding in a compartment. Second, without revealing the details, they would have to explain to those people expecting to disembark in towns prior to Warsaw that they could not do so. That would be difficult on Christmas Eve. And third, every passenger older than a child was a suspect, and the conductors would have to check each and every one before that person left the train, hoping to control the process and ensure that the killer did not have some elusive escape plan. Surely, he realized that in a semiprivate compartment the body would be quickly discovered and just as surely he would have to get away. When the train failed to stop at its first destination, he'd realize they were hoping to trap him, although it was also true that he could have slipped away before the train had even left the last station. They had to take every precaution.

As the train came to a stop at the busy station in Warsaw, with many families waiting to see the faces of loved ones traveling that night to spend the holiday with them, detectives immediately boarded and told everyone to remain seated until his or her papers were checked. As they questioned each passenger, they recorded all names and looked for evidence of blood on hands or clothing, as well as a concealed weapon. The passengers talked among themselves with annoyance, anger, or curiosity as rumors flew as to what this annoying delay was all about. They wanted to get off the train and get on with their holiday. But the police were careful to check every person thoroughly, aware that any of them could be the killer. In addition, if they came upon him, he might pull a gun, take a hostage, or do any number of things that would put others in danger. They were not looking forward to dealing with a cornered killer.

As the investigators methodically went through their task, another team handled an analysis of the crime scene and the body. They talked with the sailors who had found the woman and soon cleared them of any wrongdoing. There was plenty of blood in the compartment but no weapon and no clear indication of who had committed the murder. In such a public place, hair, fibers, and fingerprints could have come from any number of passengers over the past weeks. It seemed a hopeless task. They did not even know who the victim was.

They finally removed the body to a morgue for identification and a determination of how this unfortunate young woman had died. She appeared to be only a girl, not yet out of her teens, and she'd clearly been stabbed multiple times. Her leather miniskirt had been cut many times, as had her legs and lower abdomen. However, above the waist, there was no sign of assault. The killer appeared to have been some sort of deranged sex fiend, and the energy involved in such a frenzy suggested that he was filled with a great deal of anger. It could have been a crime of passion committed by someone who knew the young woman, but there was no way to know. Investigators could only hope it was a contained situation and not the work of some maniac who might be targeting others. What they did not yet know was that this victim was not the perpetrator's first.

As the police watched the last people leave the train and move on, their worst fears were realized: the killer had gotten away. Everyone had checked out and no one had seemed suspicious. The officers surmised from the public nature of this crime that the brutal murder had been planned for effect and the killer had committed it quickly and left. It seemed he had never meant to ride the train.

Then searchers found an item on the floor of the mail car. Dropped through the slot was a note addressed to *Zycie Warsawy,* a newspaper in Warsaw. The police carefully opened it and saw thin, elegant handwriting in red ink that conveyed a simple message: "I have done it again." While they did not know if the note and murder were connected, they rushed it to a crime lab—for fingerprints, ink analysis, paper evaluation, and handwriting identification. In the event that they caught someone, whatever they learned from this process could assist them with evidence. They were also hopeful that a lead could be developed.

Further investigation revealed that the victim was a seventeen-year-old girl from Krakow named Janina Kozielska. At first, the police believed she was married, because the compartment had been reserved by a man,

Stanislav Kosielski (his last name having a slightly different spelling than hers). He had called to reserve the tickets, saying his wife would pick them up. She did so, paying
cash. The conductor recalled showing this young woman
to the train compartment, but no one was with her. She
had told him her husband would arrive soon and seemed
excited. In fact, the man did come and the same conductor had shown him to the compartment, but nothing
about either of them stood out, so the conductor, who
processed a lot of people every day, had a difficult time
recalling much about him. In addition, he'd heard nothing inside the compartment to suggest an attack of such
brutal intensity. Surely the girl had screamed at some
point, but no one reported having heard anything.

Still, it was apparent that the unfortunate victim had
been familiar with her killer, possibly was even his lover,
although from reports soon offered by her shocked family,
it was clear she was not his wife. Janina was not married
at all. She had merely pretended to be, which signaled
familiarity with this man, as well as a willingness to travel
with him in relative privacy and keep the liaison secret.
Thus her parents could offer no name or description of
anyone Janina knew who might be responsible for her
death. They had not even known that she was involved
with anyone. However, they did reveal one key piece of
information that moved the investigation closer to
resolution.

As detectives questioned Janina's parents, they learned
that her sister, fourteen-year-old Aniela, had also been
murdered. Two years earlier in Warsaw, Aniela was

attacked in a similar manner. These grieving parents had lost both daughters to murder, and it seemed impossible that the killings were unrelated. The police knew they would have to check out all family acquaintances, because the circumstances pointed to someone who had known both girls. They also indicated that this person had not been as careful as initially surmised. Victimizing sisters would have left a trail and possible witnesses that could narrow the pool of suspects.

Red Ink

Major Ciznek, the lead investigator of the Warsaw Homicide Squad, believed that the girls had been acquainted with the same maniacal killer and that he had ingratiated himself somehow with both, one at a time, with the intent of slaughtering them. He was too careful to be considered psychotic. Ciznek questioned the parents in the hope of finding a viable suspect among the acquaintances of both girls, but they could think of no one. Of course, their neighbors would have to be checked out, along with any known sex offenders from the area who might have spotted the girls. But there was one item that offered hope: the red-lettered note found on the train.

The police had seen such notes before, written and delivered on the eve of major holidays, around the time of the murders of other young women. The "Red Spider," as the press had dubbed him, seemed to have struck again, just as he'd boasted in the note. But this time, the police had some leverage. They believed he had made a crucial error and they reviewed the cases that seemed to be linked.

The first message in red ink had arrived on July 4, 1964, at the office of Marion Starzynski, editor of the Warsaw newspaper *Prezeglad Polityczny*. "There is no happiness without tears," it said, "no life without death." But it was the last line of this note that sent a chill of alarm through those who read it. "Beware! I am going to make you cry."

There was no return address, no signature, and no way to know who had sent it. But it was written in longhand, using bright red ink. The letters were thin and uneven, suggesting that it had been written in blood, although it had not dried to the dark brown color or consistency of actual blood. This killer wanted to create a dramatic effect.

Starzynski wondered if the threat was directed at him. Given the visibility of a newspaper editor, one never knew. Sometimes a person just sought publicity and looked to the newspapers; other times a reader might be angry at an item or comment in the paper and hold the editor accountable. Since these correspondents were not personal enemies, it was difficult to identify them, and Starzynski could think of no one who might have sent such a missive, even as a joke. It worried him. Instead of ignoring the ominous message, he took it to the police. They recorded the incident, but were just as helpless as the editor in determining the identity of the author.

Nothing happened in the days that followed, and on July 22, Warsaw celebrated the anniversary of its liberation from Nazi occupation. People took to the streets to watch the celebratory parades. The note was more or less forgotten. But on that day in Olsztyn, a town two hours north of the capital by train, a young woman died. Danka Maciejowitz, seventeen, had gone out to watch a parade in the city streets, saying good-bye to her parents and letting them know she would be back in a few hours. But she did not return. Her worried parents went searching for her and finally went home. She was still not there. It was not like her to be irresponsible, so they grew more concerned and filed a police report. The following day, officers sadly informed them of the reason for Danka's absence.

A gardener tending the grounds of the Park of Polish Heroes came across the nude corpse of a blond adolescent girl. She had been stabbed several times in the abdomen and had bled freely onto the ground before she was shoved under some shrubbery. She was well hidden, and no one had seen her all night. The gardener had informed the police.

They recalled the reports from the parents of Danka Maciejowitz and made the difficult trek to their home to get an identification. The father confirmed his daughter's identity. Further examination revealed that she had been raped as well as stabbed and disemboweled. This was a devastating crime for the small town, but the crime scene yielded no viable leads. Nor did further questioning. The girl had no known enemies or potentially brutal admirers, so investigators assumed that, given the festivities of the day before, some predator had spotted her walking alone and taken advantage. As the police canvassed the area to look for witnesses, another letter arrived at the Warsaw newspaper office. "I picked a juicy flower in Olsztyn," it said, "and I shall do it again somewhere else, for there is no holiday without a funeral."

This letter, too, was turned over to the police, and they contacted officials in Olsztyn. The implication was chilling: a random killer had sent a warning, traveled to this town, and made good on his threat, striking down a random victim. He'd even taken the time to use a method of communication that would produce an eerie effect, which suggested that he was not impulsive. There was small probability that he could be linked to the victim. He'd simply struck and gotten away. His apparent enjoyment of the act and his bragging afterward indicated he would do it again.

The Investigation

With two letters clearly tied to a horrendous crime and the threat of another one, it was time to start a detailed forensic analysis. Questioned document analysis had achieved some status in prior decades, as had handwriting analysis. Experts could examine the paper on which a note had been written and the type of ink used, and if they were able to acquire examples of handwriting from suspects, they could make comparisons and ascertain if certain features of the handwriting were sufficiently similar to identify the note sender. If so, the police could do a more in-depth investigation to tie the notes to the suspect in other ways. It was painstaking work, and not altogether definitive, but certainly better than nothing.

The examination of questioned documents includes any kind of crime that involves writing, writing implements, and a writing surface. Examiners might look at impressions left on the surface of a tablet or do a chemical analysis of the surface itself. First, the investigators had to decide if the document was authentic, and it certainly seemed so. Second, they hoped to learn something about the author. Third, they sought to figure out where it had been mailed. Since there had been no ransom demands or attempts at extortion, the last task was going to be the most difficult. The letters and accompanying behavior seemed the work of a demented individual hoping to taunt the police and community from afar.

Investigators analyzed the ink, because it seemed to be blood or a bloodlike simulation. Modern ink can be one of four basic types: iron salts in a suspension of gallic acid, with dyes; carbon particles suspended in gum arabic; synthetic dyes with a range of polymers and acids; and synthetic dyes or pigments in a range of solvents and additives. The questioned ink is tested through a highly technical process called microspectrophotometry, to determine the absorption spectrum, or through thin-layer chromatography, to reveal the exact chemical composition. It can then be compared on a precise level to the database of ink profiles at most central investigative agencies. Yet the ink in these letters was unusual. If it was actual blood or a blood mixture, technicians could do a serological analysis to obtain the blood type and the more individualizing protein profiles. However, the writing fluid turned out to be neither blood nor ink. It was turpentine-thinned paint, such as might be used in a print shop. That discovery helped to narrow leads, although not in a way that was useful just then.

The next item to examine would be the type of paper used, and the paper on which the letters had been written proved to be somewhat ordinary, so that analysis offered no clues. It would help only if the same type of paper was found in the killer's possession or at his workplace. Paper is classified by the materials in its composition, differing according to additives, watermarks, and surface treatments. Specialists can determine the date when a particular type of paper was introduced on the market. Paper was considered to be generic rather than unique evidence, so it proved nothing outside the context of other pieces of evidence, but taken with other circumstances, it could help support a case.

While sophisticated equipment is used for special tests, the basic tools for comparing a questioned document with a known exemplar (we know that this person scripted this piece of writing) are a magnifying lens, microscope, camera with filters, and good lighting. Since the letter writer had not used a typewriter or printer, identification via distinct machine signatures was irrelevant.

The handwriting style of these red-lettered notes was certainly individualizing, as well as cryptic, but investigators knew they would need a suspect and samples of his handwriting before they could fully exploit it. They also had experts examine the content of the notes, which suggested the author's seemingly angry frame of mind. There appeared to be no codes or cryptic references, and content analysis, which utilizes reading sources that match phrasing, had not yet been developed as an investigative tool at the time of this case. Even if it had, there was too little content available from these brief communications to do a thorough evaluation. The police knew they would have to wait for more such letters before they could develop proper leads, but getting more notes meant that someone else might also die. They did not use graphology—the extrapolation of personality traits from handwriting—because contrary to popular belief, it is not a science.

Handwriting experts study writing samples to try to determine if two (or more) documents were written by the same person and thereby to identify the known author of one sample with the unknown author of a similar one. The same odd characteristics are expected to show up across samples originating with the same person—even when he tries to disguise his writing. Analysts look at both class characteristics, which derive from the general writing system learned, and individual characteristics, which are specific to the way a person's distinctive handwriting style develops. It's the latter that plays the most important part in forensic investigation. The best exemplars will contain some of the same words or phrases as the questioned document, and thus some of the same ways of forming letters.

Most people learn to write by imitating a certain style, usually the Palmer or Zaner-Bloser method, but as they develop their own style, idiosyncrasies appear in the way they form and connect (or not) the letters. This is influenced by education, artistic ability, physiological development, and sometimes just by a specific stylistic preference. Many experts insist that no two people write alike, and the fine nuances that make the difference are identifiable to those with a great deal of experience in examining handwriting. Over time, a person's style crystallizes, showing only slight variations over the years, such that letters she wrote while in her twenties could be matched to letters she wrote thirty years later.

The goal is to collect and compare samples that have been written across fairly tight time periods. Known exemplars are the primary source, but if they are not sufficient in number for a thorough examination, the suspected author would be asked to provide more. The procedure is to sit the subject at a table where there will be no distractions. The text to be written is dictated, keeping in mind not to "lead" the subject into how to form letters or spell certain words. The subject should use materials similar to those of the document and the dictated text should match some part of that document.

While questioned document examination often comes under fire in the courtroom for subjective interpretation, rigorous training, certification, and other "objectifying" measures have won the discipline more respect. In the case of this mysterious author, the Red Spider, it would require only a few circumstances to identify him: possession of the red paint and a thinner, the same type of thin scrawl, the right kind of implement to have written the letters, the same type of paper, and the opportunity to have written these missives in privacy. And, of course, encounters with the victims and a motive to murder.

Anger Rendered in Art

Since the messages had been written with paint, the police believed the killer was employed in some manner that placed him near art supplies or other businesses related to painting, or that he'd purchased the paint specifically to make his letters look like blood. It wasn't much, but this fact provided a few clues that might assist if other items identified a suspect. By itself, it offered little to the investigation.

Several months passed and the murder went unsolved. No more notes arrived and no more bodies that had been similarly attacked turned up. Perhaps it had been a random incident. Marion Starzynski watched the mail, afraid of finding another crimson piece of correspondence. But none arrived.

Then in January 1965, a student parade was planned in Warsaw. Sixteen-year-old Anuita Kaliniak had been selected to lead it, and she proudly posed for a photograph for the local newspaper, the *Warsawy*. She was from Praga, a suburb in Warsaw's eastern zone. The parade route was quite a distance from her home, and having no transportation, she had to walk there. Still, it was a big day for her, so nothing was going to keep her from being part of this celebratory event. She arrived on time, despite her long walk, and led the parade that day, January 17. By the end of the afternoon, Anuita was exhausted. Rather than walk all the way home, she hitchhiked. A local deliveryman driving a truck picked her up. Anuita never made it home.

Her family, proud of her accomplishment, began to grow concerned as the winter day became darker and colder. They went out along the route their daughter would have taken, hoping to meet her and to assure themselves of her safety. But no matter where they looked or to whom they spoke among her friends, no one had seen Anuita since the parade. Her parents located the truck driver who had picked her up and he said he'd dropped her off two blocks from where she lived. At that time, he stated, she had seemed happy but tired. He watched her walk away but had seen no one with her. She had simply disappeared. Unbeknownst to anyone, she had met the Red Spider and had been murdered.

Her body might never have been found had not her killer sent directions in his characteristic style. Another letter arrived the day after the schoolgirl's disappearance, directing searchers to the basement of a leather factory across the street from her home. She had been within sight of it when he'd grabbed her, killing her and dragging her body into the factory through a sidewalk grate to finish his ritual. He strangled Anuita with a wire and rammed a six-inch metal spike into her vagina. Again, it was an act of sexualized anger. Perhaps he had seen her photo in the paper, learned where she lived, and waited. Or perhaps he had simply been in the neighborhood, had spotted her alone, and jumped. No one knew and he hadn't spelled it out.

This third letter possessed the same characteristics as the first two, so now the police were aware that they were dealing with a vicious predator who enjoyed mutilating young women. He was clever and prepared, because once again he left no clues behind and managed to accomplish his foul business close to the girl's home, in a residential community, without being seen.

Even so, he was careful not to make the mistake of attacking again too quickly. The people and officials of Warsaw relaxed their guard somewhat as winter passed into spring and then summer with no further incidents and no more scraggly letters. They hoped that perhaps the Red Spider had desisted or been caught and jailed for something else. They were too optimistic.

The Spider's Web

It was All Saints' Day, November 1, before the schoolgirl killer targeted another victim, but it was fairly far from Warsaw, over 150 miles away, in Pozna. This victim was a working girl, a blond receptionist named Janka Popiel-ski. Apparently she had gone to the freight terminal look-ing for a ride to another village so she could visit her boyfriend. While there, she was attacked. Dragged behind some packing crates, she was raped and then repeatedly stabbed with a screwdriver. The killer left the clothing on her upper torso, but absconded with the rest or threw it away. He then placed the body inside a crate and left the area. Local workers found the body right away and called the police. Detectives who examined the scene suspected that a man associated with the terminal had exploited the opportunity, grabbing a weapon of convenience, so they questioned every employee, but found no evidence to link anyone to the crime.

The next step was to investigate the trains for roving killers. Whoever had mutilated this woman would have blood on his clothing, and they believed if they acted quickly, they could apprehend him. They moved from one car to another, yet despite this logical plan of action, they were unable to detain anyone even remotely suspicious. The killer had successfully slipped away.

Even so, if this was the work of the Red Spider, police knew, he'd grown careless. The victim had been discovered quickly and the proximity of the workers meant he could have been caught in the act. It was possible that he'd grown more arrogant or more compulsive. Either way, he would probably make another mistake.

The police awaited his familiar message, and sure enough, on November 2, it arrived at the newspaper office in Pozna. Its single statement was a quote from a 1948 novel about post–World War II Poland, *Popil i*, by Jerzy Andrzejewski: "Only tears of sorrow can wash out the stain of shame; only pangs of suffering can blot out the fires of lust."

While the enigmatic correspondent did not take direct credit for the murder, it was clear from the location and the extreme mutilation involved in this latest lust crime that he had killed again. Officials worried about the fact that the sites of his murders were so widely dispersed; this made it difficult to anticipate his next move. But they did have one more clue: the killer was apparently a literate person who read novels and who might be political. That aligned him more with the cultural crowd—and art—than to a mere purchaser of red paint. The Red Spider appeared to be intelligent and crafty, and was probably educated. Still, that did not get the investigators any closer to solving this terrible mystery or to ensuring the safety of the young women he targeted.

He did seem to lay low for six months between each killing, so officials anticipated that there would be no more violated female corpses for a while. Even so, as Christmas approached, given the pattern of murders around holiday times, the police in Warsaw were extra watchful. To everyone's relief, the winter season of 1965 passed without an incident that spoke of the Warsaw Ripper. Yet he was not finished.

May 1 was a major holiday for the Communist Party. It was also Labor Day, a time to honor the country's workers. Once again, parades filled the streets and people celebrated. As evening closed in, a prowler went about the streets of Zoliborz, in northern Warsaw. He looked for young females alone and he found one: Marysia Galazka, seventeen, was in the yard of her own home, looking for her cat. He probably heard her calling the cat's name. The predator leaped out at her, muffling her screams and dragging her into a toolshed, where he raped her. Then he used a knife to dig into her abdomen, and as she died, he ripped through her entrails and removed them, leaving her intestines lying across her thighs. He fled just before the girl's father came out looking for her. When he saw her brutalized body, he ran inside and called the police, but the killer was long gone.

Now an organized task force was required. The police had little doubt that the same offender had committed this fourth murder. In fact, Major Ciznek, who led the investigation, decided to examine similar crimes in a wider area. Just because a murder had not been followed by a gruesome red-lettered note did not mean that the marauder had not committed it. In Ciznek's search around the country over the past several years, he'd pinpointed more than a dozen murders of young women, all of which shared some similarities with the four unsolved killings he was investigating. Since there was no central reporting facility in Poland, these murders had not been linked. He now marked them all on a map to look for patterns. Clearly, the killer, if he was responsible for even a few of them, got around. He might be driving, but it seemed more likely that he was using public transportation.

Indeed, the towns in which murders had occurred were linked by rail lines to Krakow and to Katowice. Major Ciznek wondered if the killer might be from one of these two cities, and had been careful not to attack anyone in his own neighborhood. It would be easy enough to board a train and go to another town to seek victims, and then get on another train to return home. Ciznek gave this angle a lot of thought. Since most of the murders were south of Warsaw, he surmised that Katowice was the more likely area of residence.

It was around this time that the killer made his most egregious error to date, on Christmas Eve in 1966, taking the life of the sister of an earlier victim and linking himself to the mutilation with a note. This was the victim the sailors had discovered.

The Case Breaks

The parents of the murdered sisters told police that both girls had worked as models for artists in Krakow and were members of the Art Lovers Club there. That fit with the type of person the police were seeking. They decided to examine the list of male members of this club, as well as that of the School of Plastic Arts, where the girls had modeled.

Yet even this was no easy task. The membership numbered over one hundred and many of the male members were respected professionals. That did not excuse them, but it made the investigation a bit trickier. Going painstakingly through these lists, investigators learned about the members' professions, schedules, family lives, and areas of residence. They also looked at whether or not a member was also an artist, and what kinds of work he produced. Specifically, they were looking for someone who used the same type of red paint that had been thinned down to write the letters.

One viable suspect was a young man named Lucian Staniak. He lived in Katowice, near the train line, and he worked as a translator for a government printing house, so he was educated. Twenty-six years old, he possessed a ticket for unlimited travel that allowed him to go anywhere in the country on the trains without paying extra fees. He seemed to be a good fit.

Ciznek went to the art club and ordered the manager to open Staniak's locker, where he kept his painting supplies. He hit pay dirt. While he saw knives used for mixing and placing paint on canvas, it did not require another tedious chemical analysis to see a glaring clue that placed Staniak squarely in the category of "best suspect." He liked red paint, but more to the point, his work was gruesome and bizarre. One painting, called *The Circle of Life*, showed a number of disturbing death scenes: a cow ate a flower and was then eaten by a wolf, which was shot by a hunter. A woman driving a car ran over the hunter, and she died at the hand of a mutilating sex murderer. Her abdomen was sliced open, just like all the Red Spider victims, and as she decomposed, flowers sprang up through her remains to complete the cycle of life and death.

The artistically rendered corpse was sufficient cause, on that last day of January in 1967, to bring Staniak in for interrogation. Ciznek dispatched several officers to perform this task, feeling optimistic that at last he had a very good lead. However, to his dismay, Staniak was not at home. What Ciznek did not know was that Staniak was in another town, prowling for a victim. Before the police even knocked on his door, another girl was dead.

Staniak had boarded a train that very morning and had gotten out in Lodz, a city that had a film institute. There he looked around, spotted eighteen-year-old Bozhena Raczkiewicz, and using his charm, made her acquaintance. That evening, they went together to the railway station and settled inside a shelter, where they drank some vodka and talked about art. When he sensed that the coast was clear, Staniak used the liquor bottle to knock the girl unconscious and proceeded to use his artist's knife to cut through her skirt and panties. He raped her and kept stabbing her lower torso until he exhausted his driving need to see blood and gore. Then he fled. But he'd made yet another mistake.

It's one thing to interpret a painting as a clue to a killer's MO; it's quite another to have his fingerprints on a weapon used in a murder. Staniak had inadvertently left one on the vodka bottle. This time, he'd not been so clever.

Yet he did not go home from Lodz until the following morning. Detectives waited throughout the night, and those who were at the train station spotted him when he disembarked and took him into custody. He was placed at once into an interrogation room.

It did not take long to get a confession. Staniak was apparently only too glad to take credit for the unsolved murders, and in fact claimed that he had killed as many as twenty women—just as Ciznek had surmised. He also supplied a rather bizarre motive.

In 1964, he told the police, a young blond woman was driving her car too fast on an ice-covered street. She struck his parents as they crossed the street, killing them. Although the woman was charged with reckless driving, she was acquitted. Staniak had been incensed by this lack of justice. She had taken away his entire family, but had paid no price for it. He wanted to kill her, but he knew the police would suspect him, so he had developed another plan to get his revenge. He would kill a substitute for this woman. On several occasions, when he spotted a young woman who resembled the drunk driver, he followed her and killed her. That would appease his rage for a while. But then he discovered that he enjoyed stalking and killing, so he continued doing it whenever the opportunity arose. The murder on the train, he confessed, had been committed merely because he'd been feeling neglected by the newspapers and wanted more publicity.

Despite his detailed confession, the physical evidence corroborated only six of the murders, so that's what the authorities charged him with. He was convicted of them all and given a death sentence. However, psychiatrists stated that their analysis had determined that Staniak was psychotic and had thus been insane at the time of the murders, unaware of what he had done. A judge commuted his death sentence to life in a psychiatric institution in Katowice. The victims' families were outraged, but the sentence was final.

In this case, an investigator had been sufficiently open-minded to see the value of a work of art as a psychological revelation. Because he had put together a thorough analysis of the killer's movements, he went the step further to apprehend the suspect. In only two decades, another alert cop would think outside the box during an investigation and thereby initiate events that would forever alter crime-scene analysis and suspect identification.

Sources

Lane, Brian, and Wilfred Gregg. *The Encyclopedia of Serial Killers.* New York: Berkley, 1995.

Miller, Hugh. *Proclaimed in Blood: True Crimes Solved by Forensic Science*. London: Headline, 1995.

Newton, Michael. *The Encyclopedia of Serial Killers*. Second edition. New York: Checkmark Books, 2006.

Nickell, Joe, and John Fischer. *Crime Science: Methods of Forensic Detection*. Lexington, KY: The University Press of Kentucky, 1999.

Owen, David. *Hidden Evidence: Forty True Crimes and How Forensic Science Helped Solve Them*. Buffalo, NY: Firefly Books, 2000.

Saferstein, Richard. *Criminalistics: An Introduction to Forensic Science*. Sixth edition. Englewood Cliffs, NJ: Prentice Hall, 1995.

Wilson, Colin, and Damon Wilson. *The Killers Among Us: Motives Behind Their Madness*. New York: Warner, 1995.

FIVE

COLIN PITCHFORK:
First DNA Sweep

When friends saw Lynda Mann at school on November 21, 1983, she seemed her usual bubbly self. The English village of Narborough, in Leicestershire County, was a place where people knew one another, thanks to a couple of churches, shops, and pubs, and residents were aware of small incidents worthy of gossip. The drama of crime, however, was generally absent. That was about to change.

Directly after school, Lynda walked over to a neighbor's house to babysit. She often did this to make extra money to buy clothes. She hoped one day to be a world traveler, and those who knew her were confident that she would accomplish whatever she decided to do.

Around six forty-five that evening, Lynda went to do another round of babysitting, but learned she would not be needed, so she set out to see her best friend, Karen

Blackwell. She intended to visit one more friend that day, Caroline, to retrieve a borrowed item, so she left Karen's shortly after seven. It was cold that night, but Lynda liked to keep her affairs in order and she did not mind the weather. The house in Enderby was a fifteen-minute walk away. Caroline would recall that Lynda was in and out quickly, before seven-thirty. From there, she headed for a wooded path on the west side of town known as the Black Pad. It was fenced along one side because it lay near the grounds of a psychiatric hospital. This was the quickest way for her to get home. Somewhere along this path, she met a man who killed her and left her body in the dark, under the full moon.

No one started to search for her until well into the night. Lynda's parents had gone out to a social club for the evening, and then a pub, so they did not realize their daughter was missing until they came home about 1:30 A.M. They learned from Lynda's sister Susan that Lynda was

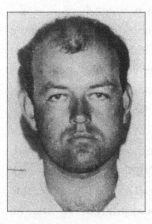

British killer Colin Pitchfork, the first man to be arrested using DNA evidence.

not home. She had promised to be there by ten and it was now three and a half hours later.

Eddie Eastwood, Lynda's stepfather, notified the police and went out to visit teenage hangouts and then walk through the neighborhood. He even trudged along the moonlit Black Pad, unaware that he passed within a few yards of Lynda's body. He also did not realize that once her murder was discovered, it would become part of a case that would grab the attention of the entire world. A scientist was busy at work on this day, unaware of his future involvement, as was the detective who would initiate one of the most important moves in the history of criminal investigation.

The Village Murders

It was too late to call her friends, but when it became increasingly clear that Lynda was nowhere nearby and had left no messages to explain her absence, her family grew frantic. City folk moved to Narborough because it was considered a safe village, and no one wanted to believe the girl had come to serious harm, but it wasn't like Lynda to be irresponsible. The fifteen-year-old was only five-foot-two and just over 112 pounds. If someone did accost her in the dark, she'd have had little defense.

The police searched as best they could, but it was not until dawn that Lynda's whereabouts were ascertained. An employee of the psychiatric hospital on his way to work came across Lynda's body at 7:20 A.M., lying on the side of the path close to the hospital grounds. At first, he thought it was a mannequin, but then realized it was a girl, partially naked. He flagged down a car, and the man, an ambulance driver for the hospital, returned with him to look at the body. The girl's jeans, shoes, and tights had been rolled up and cast aside. Her legs were extended outward and she lay partially on her side on the frost-covered grass. A scarf still covered her neck, but her jacket was pulled up and her nose bloodied. Her right leg covered a piece of wood about three feet long—possibly used to bludgeon her.

The men called in the Leicestershire constables, who were inexperienced with murder, never having received a summons for such a crime from Narborough or any other village close by. Others had to take over. The detective chief superintendent from the Criminal Investigation Division was David Baker, forty-seven, who had been a

Sir Alec Jeffreys, the British molecular biologist, whose work led to Pitchfork's apprehension—and to the exoneration of a man who had falsely confessed to Pitchfork's crimes. *Reproduced with permission from Sir Alec Jeffreys*

police officer for over a quarter of a century. He arrived at the scene and quickly notified a Home Office pathologist. A team of officers arrived with bloodhounds, while others searched for clues in the area—more clothing, a dropped item, a footprint—anything that might assist in developing a lead. Lynda's stepfather, brought to the scene, identified her.

It appeared that Lynda had been sexually violated before being killed. Her body was removed to the morgue for an autopsy, where the pathologist found that the slender girl had died from strangulation. There were bruises and scratches to her face that indicated she had been punched hard; there were also bruises on her chest, probably caused by the piece of wood. There was no indication that she had put up a fight, so it was possible she had been knocked unconscious, at least initially. However, it appeared that she had removed her shoes, probably under duress. No one would have done this in the cold. Semen stains in her pubic hair attested to an attempt at rape, which had not been completed before emission, although some penetration had occurred. Semen was recovered for antigen blood-type analysis. The rapist proved to be a secretor, with blood type A, which belonged to approximately one in ten adult males in the country. Eddie Eastwood was not among them.

Suspicion fell on hospital inmates, but the hospital assured the community that no one had left the building that night. There were no other leads, so the case went cold.

Inspector Derek Pearce, thirty-three, was known as the smartest detective in the area, and he received the assignment to head the Lynda Mann murder squad. While many officers were optimistic about a quick solution, as the months rolled by, this "squad" would grow to well over one hundred members.

In Narborough, residents stopped going out at night and demanded that the Black Pad be better protected. The county should consider spending the money to light it, they argued, because several other assaults had occurred there. Using a new and confusing computer system, the police looked up records of men convicted of criminal assaults, while other officers knocked on the doors of every residence in the village to ask questions. They wanted to know all the places Lynda had frequented, because at any of these she might have attracted the attention of a man who then followed her. On the other hand, it could have been a completely random attack, wrong time and wrong place, by a stranger. To make matters worse, some ten thousand people had been in and out of the psychiatric hospital, and many were possible suspects. In addition, the police had to distinguish good leads from bad and identify people merely seeking to associate themselves with the notorious case.

The *Leicester Mercury* kept track of all reports, which included sightings on the night of the murder of young men running, but little came of it, aside from more calls with more leads that went nowhere. By April 1984, the murder squad had been reduced to only eight investigators, and soon there were just two. Blood tests given to all suspects had turned up negative, and psychics who'd visited the family provided only vague ideas. All of them warned that this man would kill again, but the police were already aware of that possibility.

Nearly two years later, in a village just east of Narborough, a sixteen-year-old hairdresser went home one night, crossing an unlit footbridge, and a man accosted her, forcing her to give him oral sex. She told a friend the next day, who alerted the police, but they could not apprehend the perpetrator. They could only wait for the next strike, which was sure to come.

Second Victim

The village of Enderby was connected to Narborough by a shortcut called Green Lane, or Ten Pound Lane. On July 31, 1986, Dawn Ashworth, fifteen, took this lane to visit friends in Narborough. Her mother had told her to be home by 7 P.M., but she did not arrive. The family went looking for her, asking her friends what they knew and walking along both the Black Pad and Ten Pound Lane. Several witnesses had seen Dawn at various times that afternoon as she went to the homes of two friends. She had gone back to Enderby at twenty minutes to five and had been spotted going through the wooden gate to the footpath.

By late evening, Dawn's parents phoned the police. Lynda Mann was on everyone's mind. There was little they could do in the dark, but the next morning, swarms of police searched the area with tracker dogs. After hours of searching, they found nothing. The Ashworths received several phone calls in which the caller refused to talk, but by the end of that day they still did not know the whereabouts of their daughter. They feared the worst.

On the second day of the search, August 2, more than sixty police officers joined in. They picked up a blue denim jacket, similar to the one Dawn had been wearing when last seen. It was near a footbridge not far from Ten Pound Lane. By noon, they had found a clump of weeds and bushes in a field. From this protruded the fingers of a hand. They knew they had found the body of Dawn Ashworth. The footpath killer had struck again.

Like Lynda, Dawn had been stripped from the waist down, although her white shoes were still on her feet. She lay on her left side, with her knees pulled up, and blood trickled from her vagina. From scratches on her body it appeared that she had been dragged to this area, through thorns and nettles. Flies had already deposited eggs in her nostrils and ears. The autopsy found that Dawn had been penetrated vaginally and anally, at or near death, and had died from manual strangulation. She had been hit, and her mouth had been roughly held, possibly to prevent her from screaming.

No one doubted that the two sex-murder cases were linked to a single perpetrator. Dawn's body was barely half a mile from where Lynda had been attacked. Semen removed from the bodies revealed the same blood type. Since Dawn appeared to have struggled a little, newspaper reports asked the public to watch for a man with a fresh scratch. More than two hundred police officers were assigned to this task force.

A local psychiatrist stated that the offender was more likely to be a local man whom no one would suspect than a patient from the hospital. "He may be regarded by his family as a quiet, even timid man." He probably kept tight control over his lust, so people who knew him would be unaware of it. However, once accomplished, the crime would become part of an entertaining fantasy, triggering a future episode. Even with just two murders, he could be viewed as a serial killer, because it was unlikely that, unless caught, he would stop.

An officer learned that a seventeen-year-old kitchen porter from the hospital had been seen loitering in the area of Ten Pound Lane, sitting on his motorcycle, just after the police had taped it off as a potential crime scene. He appeared to watch the activity with great interest, so he became a primary suspect.

Confession

This young man, R.B., approached an officer to say that he had seen Dawn walking toward the gate on Thursday evening. He also told a fellow employee that Dawn's body had been found hanging from a tree—and this was before it was actually located. Although he was wrong about the body's condition, he seemed to know long before the police did that she was dead.

R.B. was summarily arrested on August 8. Mentally

slow for his age, his answers to questions concerning his whereabouts and his association with Dawn were inconsistent. He kept saying he could not remember, although the incident had occurred only a week earlier. He finally admitted that he had talked with Dawn and had even accompanied her partway along the lane before returning to his bike and going home. He did admit to sexual contact with another girl when he was fourteen, and had even gotten rough with her and forced himself on her for anal penetration. He watched pornography and viewed girls derogatorily as "slags." Later, R.B. added another detail: he had seen a man carrying a stick, following Dawn. Yet when the officers told him they suspected he had been involved, he quickly capitulated. He had liked her from afar and "probably went mad." He then said he'd been drunk. It was all an accident. He hadn't meant to kill her. He thought he'd been in some kind of trance, because he couldn't remember anything. Then just as abruptly as he'd begun to confess, he denied everything.

His interrogators tried again. They got him as far as admitting he had been with Dawn and that he had seen her lying on her side, under a hedge. He also said he had grabbed her around the throat and squeezed. He then had sex with the body. He added other details, but not everything he said matched the condition of the body.

It had taken about fifteen hours, but the police believed they had a confession to the assault and murder of Dawn Ashworth that would hold up. After R.B. had provided details that had not been published in the newspapers, investigators felt sure he was good for both murders. However, he would not confess to the killing of Lynda Mann. Since the blood type from both incidents was the same, they had a problem. What the police did not know is that their problem would soon become much more serious.

R.B.'s mother offered an alibi, but no one listened, especially after several young girls claimed he had molested them. His father had read an article about the discovery of DNA testing in nearby Leicester, so he asked his son's attorney about it. This man brought it to the attention of Superintendent Tony Painter, who had interrogated R.B., but Chief Superintendent David Baker was already aware of the tests and had decided to contact Dr. Alec Jeffreys. The university where the discovery occurred was nearby and there was no harm in asking. If such a test could prove that R.B. had assaulted and killed both girls, then the problem with his confession to one murder but not the other would be moot. In addition, the police would solve both cases at once and clear the books.

Science and Murder

In 1984, Dr. Alec Jeffreys, a British molecular biologist, had used Restriction Fragment Length Polymorphism (RFLP) as the DNA-typing protocol to dissolve an immigration dispute over a boy from Ghana who claimed he had a British mother and wanted to live with her. Dr. Jeffreys also resolved another paternity case, proving that a French adolescent was the father of a British-born child.

He was able to assist in these cases because of his ground-breaking work in the lab at the University of Leicester. There he had looked for the small percentage of human DNA that shows individual variation, because that would provide a marker for definitive identification. Blood testing, even with all the protein profiles that could be identified, was still fairly fuzzy in this regard.

"I'd been working in Amsterdam with Dick Flavell," Jeffreys said in an interview with *The Human Genome*. "We'd got to the point where we could detect single copies of human genes. But when I came to Leicester in 1977, I wanted to move away from the study of split genes, and to marry new techniques of molecular biology with human genetics." He looked at the structure of genes to understand inherited variations among individuals, isolating a single nucleotide polymorphism (SNP) of DNA in 1978, then started to look for areas of DNA that would be more variable. This drew him to tandem repeat DNA, where a short sequence of DNA was repeated many times in a row. It seemed that these sequences would be open to duplication and recombination.

His task proved difficult at first, but Jeffreys's work on the myoglobin gene, which produces the oxygen-carrying protein in muscle, yielded results. First he examined seal genes and then human, and there he identified a "minisatellite"—tandem repeat DNA. Jeffreys's team used this to identify more minisatellites, through which they discovered a core sequence—part of DNA that remained constant throughout. They made a radioactive probe that contained the core sequences, which latched onto the diverse minisatellites simultaneously. Then they placed the results from different people on a blot. This was in September 1984, and when the blot was ready, Jeffreys and his colleague Vicky Wilson developed an X-ray of it. To their surprise, they discovered patterns, similar in appearance to grocery-store bar codes, that distinguished each subject from the others.

"There was a level of individual specificity," said Dr. Jeffreys, "that was light years beyond anything that had been seen before." He called this a "Eureka!" moment, and so it was. "Standing in front of these pictures in the darkroom, my life took a complete turn." He set to work to refine the process and make it more manageable for identifying idiotypes, or patterns specific to all individuals except identical twins. He knew it could soon be used as a human identification system, what he called a genetic fingerprint.

For this work, Jeffreys and his colleagues received many public honors and in a paper published in *Nature* in 1985 (written with Drs. Peter Gill and David Werrett), they stated that an individual's identifiable DNA pattern was unique and would not be found in any past, present, or future person. This put the doctor in demand for more paternity cases, a natural for this type of analysis. Yet he had a greater vision. Two years after the Lynda Mann murder, Dr. Jeffreys had stated to a Leicester newspaper reporter that "the new technique could mean a breakthrough in many areas, including the identification of criminals from a small sample of blood at the scene of the crime." It was likely that officers on the task force had read the resulting article at the time of its publication, but it was the second incident that mobilized them to act on the information it contained.

Jeffreys had read newspaper stories about both victims, so he eagerly agreed to test the semen samples the police had obtained. They were packaged and sent to his lab, along with a blood sample from the suspect. Jeffreys had never tried genetic fingerprinting in a criminal case, but everyone on the police force felt certain that R.B.'s semen would prove their case, as well as confirm the technique's viability. Since the sample from the Mann murder was fairly degraded, Jeffreys was uncertain about what to expect, but he put it through the lengthy RFLP process anyway and awaited the results.

In RFLP testing at this time, the extracted DNA was cut into fragments, then the fragments were covered in a gel to separate them into single strands. An electrical current was applied to push the negatively charged fragments through the gel at speeds relative to their length toward the positive pole, with the shorter pieces migrating faster. There they lined up according to size. The pieces were removed from the gel with a nylon membrane, called a Southern Blot, and the DNA fragments were fixed to the membrane. This process exposed the A, T, C, and G protein bases, which could then be treated with a radioactive genetic probe. The single-strand probe would bind to its complementary base, revealing the DNA pattern, and a multilocus probe would bind to multiple points on multiple chromosomes. The probe identified specific areas of the DNA with dark bands, as revealed by an X-ray (autoradiograph or autorad) of the membrane. Then a print of the polymorphic sequences could be compared to prints from other specimens. The interpretation of a sample was based on statistical probability.

At the culmination of the analysis, the genetic profile of Lynda Mann's rapist was revealed, but when it was compared to R.B.'s sample there was no match. However, the work continued for the next "nail-biting" week on the semen removed from Dawn Ashworth, which was then compared to that from Lynda Mann. This time there *was* a match, but not the one expected. The samples matched each other, so while the same person had committed both crimes, neither sample implicated the suspect, R. B. Despite his confession, he was not their man.

The test was done again, with similar results, making R.B. the first person in criminal history to be exonerated by a DNA test. If not for science, Jeffreys would later say, an innocent person might have been found guilty and imprisoned.

The police who had worked long hours on the case wanted to challenge this finding, because it made no sense to them, but they were not able to do so. Jeffreys knew what he was talking about. The officers could only admit that they had made a mistake. Yet there was still the matter of the confession. When asked why he had admitted to rape and murder, R.B. said that he'd felt pressured. Yet he'd known unpublished facts about the crime scene, so the detectives surmised that he'd discovered the body before the police. (Others have suggested that during the interrogation, they inadvertently fed him the details, a common error.)

While the investigation continued, Jeffreys traveled to the FBI's academy at Quantico to show them what the process involved, and at the age of thirty-six he became a renowned scientist. He would soon become famous all over the world.

Square One

Back in England, R.B. was released and investigators were determined to find the right perpetrator, so the men of Narborough and villages nearby within a certain age range, fourteen to thirty-one in 1983, were asked to voluntarily provide a blood sample. More than 4,500 men agreed to do it and most were eliminated via conventional blood tests (since DNA analysis was expensive and time-consuming). The goal was to ferret out any man who would not willingly submit to a test, because that man might have something to hide.

Each man came for his "blooding," showed an identity card if he had one, and was interviewed. However, since the ID cards contained no photos, it was impossible to know if a man was really who he said he was. Some had passports and others had employment cards, but the process was less than airtight. If the subject was not a PGM 1+, type A secretor, he was free and clear. If he did have this blood type, his sample would be analyzed for a DNA profile. Yet, after all this processing, no new suspects turned up. Then, in September 1987, just the sort of suspicious incident the police had been expecting was reported.

A woman told them she had overheard a baker named Ian Kelly claim that he'd provided his own blood sample as a substitute for a fellow baker, Colin Pitchfork. The twenty-eight-year-old Pitchfork had a wife and child, but he was also a known thief and convicted flasher. When Pitchfork was questioned after the Lynda Mann murder, he claimed he had been babysitting his child while his wife was at school. This had checked out. When he heard about the community-wide blood test, he'd persuaded Kelly to go to the test site in his place. (He had approached three others, but they had refused.) He'd already received two notifications to show up, but said he was afraid that his past record would mark him as a likely suspect. He then fabricated a story that he'd already substituted himself to cover for another man, so he'd get into trouble if he showed up again. Kelly finally agreed and Pitchfork had given him a fake passport.

But Kelly had a big mouth. When he bragged about what he did to coworkers at a Leicester pub, one of them informed the police. That placed the spotlight dead on Pitchfork.

Before arresting him, detectives compared the signature from the blooding form, ostensibly signed by Pitchfork, with his signature on another form. There was no match. Despite its expense, the dragnet had worked: Pitchfork was a prime suspect. The police questioned other employees who had heard Kelly's admission at the pub, and confirmed the story, so on September 18, they arrested Kelly for conspiracy to pervert the course of justice. He ratted out Pitchfork, acknowledging that his cover for a friend had delayed the investigation by eight months. He wasn't going to get off lightly.

That night, the police arrested Colin Pitchfork at home. He confessed before he even got out the door, saying he had killed out of mere opportunity. About Lynda Mann, he said he'd initially decided to just flash her, but the excitement of the act had aroused him so much he decided to rape her. She'd run onto the dark path and he followed her, but then realized he would have to kill her or she'd identify him. He forced her into intercourse and then strangled her. Throughout all of his, his baby slept in his car. He returned and drove home, washed up, and then picked up his wife.

His tone grew contentious when he was discussing the second murder. The police insisted that he had anally penetrated Dawn Ashworth, but he claimed he had not. Nor did he hide her as thoroughly as he had hidden Lynda Mann, raising the possibility that someone else might have found her after the murder and sexually penetrated her. Or Pitchfork found the act too shameful to admit.

He confessed to attempting to take a third girl off into the fields to rape, but changing his mind. That girl had not told anyone. He also said he'd considered different ways of killing Ian Kelly to keep him from talking, but had feared this murder would be traced to him. The only time during his interview when he showed emotion was when he spoke enthusiastically about flashing. Otherwise, he was stone cold.

During his confession, he revealed a lot about himself. As a child, he'd felt inadequate and had been teased at school. At age eleven, he started showing his genitals to girls because he enjoyed the feeling of power it gave him. Eventually he was caught and had to go to court. He dropped out of school and found a job taking care of the handicapped, but eventually he needed the high he derived from exposing himself and went out to do it again. By this time he was married, and his wife was humiliated by his arrests. Still, she believed he'd eventually outgrow it. Colin found work as a baker and seemed to thrive in his job. He had an affair that nearly ended his marriage, but then he and his wife had a baby. After they changed their residence, he had another affair and conceived a child with the woman. He continued to look for opportunities to flash, and had nearly raped another girl. In essence, Pitchfork was a psychopath who looked for personal thrills and thought nothing of the harm he did to others.

To ensure that he would not try to recant what he had said, the police sent Pitchfork's blood for DNA testing, and the results proved that his genetic profile was indistinguishable from that of both semen samples. He became the first person in the world to be convicted of murder based on Jeffreys's method of genetic fingerprinting. On January 22, 1988, Pitchfork drew double life sentences, while Kelly received a suspended sentence for obstructing the investigation.

The Pitchfork case sparked headlines around the world, inspiring a great deal of attention from the law enforcement community. It seemed that a potentially foolproof method had been found for solving crimes in which biological evidence was crucial. The rush was on in many places to apply DNA technology to more crimes. Lifecodes, located near Westchester, New York, became the first private lab in the United States to offer RFLP testing for criminal incidents that involved biological evidence. Dr. Jeffreys forever altered the investigation of such crimes and he was knighted for his work. In 2004, he received a "Pride of Britain" award. Thankfully, the investigators on these cases were open to breakthroughs in science and the scientists were eager to apply their tools in the forensic arena. Although Pitchfork received a sentence that allowed for parole, he remains in prison at this writing.

Even as DNA revolutionized crime fighting in many countries, some law enforcement agencies continued to rely on older, less precise methods, and as a result many serial killers slipped through the cracks. Yet, concurrent with Jeffreys's work in biology, a psychological approach was also gaining in popularity, and where low crime-lab resources precluded the use of DNA testing, there were often specialists in behavioral analysis. Because of this, one investigator in the Soviet Union made a bold move.

Sources

"An Interview with Sir Alec Jeffreys on DNA Profiling and Minisatellites," ScienceWatch.com, retrieved December 4, 2007.

Jeffreys, A. J., V. Wilson, and S. L. Thein. "Individual-Specific 'Fingerprints' of Human DNA." *Nature* 37, 1985.

Levy, Harlan. *And the Blood Cried Out: A Prosecutor's Spellbinding Account of the Power of DNA.* New York: Basic Books, 1996.

Lee, Henry, and Frank Tirnady. *Blood Evidence: How DNA Is Revolutionizing the Way We Solve Crimes.* Cambridge, MA: Perseus, 2003.

Newton, Giles. "Discovering DNA Fingerprinting," genome.wellcome.ac.uk, retrieved December 4, 2007.

Wambaugh, Joseph. *The Blooding: The True Story of the Narborough Village Murders.* New York: William Morrow, 1989.

SIX

ANDREI CHIKATILO:
Lured into the Mirror

In the film *Citizen X*, a psychiatrist named Alexandr Bukhanovsky asks Andrei Chikatilo, recently arrested for numerous murders, to help him on some aspects of the profile about which he is not quite certain. In a quiet voice, he reads the relevant pages. Chikatilo listens, sometimes nodding, as if alert to the only person who seems to have understood him. He's transfixed as the reading continues.

Outside, impatient police officials are aware that without a confession, they must release this alleged offender. They've held him for nearly the maximum number of days, without cracking him, and the psychiatrist's profile is their last resort. The lead investigator, Viktor Burakov, has studied the FBI's criminal profiling program and he's convinced of its viability. Yet he, too, cannot be sure that Chikatilo will acknowledge any guilt.

Bukhanovsky's description delves into the nature of Chikatilo's mental illness and sexual perversions, suggesting reasons for it. As Chikatilo hears his secret life described so clearly, he begins to tremble. Tears come to his eyes. Finally he confirms what the psychiatrist is saying, breaks down, and admits that it's all true. He has done these horrible things.

Chikatilo reads the statement of charges for thirty-six murders and admits his guilt. He offers to tell the truth about his life and these crimes. As investigators listen, they're astonished to learn that their estimate of the number of his victims was far too low.

First Hints

A man looking for wood in the *lesopolosa,* a forested strip of land planted to prevent erosion, found some skeletal remains of a corpse. He reported them to the *militsia,* the local authorities. They discovered that the corpse had had no identifying clothing and had been left on its back, its head turned to the left. The ears were still sufficiently intact to see tiny holes for earrings, which, along with the length of hair remnants, suggested that the victim had been female. It appeared that two ribs had been broken and closer inspection indicated numerous stab wounds into the bone. A knife had apparently cut into the eye sockets, too, as if to remove the eyes, and similar gouges were viewed in the pelvic region. Whoever had committed this crime, the police thought, had been a frenzied beast. They found a report about a missing thirteen-year-old girl, Lyubov Biryuk, from Novocherkassk, a village nearby. A few items of clothing in the area linked the remains to this girl.

Major Mikhail Fetisov arrived from *militsia* headquarters in Rostov-on-Don. He was the leading detective, or *syshchik*, for the entire region. He asked for a search for any other records of people reported missing and ordered military cadets to scrutinize the entire area. Despite a thorough search, no evidence was produced that could help to identify the killer.

The autopsy report showed that Lyubov had been attacked from behind and hit hard in the head with both the handle and the blade of a knife. She had been stabbed at least twenty-two separate times. As a result, the police looked for people in the region with a history of mental illness, juvenile delinquents, or offenders with a history of sex crimes. They tried to find out whom Lyubov had known and how she might have encountered this killer.

One man, convicted in another rape, learned that he was a suspect and promptly hanged himself. That seemed to put an end to the investigation, as there were no other viable suspects, but two months later another victim was discovered.

The Division of Especially Serious Crimes

A railroad worker walking near the train station in Shakhty, a small industrial town twenty miles away, came across another set of skeletal remains, several weeks old, adult, and female. The body had been stripped, left face-down, with the legs pulled apart. Investigators spotted a key similarity with the murder of Lyubov: multiple stab wounds and lacerated eye sockets.

Only a month later, a soldier gathering wood about ten miles south of that spot came across more remains, also of a woman lying facedown. She had been covered with branches, but close inspection showed a pattern of knife wounds and damage to the eye sockets.

The link among the victims was obvious. They had a serial killer in the area, but the police were not admitting this, especially to the press. Police in the Soviet Union were careful about acknowledging the existence of serial killers, believing this was a symptom of the decadent Western cultures like that of the United States. Officially, they had three separate unsolved murders.

Major Fetisov organized a task force of ten men to start an investigation. Among them was a second lieutenant from the criminology laboratory, Viktor Burakov, age thirty-seven. He was the best man they had for the analysis of such physical evidence as fingerprints, footprints, and trace evidence, and he was an expert in both police science and martial arts. In January 1983, he was invited to join what was known as the Division of Especially Serious Crimes.

Around this time, a fourth victim was found. She appeared to have been killed six months earlier and her body was near the area where the second set of remains was discovered. It bore the familiar knife-wound patterns.

At this point police knew that the killer—the "Maniac," as he was called—did not smoke (or he'd have taken the cigarettes found near Lyubov) and that he was male. He had an issue with eyes, and his gouging of them indicated that he spent time with the victims after they were dead, even in high-risk areas.

With no definite leads, the unit decided to look at older unsolved cases, but Burakov's primary task was to head an investigation in Novoshakhtinsk, a farming and mining town in the general area. There, a ten-year-old girl had just been reported missing. Olga Stalmachenok had gone to a local conservancy for a piano lesson on December 10, 1982, and that was the last time anyone saw her. Burakov questioned her parents and learned that she got along with them and had no cause to run away. However, the parents had received a strange postcard that was signed "Sadist-Black Cat" telling them their daughter was in the woods and warning that there would be ten more victims that coming year.

On April 14, 1983, four months later, Olga was found in a field, along with some of her things buried apart from her body. Since she was killed during the winter, cold and snow had preserved her, so the pattern of knife wounds on her skull and chest was clearly visible on her bluish-white skin. The knife had been inserted dozens of times, as if in a frenzy, especially to the heart, lungs, and sexual organs.

Burakov knew he was looking for a vicious, sexually motivated serial killer who was attacking victims at an escalating rate, drawing no attention and leaving no evidence. But given the attitude of the regime in power,

Burakov had few resources to help him find the killer. Men who killed in this manner were few and only top-ranking Soviet officials knew the details of the investigations of their crimes. It was like an unpleasant family secret known only to select relatives.

Burakov followed the three-mile route from the conservancy to the place where Olga's body was left, deducing that the killer had a car. He was also certain the man did not frighten people when he approached. That would make him harder to find, though Burakov was sure the man had some kind of mental disorder that someone had noticed.

He and his team decided to focus on known sex offenders in the area, specifically on their whereabouts on December 11. Then they looked at released mental patients, as well as men who lived or worked around the conservancy who owned or used a car. Handwriting experts examined the Black Cat card against samples from the entire population of that town, but nothing of interest turned up.

Then in another wooded *lesopolosa* near Rostov-on-Don, a group of boys found bones in a gully. An examination of them linked this crime with the others. The next discovery was an eight-year-old male in a wooded area near Rostov's airport, two miles from the sixth victim. Missing since August 9, the boy had been stabbed, like the others, including his eyes.

This new development puzzled everyone. Serial sex killers, it was assumed, always attacked the same type of victim, but this offender had killed grown women and young children, girls and boys. The investigators wondered if they might have more than one killer doing the same kind of perverse ritual. It seemed impossible, but so did the idea that so many victim types could trigger the same sexual violence from one person.

Through a tip, the police interrogated Yuri Kalenik, nineteen, who lived in a home for retarded children. At first he denied everything, but interrogators kept him for several days, believing that a guilty man would inevitably confess. They beat him, so he finally told them what they wanted to hear. He confessed to all seven murders, and added four more to his list. Yuri seemed a viable suspect, because he had a mental disorder and he used public transportation, as did many of the victims. At the time, there was little understanding of the psychology of false confessions. People of lower intelligence tend to be more susceptible to suggestion or coercion, especially when fatigued, and they may tell interrogators whatever pleases them—usually supplying items they hear from the interrogator.

When Burakov asked the boy to take them to a murder site, he saw that Kalenik did not go straight to the place, even when he was close, but appeared to wander around until he picked up clues from the police about where they expected him to go. Burakov did not consider this to be a good test. Upon examining the written confession, he was even less convinced. It was clear to him that Kalenik, intimidated, had been given most of the information he finally provided. He was soon cleared.

Operation *Lesopolosa*

In another wooded area, the mutilated remains of a young woman were found. Her nipples had been removed—possibly with teeth—her abdomen was slashed open, and one eye socket was damaged. She had been there for months and her clothing was missing. Another victim found on October 20 bore wounds similar to those of the other victims, but though her eyes remained intact, this victim was entirely disemboweled and the missing organs were nowhere to be found. Perhaps the killer had changed his method.

Just after the start of 1984, a dead boy turned up near the railroad tracks—Sergei Markov, a fourteen-year-old, missing since December 27. For the first time, thanks to winter's preservative effects, the detectives were able to see just what the killer did to these young people. He had stabbed the boy in the neck dozens of times—the final count would be seventy—and he had then cut into the boy's genitals and removed everything from the pubic area. In addition, he had violated the victim anally. Then it appeared that he had gone to a spot nearby to have a bowel movement.

Fetisov decided to retrace the boy's steps on the day he had disappeared. Beginning in a town called Gukovo, he'd boarded the *elechtrichka*, or local train. In the same town was a home for the mentally retarded and the teachers there reported that a former student had left around the same time as the boy and had taken the train. Once again, the police got a confession. Once again, they made a mistake.

Finally, though, they had their first piece of good evidence. The medical examiner found semen in Markov's anus. When they did apprehend the killer, a secretor, they could compare the blood antigens. This would not afford a precise match, but could at least eliminate suspects. In fact, it eliminated all of the young men who had confessed thus far. (As yet, there was no DNA analysis available, but even when there was, the Soviet Union's political instability during the late 1980s would preclude such analysis.)

In 1984, numerous victims were discovered in wooded areas, some of them quite close to where previous bodies had lain. Investigators acquired one more piece of evidence: a shoe print left in the mud, size thirteen. On the victim's clothing were traces of semen and blood.

The killer struck that March in Novoshakhtinsk, grabbing ten-year-old Dmitri Ptashnikov, who was later found mutilated and stabbed. The tip of his tongue and his penis were missing. The semen on his shirt linked him to the previous two crimes, and this time, there were witnesses. The boy was seen following a tall, hollow-cheeked man with stiff knees and large feet, wearing glasses. No one had recognized him.

By the end of the summer of 1984, police counted twenty-four victims probably murdered by the same man. Whenever semen was left behind, it proved to have the same AB antigen. There was also a single gray hair on one victim, and some scraps of clothing. The killer had also shifted his pattern again. He now removed the upper lip, and sometimes the nose, and these he would leave in the victim's mouth or ripped-open stomach. He had stepped up his pace from five victims the first year (they believed) to one nearly every two weeks. Investigators had no way of knowing that they had not yet found the earliest victims.

Given the escalation in victims, the Soviet minister of the interior appointed a dozen new detectives to the case, and with Burakov heading it, a task force of some two hundred men and women was assigned to the investigation. Officers worked undercover at bus and train stations, looking for a man between twenty-five and thirty years of age, tall, well built, with type AB blood. They believed he was cautious, of average intelligence, and verbally persuasive. He traveled on public transportation and probably lived with either his mother or a wife. He might be a former psychiatric patient, or a substance abuser, and he might have some knowledge of anatomy and skill with a knife.

One undercover officer spotted an older man in the Rostov bus station, speaking with a female adolescent, and when she got on her bus, noticed him sit next to another young woman. Under questioning, officials learned his name: Andrei Chikatilo. He managed a machinery supply company and was on a business trip, but he lived in Shakhty. He said he had once been a teacher and he missed talking to young people, so the officer let him go. But another agent followed him and watched him accost various women. When he solicited a prostitute,

Chikatilo was arrested for indecent behavior. A search of his briefcase turned up a jar of Vaseline, a long kitchen knife, a piece of rope, and a dirty towel—nothing needed for the alleged business trip. Yet he had type A blood, not AB. He was also a member of the Communist Party, with a good character reference. Since there was nothing in his background to raise suspicion, he was released.

At his wit's end, Burakov decided to breach protocol and consult with psychiatric experts in Moscow. Most were either uninterested in making an analysis or refused to say much, but Dr. Alexandr Bukhanovsky agreed to study the few known details. He also read everything he could find on sexual pathologies and schizophrenia and wrote a seven-page report. The killer, he said, was a sexual deviate, twenty-five to fifty years old, around five feet ten inches tall. He thought the man suffered from feelings of sexual inadequacy and he blinded his victims to prevent them from looking at him or from retaining his image on their eyeballs. He also brutalized their corpses, partially out of frustration and partially to enhance his arousal. He was a sadist and had difficulty achieving release without cruelty. He was also compulsive, following the goading of his need, and would be depressed until he could kill. He might even have headaches that urged him to act out for relief. A loner, he was not retarded or schizophrenic. He could work out a plan and follow it.

None of this helped to identify a specific person, so Burakov looked up records of men convicted of homosexual crimes and came across Valery Ivanenko, who had committed several acts of "perversion." He also had a charismatic personality and once had been a teacher. At age forty-six, he was tall and wore glasses. In short, he sounded too good to be true. He was the perfect suspect.

Staking out the apartment where the man's invalid mother resided, Burakov caught and arrested him. Yet his blood type was A. In a deal, Burakov enlisted his assistance in investigating the gay population of the area in return for allowing him to function as a homosexual without fear of reprisals. Ivanenko proved quite good at getting secret information, which in turn led to others providing even more information under pressure. Burakov soon knew quite a bit about Rostov's underworld of perversion and violence, but he was no closer to catching the killer. This frustrated him.

Killer X

Over the next ten months only one body turned up—that of a young woman—but she was killed near Moscow. Burakov went there to study the photos of this victim. The treatment of the corpse was so similar that he was convinced that the Maniac had traveled to the city. He checked flight rosters and had officers go painstakingly through all the handwritten tickets, but nothing was found. In fact, there was a significant clue, but they failed to see it. Meanwhile, three young boys were raped and killed in the area.

But the Rostov crew was quickly drawn back to Shakhty. In a grove of trees near the bus depot, a homeless, eighteen-year-old girl lay dead, her mouth stuffed with leaves. This was the same signature that was found on the girl in Moscow some weeks earlier. A red and a blue thread were found under her fingernails, and the sweat near her wounds typed as AB—different from her own type O blood. Between her fingers was a single strand of gray hair. This was the most evidence left thus far at a crime scene linked to the killer.

A special procurator, Issa Kostoyev, was appointed to look into the *lesopolosa* murders. By this time, they had fifteen procurators and twenty-nine detectives involved. Kostoyev looked over the investigative work done thus far and dismissed it. He believed they'd already come across the man they were after and just hadn't known it. To try to learn more about the type of killer who would be so raw and brutal, Kostoyev had the classic nineteenth-century work on sexual predators by Richard von Krafft-Ebing translated into Russian. He also discovered a rare edition of *Crimes and Criminals in Western Culture*, by B. Utevsky, which included a chapter detailing cases of dismemberment and disfiguring of victims. He saw that some killers were driven merely by arrogance and the idea that their victims were objects that belonged to them to do with as they pleased. Kostoyev used this information to inform the team.

Burakov turned again to Dr. Bukhanovsky, allowing him to see all the crime-scene reports so he could write a more detailed profile. This, he thought, might help detectives to narrow the leads, as per the FBI's profiling protocol. Bukhanovsky spent months on the task, this time turning out sixty-five pages. He labeled the unknown suspect "Killer X."

The details, briefly, were as follows: X was not psychotic, because he was in control of what he did; he was narcissistic and considered himself gifted, but was not unduly intelligent. He was heterosexual, so boys were merely a "vicarious surrogate." He was a "necrosadist," needing to watch people die in order to achieve sexual gratification. The multiple stabbing was a way to "enter" them sexually, and he either sat astride them or squatted next to them. The deepest cuts were made at the height of his pleasure, and he might masturbate. There were many reasons why he might cut out the eyes: he could be excited by eyes or might believe his image was left on them, a superstition of unenlightened people. Cutting into the sexual organs was a display of power over women. He might keep the missing organs or eat them.

An interesting twist in the profile was the hypothesis that X responded to changes in weather patterns. Before most of the murders, the barometer had dropped. That might be his trigger, especially if it coincided with other stressors at home or work. Most of the killings were also done midweek, from Tuesday to Thursday.

While the psychiatrist was vague about height and occupation, he now thought X's age was between forty-five and fifty, the age at which sexual perversions are most developed. It was likely that the suspect had had a difficult childhood. He was conflicted and probably kept to himself. He had a rich fantasy life, but an abnormal response to sexuality, to put it mildly. Bukhanovsky could not say if the man was married or had fathered children, but if he was married, his wife let him keep his own hours and did not ask much of him. His killing was compulsive and might stop temporarily if he sensed he was in danger of discovery, but would not stop altogether until he died or was caught.

Despite the length and detail of this psychological report, Burakov still found nothing of practical use for the investigation. Having learned about the way FBI profilers conducted prison interviews to acquire a database about behaviors and sexual fantasies of killers, he decided to try another method.

Burakov talked with Anatoly Slivko, a man who faced execution for the sex murders of seven boys. Slivko was willing to talk and he attributed such acts to an inability to engage in normal sexual arousal and satisfaction. Sexual murderers have endless fantasies in which they go through the murder scenario step-by-step, and feel the urge for action, and the act of planning their crimes has its own satisfaction. Slivko, too, offered nothing of practical use for the investigation, but his answers to questions revealed the paradoxically compartmentalized mind of a man who could kill boys, on the one hand, and feel morally indignant about using alcohol in front of children, on the other. That meant he could live in society in a way that hid his true propensities. Only hours after this interview, Slivko was executed.

The investigators believed that "X" was similar in psychological makeup to Slivko, and that meant he would be next to impossible to catch. At this time, the killing seemed to stop.

Frustration

Only one dead woman turned up in 1985 in Rostov, and nothing happened that winter or the next spring. Then on July 23, 1986, the body of a thirty-three-year-old female was found, but it bore none of the markings of the serial killer, except that the victim had been repeatedly stabbed. Burakov had doubts about her being part of the series, but this was not so with the young woman found on August 18. All of the disturbing wounds were present, but she had been mostly buried, save for a hand sticking out of the dirt—a new twist. Now police had to wonder whether there were others not yet found because they, too, were buried.

At the end of 1986, Viktor Burakov finally had a nervous breakdown. He was weak and exhausted, and could not sleep, so he went to a hospital for a month, then rested for another month. Four years of intense work had brought him to this. But he would not give up. In fact, his ordeal had given him some perspective.

The winter of 1988 had melted into spring before a railroad worker found a woman's nude body in a weedy area near the tracks on April 6. Her hands were bound behind her, she had been stabbed multiple times, the tip of her nose was gone, and her skull had been bashed in. A large footprint was found nearby. Then, only a month later, on May 17, the body of a nine-year-old boy was discovered in the woods not far from a train station. He'd been sodomized and then his orifices were stuffed with dirt. He also bore numerous knife wounds and a blow to the skull, and his penis had been removed. He was identified as Aleksei Voronko, and a classmate had seen him with a middle-aged man with gold teeth, a mustache, and a sports bag. They had gone together to the woods.

This was a strong lead, one that could be followed up among local dentists. Few adults in the area could afford gold crowns for their teeth. Yet by the end of that year, after visiting many dentists, investigators had turned up nothing. To their astonishment, the Ministry of Health issued a statement about a mistake that had been made in typing blood in other biological secretions. There were rare "paradoxical" cases, the lab report stated, in which the results did not match the actual blood type. In other words, any of the suspects that had supposedly been eliminated based on blood type could have been the killer.

While this was frustrating news and made the investigation more difficult in many ways, it also reopened a few doors from the past. However, to fully undo the mistakes of the past, semen samples, not blood, would have to be obtained, and this had to be done voluntarily. Four years' worth of work would have to be redone. The idea was overwhelming. The only method of investigation that seemed viable now was to post more men to watch the public transportation stations. But Procurator Kostoyev insisted on better accountability and efficiency. He did not like wasting all the manpower at the train stations. Another hurdle.

Still, it was April 1989 before investigators came across another victim who could be added to the *lesopolosa* series—a sixteen-year-old boy, stabbed repeatedly and genitally mutilated. This crime was followed by the murders of five more boys and a woman. Since Mikhail Gorbachev had made changes in party leadership, decreased government censorship of information, and instituted the policy of glasnost, which allowed greater access to information, journalists were at last writing openly about the murders. They knew a serial killer was operating and they pressured officials to put an end to the murders. Few reporters realized that there were now thirty-two victims.

Desperate, Burakov decided on a new plan. He would select the most likely train stations for undercover efforts, and make surveillance overt in the others, so that only those stations where plainclothes officers were patrolling would seem safe to the killer. In other words, the police would try to lure the killer toward places where he'd be likely to pick up another victim. In those places, they would record the names of every man who came and went. They would also place people in the forests nearby, dressed as farmers. It was a major effort, involving over 350 officers, but it was their last hope.

The train station in Donleskhoz was considered a good place to set up a post, since two of the victims had been found near there. Mushroom pickers generally used the station during the summer, but otherwise it was relatively uncrowded. Two other stations were selected as well. But even before the plan was put into effect, the killer chose a victim at the Donleskhoz station, a sixteen-year-old retarded boy. Part of his tongue was missing, as were his testicles, and one eye had been stabbed. When his identity was established, officers learned that he'd spent most of his travel time on the *electrichka*, the slow-moving train, but no one had seen him exit with anyone.

Burakov was in despair. They'd formed a good plan, and had it been in place, they might have caught the Maniac!

When another missing boy was found dead near the Shakhty railroad station, Burakov got moving. He set the snare, with everyone in place, but, undetected, the killer grabbed a young woman—number thirty-six. Burakov was beginning to think they were chasing the devil himself.

Yet there were reports of men who had been at the train station near this crime scene. One name stood out. In fact, the very sight of it chilled Burakov to the bone. Over half a million people had been investigated by this time, but this particular man had been interrogated and released only because his blood type had not matched that of the semen samples. This man had to be the killer. Burakov was sure of it. The man fit the descriptions, he had gray hair, and he'd been carrying a knife and a rope in his briefcase.

Endgame

Andrei Romanovich Chikatilo, fifty-four, had been at the Donleskhoz train station on November 6. A witness said he'd emerged from the woods, a red smear on his face, and washed his hands at a pump.

Burakov placed him under surveillance and did a thorough background review. He was married with two children, and had been accused of molesting a student, which forced him to resign from a teaching post. So he had sexual problems. He had then worked for a company at a job that allowed him to travel, but was fired when he failed to return from business trips with the supplies he was sent to get. He had spent three months in jail for a petty offense, and during that time, there had been no murders. In addition, records showed that his trips coincided with other murders—including the one in Moscow. He had once been a member in good standing in the Communist Party, but had ultimately been expelled.

Yet even with all this documentation, Burakov knew his case was weak. They would need to catch Chikatilo in the act or get him to confess, but allowing him to freely roam risked letting him kill someone else. Kostoyev ordered his arrest, believing he could get a confession out of him.

On November 20, 1990, three officers dressed in street clothes surrounded Chikatilo and brought him in for interrogation. They noticed that he did not have a mouth full of gold teeth, as one witness had stated, but in his satchel was a pocketknife. Chikatilo was put into a cell where a gifted informant had been placed, but this strategy failed. A search of Chikatilo's home produced no items that had belonged to any of the victims, but did yield no fewer than twenty-three knives. A medical examination indicated that Chikatilo's semen supposedly had a weak B antibody, making it appear that his blood

THE DEVIL'S DOZEN   153

type was AB. The lab personnel called him the "paradoxical" rare case. More likely, the lab had screwed up in the first place and then tried to cover up the mistake.

Kostoyev decided to handle the interrogation himself, in the presence of Chikatilo's court-appointed lawyer. He wanted the room to be spartan, with only a table, chairs, and a safe that would hint of the presence of incriminating evidence. Kostoyev had failed to obtain a confession in only three out of the hundreds of interrogations he had conducted. He reputedly had a knack for getting inside a suspect's head, figuring out how he thought, and getting him to talk. All guilty men eventually confessed, he believed: they had to. In any event, he knew he had a full ten days, and in addition, he had some bait.

When Chikatilo was brought in, Kostoyev could see that he was a tall, older man with a long neck, sloping shoulders, oversize glasses, and gray hair. He walked with a shuffling gait, like a weary elderly person, but Kostoyev was not fooled. He believed Chikatilo was a calculating killer with plenty of energy available when he needed it.

Chikatilo insisted that his arrest had been a mistake. He denied that he had been at a train station on November 6 and did not know why this had been reported. He said little else, but the next day, he waived his right to legal counsel. He wrote a three-page document in which he confessed to "sexual weakness"—the words he had used before. He hinted at "perverse sexual activity," but did not specify what this meant, and said that he was out of control. Then he wrote another, longer essay in which he said that he had moved around in train stations and had seen how young people there fell victim to homeless beggars. He also admitted that he was impotent.

Kostoyev told him that his only hope would be to confess everything in a way that showed he had mental problems, so that an examination could affirm that he was, in fact, legally insane. Otherwise the evidence would surely convict him without a confession. That was Kostoyev's bait.

Chikatilo asked for a few days to collect himself and said he would submit to an interrogation. Everyone expected him to confess, but when the day arrived, he insisted that he was guilty of no crimes. For each crucial time period involving a murder, he claimed that he was at home with his wife.

The next day, he revised his statements. In 1977, he had fondled some female students who had aroused him. He had difficulty controlling himself around children, but there were only two instances in which he had lost control.

Nine days elapsed and Kostoyev had gotten no closer to his goal. Clearly, he had met his match. He could think of no other approach to take to pressure this man to finally open up. He brought in photographers and said they had witnesses to whom they were going to show these photographs. Still, Chikatilo did not yield.

It was looking as if they might have to let him go, which would be disastrous. Burakov thought they should try another interrogator—Dr. Bukhanovsky. Kostoyev initially resisted, but finally had to admit he was getting nowhere. He agreed to let the psychiatrist see what he could do.

The Psychiatrist and the Murderer

Bukhanovsky agreed to question Chikatilo, but only out of professional interest. He was soon alone in a closed room with the likeliest suspect in the *lesopolosa* murders. The psychiatrist saw right away that Chikatilo was the type of man he had described in his profile: ordinary, solitary, ostensibly nonthreatening. He introduced himself and then showed Chikatilo the profile. He sensed that the offender wanted to talk about his rage and his humiliation, so it was best to show sympathy. He listened for a while before he discussed the crimes. Discussing his report, he spoke for some time, in rich detail, and as Chikatilo listened, he seemed affected by the psychiatrist's analysis and finally surrendered, saying he would tell everything. His story was even more perverse than anyone had realized.

Among his admissions was that his first murder had occurred in 1978, before the police had begun to keep track of them. He had killed a little girl. This was alarming, since a man had already been arrested, tried, and executed for that murder. But Chikatilo said that he had moved to Shakhty that year to teach. He spent time watching children and feeling a strong desire to see them naked. To maintain his privacy, he purchased a hut on a dark, dirty street. When he went to it one day, he encountered the girl, so he took her inside and attacked her. When he could not achieve an erection, he used his knife as a substitute for his penis. After she died, he tossed her body into a nearby river.

Kostoyev asked him to explain the blindfolds he had used, and just as investigators had suspected, Chikatilo admitted that he had heard that the image of a killer remains in the eyes of a victim. That was why he had stabbed so many of his victims in the eyes. Then he had decided it was not true, so he stopped doing it (explaining the change in pattern).

Chikatilo had grown obsessed with reliving the crime, and this was compounded by anger over an injustice he believed he had suffered. His fantasies became more violent. In 1981, he attacked a girl who was begging for money, and used his teeth to bite off one of her nipples and swallow it. This, he found, made him ejaculate. He covered the body with newspaper and took her sexual organs away with him.

The killer went on and on. He remembered the details of each of the thirty-six *lesopolosa* murders. Sometimes he acted as a predator, learning someone's routes and habits. Others were victims of opportunity. The stabbing almost always was a substitute for sexual intercourse, and he had learned how to squat beside victims in such a way as to avoid getting their blood on his clothing. His impotence generally triggered his rage, especially if a woman ridiculed him. He soon understood that he could not get aroused without violence and blood.

With the boys, Chikatilo would fantasize that they were

his captives and that he was some kind of hero for torturing them. He could not give a reason for cutting off their tongues and penises, although at one point he said he was getting revenge against life. With grown women, Chikatilo would place his semen inside a uterus that he had removed, and as he walked along, he would chew on it—"the truffle of sexual murder." He said it gave him an "animal satisfaction" to chew or swallow nipples or testicles.

To corroborate what he was saying, he drew sketches of the crime scenes, and what he said fit the known facts. Then he confirmed what everyone had feared—he added more victims to the list. Many more. One boy he had killed in a cemetery and placed in a shallow grave. He took the interrogators there and they recovered the body. Another was killed in a field, and she was located. On and on it went, murders here and there, and the bodies were always left right where they were killed, except for one. Chikatilo described a murder in an empty apartment; in order to get the body out, he'd had to dismember it and dump the parts down a sewer.

In the end, he confessed to fifty-six murders, although there was corroboration for only fifty-three: thirty-one females and twenty-two males. The police now had sufficient evidence to take this man to court.

The Roots of Perversity

Chikatilo was born in 1936 in a small Ukrainian village; his head was misshapen as a result of water on the brain. His father was a POW in World War II and had been sent to a prison camp in Russia, so his mother raised him and his younger sister on her own.

During the early part of the twentieth century, citizens of the former Soviet Union were often subjected to famines, especially in the Ukraine, after Stalin crushed independent farmers and sent many citizens to the Siberian gulag. Some six million people died of starvation, and desperate people were known to strip meat from corpses in order to survive. Sometimes they went to a cemetery, where corpses were stacked for burial, and sometimes (legend has it) they grabbed someone on the street. Human flesh was bought and sold, or just hoarded.

Children saw disfigured corpses and heard terrible tales of hardship. Chikatilo had grown up during several of these famines; according to his mother, he had once had an older brother, Stepan, who had been killed. In a prison interview, he said, "Many people went crazy, attacked people, ate people. So they caught my brother, who was ten, and ate him." He might simply have died and been consumed, if he even existed (which could not be corroborated in any records), but Chikatilo's mother used to warn him to stay in the yard or he might get eaten as well.

Most of his childhood was spent alone, living in his fantasies. Other children mocked him for his awkwardness, so to entertain and empower himself, he dreamed up images of torture, which remained a feature of his killings later in life. He had his first sexual experience as an adolescent when he struggled with a ten-year-old friend of his sister's and ejaculated. That impressed itself

on him, especially as he grew older and realized he was
unable to get an erection but able to ejaculate.

When he returned from the army ready to settle down
with a wife, he found he was still unable to perform sexually.
A girl spread this information around, humiliating him,
and he dreamed about catching her and tearing her to
pieces. His sister arranged a marriage for him with a woman
who belittled him, but he could only impregnate her by
ejaculating outside her and pushing his semen in by hand.
He became a teacher and soon found himself attracted to
young girls. Molesting them gave him satisfaction, but when
such incidents were reported, they were covered up and
denied instead of leading to prosecution.

For true satisfaction, Chikatilo needed violence, so he
started to commit murder. Since he was on the road quite
often as a parts supply liaison, it was easy to find vulnerable strangers. Chikatilo believed he suffered from an
illness that caused his uncontrollable transgressions. He
asked to see specialists in sexual deviance, so he was sent
to Moscow's Serbsky Institute for two months. Neurolo-
gists there determined that his brain had been damaged
at birth, and this had affected his ability to control his
bladder and emissions of semen. However, he was found
to be sane: he knew what he was doing and he could have
controlled it. That was good enough for the prosecutor.

Brought back to Rostov, Chikatilo went to trial on
April 14, 1992, placed inside a large iron cage. The judge
sat at a dais and two citizens on either side acted as jurors.
There were 225 volumes of information against him.

Since the press spread the word about the Maniac's trial, the courtroom was filled with relatives of his victims. When he entered, they screamed at him. Now bald and without his glasses, he looked slightly psychotic, especially when he drooled and rolled his eyes or dropped his trousers.

That he would be found guilty of murder was a foregone conclusion, but there was a chance that his psychological problems could save him from execution. However, his lawyer, Marat Khabibulin, was not allowed to call psychiatric experts; he could only cross-examine those experts that the prosecution put on the stand, and since he had not been appointed until after Chikatilo had fully confessed, he was at a serious disadvantage.

Judge Leonid Akubzhanov asked sharp questions and tossed off demeaning comments at the prisoner. Chikatilo challenged him, claiming to be a victim of the former Soviet system and calling himself a "mad beast." He also stated that he had murdered seventy people, not fifty-three.

The trial dragged on into August. The defense summed up its case by saying that the evidence and psychiatric analyses were flawed and the confessions had been coerced. Chikatilo's lawyer pleaded for a not-guilty verdict. The next day, Chikatilo broke into song from his cage and then muttered a string of nonsense, with accusations that he was being "radiated." He was taken out of the courtroom before the prosecutor began his final argument, in which he asked for the death penalty. On October 14, Andrei

Chikatilo was found guilty of five counts of molestation and fifty-two counts of murder. Chikatilo cried out incoherently, shouting, "Swindlers!" and throwing his bench while demanding to see the corpses. The judge sentenced him to be executed. He appealed, but it was denied, so on February 15, 1994, Andrei Chikatilo, the *Lesopolosa* Maniac, was taken to a soundproof room and shot behind the right ear, ending his life. For Burakov, it was the resolution of a long and difficult investigation, but like other good detectives, he had stayed the course, devised inventive methods, educated himself beyond what was expected, and finally saw results.

Criminal profiling played an important role in many serial-killer investigations during the 1990s, but it has often been disparaged as "mere" psychology. In fact, profiling from crime scenes is only one aspect of the FBI's Criminal Investigative Analysis, which offers other types of behavioral analysis. One of them was instrumental in our next story.

Sources

Cannibal: The Real Hannibal Lecters. HBO, February 2003.

Conti, Richard P. "The Psychology of False Confessions." *Journal of Credibility Assessment and Witness Psychology* 2 : 1 (1999), 14–36.

Cullen, Robert. *The Killer Department: Detective Viktor Burakov's Eight-Year Hunt for the Most Savage Serial Killer in Russian History.* New York: Pantheon Books, 1993.

Krivich, Mikhail, and Ol'gert Ol'gin. *Comrade Chikatilo: The Psychopathology of Russia's Notorious Serial Killer.* Fort Lee, NJ: Barricade Books, 1993.

Lourie, Richard. *Hunting the Devil: The Pursuit, Capture and Confession of the Most Savage Serial Killer in History.* New York: HarperCollins, 1993.

Matthews, Owen. "A Crime-Fighting MD and the Twisted Citizens of the Capital of Serial Crime: City of the Dead." *Newsweek,* January 25, 1999.

SEVEN

JACK UNTERWEGER:
Linkage Analysis and the Detective's Database

Three deputy U.S. marshals and an agent from the Bureau of Alcohol, Tobacco and Firearms kept surveillance on a Western Union office on Collins Avenue in Florida's South Beach. It might have seemed like a cushy assignment, sitting there watching scantily clad people enjoying the sun, but the team was waiting for a desperate fugitive and suspected serial killer named Jack Unterweger. He had fled from Austria and established himself in Florida, but telegrams sent by Austrian officials pinpointed his whereabouts and allowed police to set a trap.

Armed with a photograph of Unterweger, the agents watched for his approach. Since he had lied to customs about his criminal record, they had cause for arrest, although it was only a reason to detain him until they had the paperwork for more serious charges.

Eventually Unterweger approached, in the company of his girlfriend, Bianca Mrak. "He looked like a normal tourist," Shawn Conboy later told a reporter, although his distinctly European clothing, pale skin, and the prison tattoos covering his arms gave him away. The agents could hardly believe that this short, scrawny guy was responsible for a dozen murders, but it wasn't their job to make that call. They just had to keep an eye on him.

Bianca entered the money-exchange area of the office while Unterweger waited outside. When she returned, they started to walk away and the marshals fell in behind them. But Unterweger, alert, noticed them and took off running. One agent stayed with Bianca while the others chased Unterweger.

He ran down an alley off Collins Avenue and into a restaurant, moving through it as fast as he could, and then ducked out the back. But the agents were faster and they managed to corner him in a parking structure as squad cars pulled up. The little Austrian had no choice but to surrender and they slipped handcuffs on his wrists, put him into a car, and took him to downtown Miami. Unterweger, a former convict freed under unusual circumstances, had vowed that he would never spend another night in prison. He acted confident that he would not be found guilty of any of the crimes of which he was accused. He did not realize that in addition to the Austrian officials who were interested in questioning him, there were detectives from Los Angeles as well. He was a suspect in a case that involved an international crime spree, and since authorities had no witnesses or direct physical evidence, it would take an impressive database and sophisticated behavioral assessment to nail him.

Alert Detective

It was a retired Austrian detective, August Schenner, who made the first connection. He watched the newspapers during the early 1990s as a string of murders was reported that bore an eerie likeness to two murders he had once investigated. What he did not know was that the murders in Austria were just more in a series that had begun near Prague.

On a chilly September morning in 1990, a woman's body was found along the bank of the Vltava River in Czechoslovakia. She was lying on her back, naked, except for a pair of gray stockings. Left in a sexually suggestive position with her legs open, she was covered with leaves, grass, and twigs. On her finger was a gold ring. This victim had been recently strangled, as well as stabbed in the buttocks and beaten. There were bruises all over her, signaling quite a struggle, but no sign of sexual assault.

A search along the river turned up female clothing that appeared to be the right size for the body, along with a wallet containing identification. The victim's name was Blanka Bockova. She was thirty years old, married, and had worked at a butcher shop in Prague. She had left the shop on September 14, the day before her body turned up, going to Wenceslas Square for a drink with friends. They left just before midnight, but she wanted to stay. They saw her talking with a well-dressed man around forty years of age. He was not a regular, and no one knew his name or where he was from, so he was never picked up for questioning and the case went unsolved.

Sometime after October 26, 1990, in Graz, Austria, a prostitute named Brunhilde Masser vanished. Prostitution was legal in Austria, where prostitute murders averaged about one per year. Thus there was reason for concern over this unusual crime, and that concern increased on December 5 when another prostitute, Heidemarie Hammerer, disappeared from Bregenz, an Austrian tourist city that borders Switzerland and Germany.

On New Year's Eve, hikers came across Hammerer's fully clothed body. Upon closer inspection, it appeared that she had been killed and then re-dressed, after which she had been dragged through the woods. She still wore her jewelry, so robbery did not seem to be a motive. Her legs were bare and a piece of fabric had been cut from her slip with a sharp instrument, like a knife. This piece was found in her mouth.

Cold weather had helped to preserve the remains, so the pathologist determined that Hammerer had been strangled with a pair of panty hose, presumably her own. In addition, there were bruises on her wrists that bore the marks of some kind of restraint, such as handcuffs or tight ligatures. She had bruises on other areas of her body as well, as if she had been beaten. No sexual discharge was present on or around the body. One potential piece of evidence was the presence of several foreign red fibers on her clothing. The regional office of the Austrian Federal Police began an immediate investigation.

Five days after Hammerer's body was discovered in Bregenz, hikers came across some badly decomposed remains of a woman in an isolated forest north of Graz. The local pathologist determined that the killer had stabbed her and possibly strangled her with her own panty hose. Her clothing, handbag, and other personal property were missing, yet she still had her jewelry. The police soon identified her as Brunhilde Masser.

The Austrian Federal Police assigned to the Styrian region took over this investigation, but they found no one who knew about Hammerer's or Masser's last customers. Someone had seen a man in a leather jacket with Hammerer but could not identify him.

Three months later, on March 17, in Graz, Elfriede Schrempf vanished from her usual corner. Soon, a stranger called Schrempf's family. He mentioned her by name, made threatening comments, and hung up. He called once more with the same message, but the family could not identify him. While the Austrian police did not yet know about the murder of Blanka Bockova in Prague, they did have two disturbing murders and one missing-person case that bore similar associations.

There were no real leads, although the police kept on the case for several months. Then, just as the investigation began to fade, on October 5, hikers called in a set of skeletonized remains that they'd found in a forested area outside Graz. These remains suggested a woman about the size of Schrempf, who was soon identified as the victim.

Then, over the course of a month, Silvia Zagler, Sabine

Moitzi, Regina Prem, and Karin Eroglu, all prostitutes, vanished from the streets of Vienna. It appeared that the killer had selected a specific victim group, workers in the sex trade, but there was no evidence of sexual violation or ejaculation on or near the bodies. The victims' bruises indicated anger, so this man might have been committing murder in frustration. A team of investigators from the various relevant jurisdictions came together to discuss the crimes, but concluded that they did not have a serial killer on their hands. There were similarities, yes, but there were also differences.

On May 20, Sabine Moitzi's body turned up, and three days later, so did the remains of Karin Eroglu. Both had been dumped in forested areas outside of Vienna, lying prone, and both had been strangled with an article of their own clothing. Eroglu's body was naked except for her jewelry and Moitzi wore only a jersey, pulled up. Moitzi's money was missing, but her clothing and handbag were found a few yards away from her body. Eroglu had been subjected to blunt-force trauma to the face. Her handbag and clothing were missing, except for her shoes and a body stocking, which her killer had forced down her throat. The press began printing articles about a serial killer, dubbing him "the Vienna Courier" and "the Vienna Woods Killer."

It was around this time that August Schenner, retired from the Criminal Investigation Department in Salzburg, made a call to his former colleagues. He asked about the status of a convicted killer named Johann "Jack"

Unterweger. Something about the prostitute killer's MO reminded Schenner of this man.

Back in 1974, he said, he had investigated two murders. Margaret Schaefer, eighteen, had been strangled and left in the woods. She was a friend of Barbara Scholz, a prostitute who had been involved in the killing. Scholz and Unterweger had robbed Schaefer's house and then took her into the woods. With a belt from her coat, Unterweger tied her hands behind her back, beat her, removed her clothes, and demanded sex. She refused, so he hit her in the head with a steel pipe. Then he used her bra to strangle her to death, leaving her nude body faceup in the forest, covered with leaves.

When the police questioned Unterweger, he broke down and confessed. In court, he defended himself by claiming that as he had hit Fräulein Schaefer, he had envisioned his mother in front of him. His anger was such that he could not stop. (It seems likely that he borrowed this notion from a psychiatrist who had interviewed him.)

Dr. Klaus Jarosch pronounced him a sexually sadistic psychopath with narcissistic and histrionic tendencies. "He tends to sudden fits of rage and anger," Jarosch wrote. "His physical activities are enormously aggressive with sexually sadistic perversion . . . He is an incorrigible perpetrator."

The second murdered woman, Schenner said, was Marcia Horveth, a prostitute, who was strangled with her stockings and a necktie. Adhesive tape was applied to her mouth, and her body was thrown into Lake Salzachsee near Salzburg. The police did not investigate Unterweger for this murder, because he was already in prison for life. It had seemed a waste of resources. Yet Schenner, convinced that Unterweger was responsible, interviewed him, finding him quite vehement in his denials.

While at the prison, Schenner had the impression that the charming convict was running the place. That was reason enough to suspect that, despite a life sentence, he had persuaded officials to give him a parole hearing, where he could then strut his best stuff. Schenner learned that fifteen years into his sentence—just a few months before Brunhilde Masser was murdered—Jack Unterweger had indeed been paroled. Not only was he free, he was a national celebrity.

A Voice from Prison

Unterweger had signed up for writing courses, and was soon editing a prison newspaper and literary review. Eventually he was writing poems, short stories, and plays that won him some attention in the outside world. In 1984, his prison autobiography, *Fegefeuer* (Purgatory), was a bestseller and his rage-filled tale "Endstation Zuchthaus" (Terminus Prison) won a prestigious literary prize. In his writings, he admitted that by the time he had committed the murder that sent him to prison for life, he had fifteen prior convictions for such crimes as rape and burglary. "I wielded my steel rod among prostitutes in Hamburg, Munich and Marseilles," he wrote. "I had enemies and I conquered them through my inner hatred."

His memoir begins with a tone of existential despair.

"My sweaty hands were bound behind my back," he wrote in *Fegefeuer,* "with steel chains snapped around my wrists. The hard pressure on my legs and back makes me realize that my only escape is to end it. I lay awake, removed from the liberating unconsciousness of the sheep. Bathed in shit, trembling. My miserable small dreams are a daily reminder. Anxiously I stare into the unknown darkness of the still night outside. There's security in darkness. I try to divert my thoughts from wondering about the time. I ask only for the immediate moment, for in that lies my strength. It's still night, already late into the night, getting closer to morning."

Unterweger gave the impression that he was himself a victim, and he lied about his rough life. He falsely claimed his mother and her sister had been prostitutes, that an aunt (who didn't even exist) had been murdered, and that he'd been forced to live with an abusive, alcoholic grandfather. (Unterweger's stepsister insisted that this was inaccurate.) Critics and prison reformers embraced his supposed honesty and hailed him as an example of how art can redeem a criminal. Journalists contacted him for interviews and it wasn't long before support swelled among café intellectuals—*Literarniks*—to set him free. It seemed clear from his ideas and ability to write that he could contribute to the betterment of society. In fact, a prominent sex researcher said that Unterweger was remorseful, understood his past actions, and could keep himself from relapsing.

On May 23, 1990, just before his fortieth birthday, he won parole. He was granted a generous government subsidy to assist him in making the transition from prison to the world. "That life is over now," he told the press. "Let's get on with the new." What he meant was that he was ready to kill again.

In his new life, Unterweger became the darling of Viennese intellectuals. He was much in demand, attending book launches, literary soirees, and opening nights. *Fegefeuer* was made into a movie, and the former convict was a frequent guest on talk shows. A traveling theater troupe presented his plays, inviting him to the openings, where he presented himself as a suave and stylish figure in white suits, silk shirts, and gold chains. He purchased several flashy cars, and whenever he showed up in Vienna's trendy champagne bars, he charmed the women.

Unterweger was good at sniffing out stories that the public craved to read. It wasn't long before someone thought he ought to be writing about murder, since he knew that subject firsthand, so he avidly pursued such cases, wrote about them, and talked about them on television. Regarding the recent string of prostitute murders, he hounded investigators in print about their failure to arrest someone. He interviewed prostitutes in the streets, wrote forcefully about "the Courier," and alerted the public that, contrary to what the police said, their worst fears were true: Austria had a serial killer.

Clandestine Investigation

Eventually, investigators began to view him as a suspect, given his background. He had started early, stealing cars and breaking into businesses. He seemed to despise prostitutes and had once forced a young woman into acts of prostitution and taken her money—a way to degrade her. But their first task was to ensure that it was physically possible for Unterweger to commit any of the crimes.

They instituted a discreet surveillance of him, but he did not act in a suspicious manner. He went about his business, meeting literary colleagues and dining with various women. Then on June 11, 1991, three days into the surveillance, he flew to Los Angeles to write a series of freelance articles about crime in that city for an Austrian magazine.

During the five weeks that Unterweger was in Los Angeles, the murders in Austria stopped. Dr. Ernst Geiger, the number two man in the Austrian Federal Police and the most experienced detective on the force, took charge of the investigation. He knew he had to build a clear case against Unterweger or eliminate him and move on, because the public would turn on the police if they falsely accused such a popular figure. Through credit-card receipts at hotels, restaurants, and rental-car agencies, investigators pieced together Unterweger's movements. They placed him in Graz in October when Brunhilde Masser was murdered and again in March when Elfriede Schrempf disappeared. He was in Bregenz in December when Heidemarie Hammerer was taken, and a witness said that Unterweger resembled the man with whom Hammerer was last seen. On that night, this witness said, the man had worn a brown leather jacket and red knit scarf. The police listed these items on a warrant.

They also determined that Unterweger had been in

Prague the previous September. Contacting authorities there, they learned that his visit had coincided with the unsolved murder of Blanka Bockova, and during the times when the four victims were abducted in Vienna, Unterweger was there as well. They had enough evidence to warrant an interview with the famous writer.

On October 22, 1991, officers of the Criminal Investigation Bureau in Vienna questioned Unterweger about the Austrian murders. The lead interviewer already knew his suspect, because as a journalist, Unterweger had questioned *him* about the series of murders for an article. There was the chance that the bureau's interest in him might pressure him to confess, but while he admitted seeing hookers, he denied knowing any of the victims. Although Unterweger had no alibis, investigators had no evidence, so they had to give up.

In retaliation, Unterweger wrote more articles about the mishandling of the investigation. Many of his new cronies supported him, taking up the cause that he was being targeted and persecuted.

Around this time, the missing Regina Prem's husband and son, who had unlisted numbers, received telephone calls from a man who claimed to be her killer. He accurately described what she was wearing the night she disappeared. He was her executioner, he said, and God had ordered him to do it. She had been left in "a place of sacrifice" with her face "turned toward hell." He also said, "I gave eleven of them the punishment they deserved." Three months later, in January 1992, Prem's husband found five empty cigarette packs of the brand that she preferred rolled up in his mailbox. Among these packs was a passport photo that Regina had carried of her son.

Geiger questioned Austrian prostitutes, who described Unterweger's desire that they wear handcuffs during sex. That was consistent enough with the killer, so the police continued their surveillance. Geiger also tracked down the BMW that Unterweger had purchased upon his release from prison. He'd replaced it with a VW Passat, but its new owner allowed the police to go through it. They found a hair fragment, which might or might not help, but which they sent for analysis.

In February 1992, the Interior Ministry created a special commission for further investigation, which involved investigators from Vienna, Graz, and lower Austria, with Geiger leading it. He was determined to rearrest Unterweger and hoped for useful results from the lab analysis.

Manfred Hochmeister, at the Institut für Rechtsmedizin in Berne, Switzerland, found sufficient skin on the root of the hair shaft from the car to perform a DNA analysis using the PCR technique. They compared it to the DNA of each of the victims and found that it matched the first victim, Blanka Bockova, from Prague. That placed the strangled woman with Jack Unterweger, since he had driven the car at the time, and made it possible for police to get a warrant to search Unterweger's apartment in Vienna.

When investigators arrived, he was not at home, but their hunch about him inspired a comprehensive search. They discovered a menu and receipts from a seafood restaurant in Malibu, California, as well as photographs of

Unterweger posing with female members of the Los Angeles Police Department. Opening a closet, they received a nice surprise: a brown leather jacket and red knit scarf, which they seized.

Geiger contacted the LAPD to ask about unsolved murders in the city and discovered that they were investigating three seemingly linked murders of prostitutes. Geiger pressed for details: all had been left out in the open, strangled with their bras, and killed during the time when Unterweger had been in the city. Shannon Exley, thirty-five, was found on June 20, 1991, on a hill near the Pomona Freeway in the Boyle Heights area; on June 30, Irene Rodriguez was dumped on pavement on First and Myers streets in Boyle Heights; and then twenty-six-year-old Peggi Jean Booth (aka Sherri Ann Long) was strangled and left in brushland on Corral Canyon Road in the Malibu Hills. Her body was discovered on July 10.

Geiger mentioned Unterweger being there and learned that the L.A. cops were familiar with him. He had introduced himself as a European journalist and said he was working on an article about prostitution in L.A., so he needed to know where these women might be found. Using the receipts recovered at Unterweger's apartment, Geiger realized that the places where each victim was last seen alive were near one of the seedy, twenty-five-dollar-a-night hotels in which Unterweger had stayed. Now, for the first time, the LAPD had a viable suspect for their serial killings and Geiger had even more supporting information for his own case. He also found the two articles that Unterweger had published upon his return from

California. "Real life in L.A.," Unterweger had written, "is dominated by a tough struggle for survival, by the broken dreams of thousands who come to the city and an equal number who leave, sometimes dead."

In Switzerland, analysts at the University of Berne had finished their examination of the leather jacket and red scarf from Unterweger's apartment. Fibers from these items were consistent with those found on the body of Heidemarie Hammerer. No one could definitely identify the scarf as the source of the evidence, but it could not be eliminated either, and it allowed Geiger to obtain an arrest warrant. Once again, when the police arrived at Unterweger's apartment, he was gone—off on a holiday with his girlfriend, Bianca Mrak, a pretty eighteen-year-old who had met him in a wine bar where she worked as a waitress.

Meanwhile, Unterweger's friends told him that the police were seeking information about him, so he fled the country, with Bianca in tow. The couple ended up in South Beach. From there, Unterweger called Austrian papers to insist that he was being framed and asked his friends for support. The authorities learned that Bianca's mother was sending money via wire transfers, so they contacted her to tell her their suspicions about the man who was with her daughter. She agreed to help.

Unterweger offered a deal: he promised to return and answer questions if the arrest warrants were withdrawn. He wrote a letter in his defense to Austrian officials, which he wanted published in newspapers so the public would read his claim and decide for themselves about his innocence.

"My flight was and is no confession," he insisted. "It is a different type of despair." He went on to point out that there was no way to prove anything against him. "I was doing well," he wrote, "perhaps too good—and fate decided to punish me once more for my debt from the past. But in the moment, I still have something to say. If a fair, neutral official of justice is invited to determine that the warrant against me is unjust, I am ready to place myself at this person's disposal."

One magazine, *Erfolg*, offered him a substantial fee for the exclusive story of his escape. He agreed to do it, happy for both the money and the publicity, and gave its editors an address. They passed this along to Geiger.

To everyone, Unterweger made the same claim: he had an alibi for every one of the murders. The police were giving out a "controlled history." They had singled him out as a scapegoat because they were upset over his parole and his published criticism of them, and were intent on sending him back to prison. Until he could get a fair hearing, he said, he would remain on the run.

Bianca wired her mother to send cash, providing a Miami address, and Mrs. Mrak informed the police. (By some accounts, the editor of *Erfolg* only pretended to hire him so that he would go to the money-exchange office and into the hands of police.) The information was conveyed to Interpol, which alerted U.S. officials. The U.S. marshals took it from there. They arrested Unterweger, while an agent accompanied Bianca to the place where she and Unterweger were staying. A search of their rooms turned up Unterweger's travel journal, which indicated that he was contemplating murdering Bianca.

Unterweger was detained in order to await extradition, but it was unclear whether he was going to California or to Austria. Although LAPD detectives Fred Miller and Jim Harper arrived to question him, it was deemed best to turn him over to his native country. To strengthen their own case, Miller and Harper obtained a search warrant for tissue samples, so they drew Unterweger's blood and took hair samples and swabs of saliva for DNA testing. His DNA matched that found in semen from one of their victims, but she also had semen from six other men, so this case was weak. Unfortunately, there had been no discharge in or on the other two prostitutes.

The detectives told Unterweger that in California he faced the possibility of the gas chamber, so he quickly agreed to be deported. He had Austrian public opinion on his side, and the actual physical evidence the police had there was flimsy. He believed he could beat the rap. In a fairly good mood, he was sent back to Austria on May 28, 1992.

While being detained in his home country, Unterweger gave interviews freely. He claimed that he had been fully rehabilitated and asked, in *Profil* in October, "Would I be so stupid and so mad that during the luckiest phase of my life, in which I've done theater productions, played a role onstage, organized a tour, and made many wonderful female friends, I would go kill someone each week in between?" He also kept a prison journal of his thoughts and his poetry about the time he'd been free, and wrote letters to the press insisting on his innocence. He could prove it, he said, although he offered nothing to support this claim.

Then, a year after her disappearance in 1991, parts of a skeleton were found that were identified as the remains of Regina Prem, the woman whose husband had received the disturbing phone calls. She had been left in the woods, which was consistent with the pattern of killings, but no clothing or jewelry was found, and after such a long period of exposure to the elements, her manner of death could not be determined.

Although some of the eminent writers who had led the campaign to free Unterweger continued to stand by him, his most vocal early supporters issued public apologies. Jack was losing some of his appeal.

VICAP

The best hope for conviction was to demonstrate the repetitive patterns from case to case. There was no time for the Austrians to develop a database, and they knew that testimony from a mental health expert could easily be countered by defense experts. The FBI had a database and plenty of expertise in serial murder. Three of the murders were committed on U.S. soil, and since Austrian courts allowed evidence from crimes committed in other jurisdictions, Geiger knew what he had to do next.

He contacted an FBI office in Vienna, and through them, he explained what he needed to Supervisory Special Agent Gregg McCrary in the Behavioral Science Unit (BSU) at Quantico, Virginia. McCrary described their meeting and his involvement in the case in *The Unknown Darkness*. Geiger enlisted Thomas Mueller, chief of the Criminal Psychology Service in the Federal Ministry of the Interior, to go with him to the States, and for two weeks, they learned how the BSU worked on such cases. Profiling was not involved, since these cases were well beyond that stage, but the area of Criminal Investigative Analysis that was relevant was case linkage—showing that the behaviors were consistent across the cases in such a way as to prove that the same perpetrator committed them all.

"Before the Austrian investigators arrived," McCrary said, "I asked that they separate the victim files from suspect information, because we don't want to know anything about this person. As objective as we try to be, we still might spin or interpret the cases to fit. We put that aside and don't compare it until we've gone through the case and drawn our own opinion. On the other hand, I wanted a lot of information about the victims—the method and manner of their respective deaths, family history, occupation, the crime scene photos, and the full autopsy reports. I would start without any presupposition that these cases were linked and if I came to the conclusion that they were, I would tell the investigators the kind of person who was most likely to commit the crimes in question. Afterward, they could compare those characteristics to their suspect.

"The two most logical officials for me to meet made plans to come to the states: Ernst Geiger, who was in charge of the investigation, and Thomas Mueller. They told me when they expected to arrive and I blocked out my calendar for two weeks in August. They were bringing twelve boxes of reports, so I commandeered the downstairs conference room for the duration of their visit."

Since criminal profiling had not yet been utilized in Austria, McCrary carefully explained to them the concept of a signature analysis that might link several crime scenes. He looked through the eleven files they brought: seven in Austria, one in Czechoslovakia, and three in the United States. This was unusual: "Killers who travel outside their realm of familiarity are rare. In particular, while they may cross into bordering countries, such as from Austria into neighboring Czechoslovakia, we almost never see them actually fly overseas to look for new victims." Nevertheless, he knew that the human factor meant there was always room for a surprise.

McCrary examined the chronology and methods. "Examining one victim at a time, we looked at the way each had been killed, the manner of body disposal, the type of items left at the scene and the type removed. I took extensive notes to try to distill the significant factors that would help to create a timeline and a means for comparing one case to another. In particular, I was looking for an escalation of certain behaviors. I also examined the terrain and type of geography at the disposal sites and their relationship to the cities of Prague, Graz, and Vienna."

He spotted a pattern:

• The victimology and manner of disposal were similar

• All victims were left outside, and most had branches or foliage placed over them

- No semen was left on or in the bodies (except a small amount on one of the L.A. prostitutes)

- The cause of death was strangulation, usually with an undergarment or stocking

- Many had restraint bruises on their arms and wrists

- No one had seen them going with someone or getting into a car

- There was an absence of any indication of sexual assault

- The trace evidence was next to none

- The MO appeared to be calculated rather than spontaneous

"I believed that this killer acted violently, probably out of impotence. He was insecure about his masculinity and when he could not perform after being stimulated, he blamed the women for shaming him, so he killed them and left their bodies in humiliating positions. The violence itself had become erotic to him."

The next step was to put information into the FBI's Violent Criminal Apprehension Program (VICAP) database. This program was the result of the efforts of a Los Angeles–based detective named Pierce Brooks. As early as 1958, he had spearheaded the movement to develop a national database for unsolved crimes around the country. In one case he worked, he had spent his off-hours and many weekends in the library looking for similar incidents to link to the offender. He started in Los Angeles and then began to go through articles from other major cities. The task seemed hopeless, but then he found a murder in another city that was similar. He made a fingerprint match between the two cases, but the process had been time-consuming and arduous, and with the development of computers he knew it could be streamlined.

He approached his chief with the idea, but such an enterprise seemed financially extravagant. Nevertheless, Brooks knew that investigators around the country needed a centralized database and he never stopped pushing for it. It would be more than two decades before he finally realized his dream. In the early 1980s, at a Senate subcommittee meeting for the Department of Justice, he and others argued for funding for a networked computerized system that would catch serial killers earlier in their careers than had been the case up to then. Brooks said that his own method of looking up linked crimes had remained the same for twenty-five years, which was shameful in the light of advances in technology. Thus VICAP (or ViCAP) was born. The FBI was set to run it out of Quantico as part of the National Center for the Analysis of Violent Crime (NCAVC), and in 1985 Brooks became its first director.

Using standardized forms that contained a lot of questions, police departments from around the country provided detailed data about specific types of incidents: solved, unsolved, and attempted homicides (especially random or sexually oriented); unidentified bodies in which the manner of death is suspected to be homicide; sexual assault incidents; and missing-persons cases in which foul play appears to have played a part. In other words, by using the FBI-provided software and searching the database, a homicide in Los Angeles might be linked to one in Florida committed by the same person, or a murdered John Doe in Missouri could be identified as a missing-person runaway from Michigan. The database benefited large and small agencies equally, giving anyone who searched it the ability to link crimes from around the country.

In addition, VICAP also offered services in investigative support, such as off-line searches and the development of detailed time lines, case management consultation (especially multiagency), and training in crime analysis. The staff could also prepare a "VICAP alert" notice for the *Law Enforcement Bulletin* and other publications.

"At that time, we had 10,000 to 12,000 solved and unsolved homicide cases on file," said McCrary, "so we entered key words from the case analysis in order to narrow down the search field. I wanted to keep it as simple as possible, so I used a minimum number of variables from the cases: age group, the fact that they were prostitutes, the ligature strangulation, the outdoor disposal sites, how they were left mostly or partly nude, and that they had retained their jewelry."

Using the VICAP system, he ordered a multidimensional ad hoc search with fifteen cross-referenced criteria. After two days, Geiger received a report that included the eight European cases and the three from California, as well as one more in California. However, the man responsible for this last crime turned out to already be in prison.

"That was a convincing statistic," said McCrary. "Just using those variables, we excluded thousands of other cases in the database. The eleven believed to be in the series were all linked by the computer. In other words, it would be highly unusual to have more than one guy engaging in this specific type of behavior during this same time period. Even more significant, this offender had committed all these murders in less than a year."

Then it was time to open the envelope containing the information about the suspect. Unterweger's movements also formed a time line from September of 1991 through July of 1992. He proved to be a very good suspect: "We could put Unterweger at every murder location. He was either the unluckiest man in the world to have been in all those places at the wrong time or he was an excellent suspect."

The Fugitive Pleads His Case

The trial began under Judge Kurt Haas in June 1994 in Graz, Austria. As an Austrian citizen, Unterweger could be tried for the three murders in Los Angeles and the one in Prague along with the seven in Austria. Despite his many indictments, public support for him had not diminished and he continued to seek interviews in which he claimed he was innocent and bragged about how he would win. (He'd even published another book by then—*99 Hours*—that detailed his life on the run.) The prosecutors, Martin Wenzl and Karl Gasser, intended to show that he was a liar, that he had no alibi, that as a psychopath he was still dangerous, and that the evidence nailed him and only him. Unterweger was represented by Hans Lehofer, as well as by the entertainment lawyer who had assisted in winning his parole, Georg Zanger.

Detective Jim Harper arrived from Los Angeles to lay out the evidence from those cases, and Lynn Herold from the crime lab to testify about the special knots used to bind or strangle each victim. The bras from the Los Angeles prostitutes had been cut in exactly the same places in order to create a braid using the straps. Herold showed how the Austrian killer had made a similar knot with the tights and stockings belonging to the victims there.

Gregg McCrary, the first FBI profiler to testify in an Austrian court, discussed the VICAP system, the unique behavioral patterns that linked all of the crimes, and how those behaviors were associated with Unterweger's first murder. In addition, the prosecution had a psychiatric report about Unterweger's sadistic criminal nature; Blanka Bockova's hair recovered from Unterweger's car; numerous red fibers from Brunhilde Masser's body consistent with fibers from Unterweger's red scarf; and character-witness testimony from former associates and girlfriends whom he had conned.

Unterweger's attorneys had never before dealt with the FBI's criminal investigative analysis program, so they inadvertently asked questions that only strengthened the prosecution's case. They attempted to prove that the prosecution's case was irrational and illogical—Unterweger was a successful journalist and successful with women, so why would he undermine himself so badly, and why would he even need a prostitute? These questions were easily addressed by someone familiar, as McCrary was, with the compulsion and fetishes involved in serial murder. Rationality is not usually the issue, he pointed out, nor the availability of sex. Killing was a dark addiction, motivated by thrill or the need for control.

Unterweger, dressed like a dandy, argued his case before the jury. He seemed confident that his charm and good looks would deflect them from the evidence. He asked the jury not to judge him on past deeds, admitting what a "rat" he had once been, "a primitive criminal who grunted rather than talked and an inveterate liar." He "consumed women, rather than loved them." But he had changed, he insisted. He had been rehabilitated. He was no longer the bad person he once had been.

"I'm counting on your acquittal," he said, "because I am not the culprit. Your decision will affect not only me but the real killer, who is laughing up his sleeve."

The trial lasted two months, involving many witnesses, and the opinion of the press toward Unterweger began to shift, especially when they learned he had tried to persuade some people to provide a false alibi. Things looked bad for the defendant. So far he'd been unable to counter the evidence, as he'd promised to do. Perhaps the reformed criminal had not been reformed after all. Even Bianca Mrak had decided she'd had enough and abandoned him.

In the end, the evidence was convincing. The jury voted six to two to convict, which was sufficient in Austria. Jack Unterweger was found guilty of nine counts of murder—the Prague victim, all three Los Angeles victims, and five in Austria. (The remaining two Austrian victims had been too decomposed to establish a definite cause of death.) The court immediately sentenced the defendant to life in prison. His eyes filled with tears as he vowed to appeal.

This was quite a blow to a man who had assured everyone that he would never spend another day in that hellhole. Psychopathic serial killers often have issues with control, and Unterweger was no exception. Defiant to the end, he fulfilled his promise in the only manner that was left to him: when the guards were not looking, he used the string from his prison jumpsuit to hang himself. By some accounts, it was tied in the same knot he had used on the panty hose of his victims.

On a positive note, Unterweger's legacy was that Austria set up a system for criminal investigation similar to the FBI's VICAP program. As for Jack Unterweger, he was a rare and clever offender, but his case demonstrated what McCrary likes to say: "When you educate a psychopath, all you get is an educated psychopath."

Catching a serial killer usually involves the coordination of a number of resources, but rarely do investigators bait a trap with a former victim. The following case was one such success story.

Sources

Articles from German newspapers and magazines on Jack Unterweger.

Blumenthal, Ralph. "Confined, in Prisons, Literature Breaks Out." *New York Times,* August 26, 2000.

DeNevi, Don, and John H. Campbell. *Into the Minds of Madmen: How the FBI Behavioral Science Unit Revolutionized Crime Investigation*. Amherst, NY: Prometheus Books, 2004.

"Forensic Psychiatric Aspects of the Case of Jack Unterweger." *Forensische Psychiatrie und Psychotherapie*, Expenditure 4.

King, Brian, editor. *Lustmord: The Writings and Artifacts of Murderers*. Burbank, CA: Bloat, 1996.

Leake, John. *Entering Hades: The Double Life of a Serial Killer*. New York: Farrar, Straus and Giroux, 2007.

Malnic, Eric. "Following a Killing Trail." *Los Angeles Times,* March 13, 1992.

———. "Police Fight Time in Effort to Link Austrian, Killings." *Los Angeles Times,* April 3, 1992.

———. "Austrian Slayer of L.A. Prostitutes Kills Self." *Los Angeles Times,* June 30, 1994.

McCrary, Gregg, with Katherine Ramsland. *The Unknown Darkness: Profiling the Predators Among Us*. New York: William Morrow, 2003.

Unterweger, Jack. *Fegefeuer, order die Reise ins Zuchthaus*. Maro Vlg., Augsbg, 1983.

———. *Endstation Zuchthaus/Kerkerzeit*. Taschenbuch, 1984.

Wagner, Astrid. *Kannibalenzeit: Die Unterweger-Verschwörung*. Broschiert, 1996.

———. *Im Zweifel Schuldig: Der Fall der Jack Unterweger: Wenn Medien Recht Sprechen*. Broschiert, 1998.

www.fbi.gov/hq/isd/cirg/ncavc.htm

EIGHT

HARVEY ROBINSON:
A Risky Sting

It was rare for patrol officers to be in this position, but for two weeks Brian Lewis and Ed Bachert had been sitting up all night in separate houses in the hope of stopping a roving killer. At each place lived the victim of a brutal attack, and on Bachert's watch in the middle of the night, someone had banged on the door but tried nothing more. Lewis wondered if the house where he was staying would be next.

The killer had already returned to the place at least once, before the surveillance, stealing a gun. He knew that someone who lived there could identify him, so Lewis had been watching throughout the night. If no one showed up soon, the surveillance would end, but with a few nights remaining, Lewis knew he still had a chance to stop the man who had already killed three women in the area.

Allentown, Pennsylvania, in the peaceful Lehigh Valley, seemed an unlikely place for a serial killer, but during the 1980s and 1990s, such crimes had increased across the country. There had been several serial killers in Philadelphia, an hour to the south. Then, in quick succession in 1993, a man abducted a girl and also entered four different homes, killing three people and assaulting two more, including a five-year-old child. The woman Lewis was now protecting would probably have died had not a neighbor fortuitously stepped in.

It was now the twelfth night on his watch. He had a few magazines to help keep himself alert, and lights burned as enticement at the two windows left open. Around 1:20 A.M., Lewis heard a noise and tensed to listen. Someone was testing the patio door.

Harvey Robinson, whose series of rape/murders struck fear into the small town of Allentown, Pennsylvania, in 1992.
Allentown Police Department

This was it! The end of a terror spree that had started eighteen months before.

Harming the Innocent

Mary Burghardt, twenty-nine, suffered from a mental illness and could not function without assistance. On August 7, 1992, she reported that someone had cut through a screen door and entered her apartment. Two days later, she was unaware that a young man was watching her through a window as she began to undress. She entered the living room with some milk and cookies, and suddenly the same man tore through the front window screen and came at her, smacking her so hard in the head that he knocked off her glasses and spattered the wall with her blood. Although trapped, she managed to run past this intruder and get to a room where she could pound on the wall and scream for help. No one came.

The intruder turned on the television, increasing the volume. With his prey trapped and helpless, he bludgeoned her with a blunt weapon until she fell to the floor; he kept hitting her in a rage until he had delivered thirty-seven blows to her head, some so strong that strands of her hair were driven into the skull fractures. Once he was certain she was dead, he looked for a pair of her panties in a drawer and then used them to masturbate over her prostrate body. Then he left through a back door. Despite being covered in blood, he walked through a field and returned to his home, about four blocks away.

Soon he was detained for a lesser crime and sent to

juvenile detention. When he was released eight months later, on June 9, 1993, he drove back to his victim's neighborhood and spotted a girl on a bike delivering papers. He grabbed her in broad daylight.

A woman on East Gordon Street, waiting for her *Morning Call,* looked out her window and saw the newspaper cart abandoned between two parked cars. It was uncharacteristic of carrier Charlotte Schmoyer to be negligent, so the woman phoned the police. They called Schmoyer's supervisor, who said he had not heard from her and could not locate her. When officers searched the area, they located the girl's bicycle and portable radio, but not her. She was also not home.

D.A. Robert Steinberg accompanied the police as they followed a tip to a wooded area at the East Side Reservoir. They discovered a trail of blood leading from the parking lot and Steinberg noted a discarded shoe. Then one searcher called out from the woods that he had found the fifteen-year-old's body, covered with dead leaves and several heavy logs. No one had seen the incident, but a resident recalled a light blue car in the area, while someone else reported a similar vehicle at the reservoir.

An autopsy revealed that Schmoyer had been stabbed twenty-two times in the back and neck before her throat was slashed open. She had also been raped, and three superficial cuts indicated that a knife was held to her throat during her ordeal. A pubic hair was picked off her navy sweatshirt and a head hair from her knee.

Yet there were no real leads and no clues from the scene of the abduction or murder, so this shocking crime went unsolved. Residents wondered if the girl had known her abductor or if the incident had involved a stranger's random attack. No one yet realized that Charlotte Schmoyer was actually the second victim of the killer.

Early Warning

Denise Sam-Cali, thirty-seven, lived on the East Side of Allentown, not far from where Charlotte had been abducted, and she usually walked a mile each morning to the limousine and bus service she owned with her husband, John. She learned only later that a young man had spotted and followed her.

Denise and John went away for a few days and returned on June 17. To their annoyance, they found the back door to their home slightly open. John went inside to look around, but saw no immediate evidence of a burglary. Nevertheless, someone had clearly been there, as a whiskey bottle had been moved and they found a dirty footprint on the couch. Then John checked his gun collection, which he kept in a special bag in the closet, and was stunned to discover the bag gone. He phoned the police, who were unable to locate the stolen collection.

For protection, John quickly purchased two more guns, including one for Denise. He felt frightened knowing that someone not only had those guns but had also entered his home, and violated it. Denise did her best to learn how to shoot, although she hoped she'd never need to defend herself in this manner. The couple had reason to grow even more worried when another incident occurred in their neighborhood.

On June 20, an intruder entered the home of a woman who was in bed on the second floor with her boyfriend. Her five-year-old daughter slept in a bedroom nearby, and the intruder entered and choked her into unconsciousness, carrying her by her neck downstairs. She revived and tried to scream, but he dumped her headfirst into a laundry basket full of towels and dirty clothes. While she was unable to move or scream, he raped her. Then he choked her again and she passed out. At this point, he left the residence and went home, just two blocks away.

Early the following morning, the girl woke her mother to tell her what had happened, so the woman's boyfriend checked downstairs and found that a window screen had been removed. The victim's mother saw small hemorrhages in the child's eyes, a sign of asphyxia. She took her to a doctor who found that she had been choked till some blood vessels had burst and had been sexually attacked. The intruder had probably intended to kill her.

With one victim grabbed outside and two accosted inside their homes, Allentown residents were alarmed. More people began locking their doors and windows, despite the summer heat, but this did not stop the marauder. After a month, he struck again.

Failed Assault

Denise Sam-Cali was home alone on June 28, because John was on a business trip. She had come in late after visiting her aunt down the street, and gone to bed.

Although she had practiced with the new gun and was able to hold it steady, she still did not feel safe. Opening the bedroom window for some fresh air, she undressed and crawled under the sheets.

But she was restless and unable to sleep. She lay in bed listening to the night noises outside and hoping that John would come home. Suddenly she caught her breath. She was sure she'd heard something inside the house that sounded like crackling paper. She sat up and shouted, "Who's there?" She hoped whoever it was believed he had entered an empty house, like before, and that he would be startled to realize someone was home and decide to just leave. But the place was silent.

Deciding she'd be safer with a neighbor, Denise jumped out of bed, grabbed a comforter to cover herself, and ran down the hall. To her horror, a man emerged from a walk-in closet with a knife in his hand. Racing away, she went for the door, but he got there, too, and grabbed her arm. He tried to stab her in the face, cutting her lip, but she knocked the knife away and struggled to get out. Although he still had a firm grip on her arm, she managed to break free, get outside, and run. On the lawn, the man caught her by the hair and threw her to the ground. She tried to scream but nothing more than a gurgle came out. This intruder was adept at pinning a woman down while he prepared to rape her. He began to strangle her, and she later recalled being punched four times in the face. Denise bit her attacker hard and cried out, but he choked her until she blacked out.

But she was lucky. A neighbor turned on a floodlight, which frightened off the attacker. Denise regained consciousness and managed to crawl back into her home and call 911. The police arrived and took her to a hospital. It was clear from her injuries that she would need hospitalization and possibly plastic surgery. She let a nurse process her with a rape kit for evidence, although she was not certain she'd been raped. As doctors attended to her bruised face and the strangulation marks on her neck, she was aware how lucky she was to be alive. Her assailant had certainly intended to kill her. The police soon found the knife he had grabbed in the house, wrapped in a napkin and left behind on the floor.

John was horrified when he learned what had happened. He made immediate plans to secure their home but insisted that Denise stay with one of her relatives. When she was able, she gave the police a description of her attacker: he'd been white, about five-foot-seven, muscular, young, and clean-shaven. His eyes, she recalled, were filled with rage. It would take a session with a hypnotist to help her bring forth enough details from that night to realize that she had indeed been raped.

When the newspaper reported that Denise had survived the attack, she knew she would never be safe in her home as long as this killer was free. He would certainly be afraid that she would recognize him, and given the fact that most of his assaults were in her neighborhood, it was likely he lived there.

John installed an alarm system, but once again the intruder managed to break in. During the night of July

18, someone set off the alarm and left in haste by the back door before the Calis saw him. However, they found several things missing in the morning, including some luggage and a handgun left on a table.

The D.A. believed that the rapist would certainly revisit the home again to silence the witness and he wondered if he could work this to his advantage. It would mean the Calis would have to remain in the home, vulnerable, to lure the man back, but he assured them that they would have police protection every night. They bravely agreed to the plan. Denise wanted relief from the unrelenting nightmares she'd been having since her attack. This man, she believed, had victimized her and would continue to exert power over her until she did something to take it back. She figured that if the intruder managed to break in and get past the police guard, she'd be ready to blast him with her own gun. John would be there, too.

But before this plan was set in motion, another woman was killed.

The Allentown serial killer had spotted a large-boned, overweight white woman, and he'd followed her until he saw where she lived. Jessica Jean Fortney was forty-seven, and she lived with her grown daughter, son-in-law, and their seven-year-old child. On July 14, these three were asleep on the second floor, with loud fans cooling the place, when the man entered and attacked Fortney in the living room, breaking her nose with a weapon. Then he raped and strangled her, leaving her blood-covered body on the sofa beneath a blanket. But this time, there was a witness. Fortney's grandchild had seen the assault from her bedroom. Her description matched what Denise Sam-Cali had said about her attacker.

D.A. Steinberg realized there was a dangerous serial sex killer at large in Allentown who was striking quickly, and often. These crimes had all been committed in the same general area, and except for the newspaper girl, all the victims were attacked inside their homes, after the offender had entered through a window.

The police could only hope the killer would try yet again to silence the one woman who had survived. Their fear was that he would begin to roam a larger area, as his latest crime, over a mile away from the others, suggested. Allentown was close to the urban communities of Bethlehem and Easton, as well as a cluster of smaller towns within a fifteen-minute driving distance. If the killer had a car, as it seemed he did, and was feeling the heat, he might just go farther out. But on July 31, he made a major miscalculation.

The Sting

Officer Brian Lewis, a patrolman with just over three years' experience, was assigned to the Sam-Cali home, a single-story ranch house, while another officer, Ed Bachert, went to the house where the five-year-old girl had been accosted. The assignment was to last two weeks.

They generally arrived around eleven-thirty in the evening and remained until six in the morning. Lewis's routine was to go around and secure all the doors, but leave two casement windows in the front room open, because the intruder had used this entry before. No one knew if this plan would work, but the officers continued to watch, night after night. Then, on the twelfth night, around 1:20 A.M., Lewis heard a distinctive noise: someone was prying at the patio door.

"I was right inside the front door," he related, "against the wall. I knew all the doors were secure, and the patio door even had a piece of wood inserted to prevent it from opening. The rear door had a dead bolt as well. I was positioned where I could see the living room and the casement windows. When I heard a big yank on the patio door, it was probably the best adrenaline rush of my life. I knew this was it!" An outside light showed him a shadowy figure moving around, so unlike the incident a few nights before at the other house, this person was sticking around.

"My instructions were to allow him to come into the home and I would then notify others with the police radio." To accomplish this, Lewis would pull a pin out of the radio, which sent a signal to the communication center that he was in need of immediate assistance.

"I then heard the back doorknob being turned, and a few minutes later, there was another tug on the patio door. I got my gun and flashlight out, and I went to kneel behind the couch." He'd never before shot at a person, so he was understandably tense. "The next thing I saw was the doorknob turning on the front door, and I'm thinking, did I lock that? I was only about two feet away from it. But it didn't open. By that time, my adrenaline had subsided and I was thinking, we've waited this long, don't screw it up."

He saw the screen on one casement window being prodded, and he expected a knife to come through to cut it, "but it just kept getting pushed and finally it pushed in. I saw a hand with a big rubber glove like the kind that janitors use, and it lowered that screen onto the couch below."

At this point, he had not yet pulled the pin on his radio and he did not dare try to talk into it, lest he alert the intruder and scare him off.

"The next thing I see is a face coming through the window. Because the area was lit by a table lamp, I saw a profile. He had a good-size nose. Then the face turned and looked in my direction and then looked away. The next thing I saw was an arm and leg come in. I ducked behind the couch to completely hide and pulled my pin. I heard someone inside the living room, so I stood up and identified myself, and said, 'Freeze!'"

For a moment, the two of them were face-to-face in the small living room. The intruder had a gun on his waistband and he reached for it, so Lewis fired a shot from his Smith & Wesson six-shot revolver. "My flashlight fell to the floor and he dove into the kitchen area, where it was dark. I moved to the doorway and saw a muzzle flash coming back at me. I realized we were in a battle, so I stepped to the left of the doorway, which was a wall, to get some cover. I immediately stepped back to the doorway and fired a shot at where I believed he was, on the floor. By the time I'd fired, he had moved to the back door. I could hear him but I couldn't see, so I fired my next four shots at where I believed he was."

Now Lewis was out of ammo, so he had to reload. He pulled back to where he had cover, but thought, *I can't reload here. He's right there, he's got a gun.* He recalled an incident in Allentown where a sheriff's deputy was shot and killed while reloading, so he retreated toward the back bedroom. He knew the couple was in there, so he yelled out, "Don't shoot, it's me!"

Frightened by all the commotion, John and Denise were standing on either side of the bed, holding guns. Lewis got on the radio to tell other officers what was happening. He heard the intruder banging on the dead-bolted back door and kitchen walls, trying desperately to get out. The house was literally shaking. Lewis instructed the couple to stay out of the way as he reloaded and prepared to face the gunman again.

But suddenly the place went quiet. It felt too still.

Lewis edged cautiously toward the kitchen, uncertain what to expect and keeping his gun ready. As he drew closer, he anticipated that the guy might spring out at him or fire from some dark area. He neared the door to the kitchen, tense, his heart pounding, but when he still heard nothing, he wondered if the intruder had found a way out. Then he saw it: several broken windows on the wooden door. "They were just ripped out of the door."

The man had managed to force his way out and slip away. Lewis went outside, hoping the vice officers had caught him, but there had been an unfortunate delay. When his backup had heard the shots and received the emergency signal, they'd been several blocks away. Thus the intruder had eluded them.

Nevertheless, an examination of the door frame indicated that he'd left blood behind. Lewis thought that perhaps he'd winged the guy and they might have a blood trail to follow. Even better, the intruder might seek medical attention, and blood samples at the hospital would match those in the Calis' house. He also noticed that one of his shots had hit a can of baked beans, exploding its contents into the room. Another officer held up the can and said to Lewis, "You're never gonna live this one down." However, it would prove to be a fortuitous hit.

The entire episode had lasted about twenty minutes. Calls were made to the consortium of Lehigh Valley hospitals to be on the lookout for anyone coming in with a bad cut from glass or a bullet wound. This was the closest the police had come to nailing this offender and they were excited but cautious. There was no certainty in such situations.

Several hours went by without a word. It seemed that the killer had eluded them, but around 3:30 A.M., police learned that a young man had shown up at the Lehigh Valley Hospital's ER to get treated. His arm and leg were bleeding badly. He seemed to realize that he'd walked into a trap and quickly headed for an exit without talking to anyone, but he was stopped outside and detained.

Lewis arrived, but the light had been poor, so he couldn't be sure it was the same man he'd seen in the home. The shoes looked the same, but that was no way to identify someone. However, inside the cruiser car, under different lighting, he was sure. This was the man who had shot at him hours earlier. His name, it turned out, was Harvey Miguel "Miggy" Robinson and he lived on the east side of town with his mother, Barbara Brown, only a few houses from where Ed Bachert had watched during the night.

Lewis learned that Robinson, only eighteen, had told his girlfriend he'd been hurt at a party and it was she who'd insisted he get medical treatment. So he'd gone to the hospital. Since the Sam-Cali residence was on the west side and the hospital across town, he might have believed no one would link him to the break-in.

What to Do with a Serial Killer

Robinson was booked and arraigned on multiple charges, including breaking and entering, burglary, aggravated assault, and attempted homicide. He was held in lieu of $1 million bail. On September 3, Denise Sam-Cali testified at his hearing that she could identify Robinson as the man who attacked her and she fully described her ordeal. He sat throughout the hearing with a glare on his face. Other evidence against him included Officer Lewis's identification, a bite mark that Denise claimed to have made during her assault, black gloves found in his bedroom at his mother's home, and the Colt .380 handgun stolen from the Calis, along with casings that matched those from two bullets fired on July 31 in their home.

The police worked hard to find evidence for the trials. They searched two cars, a light blue Ford Tempo GL belonging to Robinson's mother, which was similar to the car seen in the neighborhood when Charlotte

Schmoyer was abducted, and Robinson's gray Dodge Laser SE. His blood was in both, indicating that he had driven them at different times on the night of the shoot-out, after he was cut. The cars were processed for finger-prints and other evidence. Searching his house, they located some baked beans from the can that Officer Lewis had shot open. They also found clothing, which Robinson had attempted to wash, that matched what Lewis had seen the intruder wearing.

For his arraignment, Robinson wore a bulletproof vest. Police had learned that between the Burghardt and Schmoyer murders, eight months apart, Robinson had been incarcerated for burglary but had no history of mental illness. Investigators believed that he had either known his victims or had stalked them in some manner before raping or killing them. He may have burglarized Burghardt's apartment a few days before he killed her.

In December 1993, just after Robinson turned nine-teen, the papers announced that DNA tests from his blood samples linked him via semen to the three rape/murders and the two rapes. In addition, his blood and hair were found on Schmoyer, and both the little girl he had raped and Denise Sam-Cali identified him as their attacker.

The Case

During a preliminary hearing on January 6, 1994, the prosecutors laid out the case against Robinson for mul-tiple rapes and murders, among other charges. Eighteen witnesses were called, including Denise Sam-Cali once again, although the trial for her rape and attempted murder would be a separate proceeding.

D.A. Steinberg led the prosecution while Robinson's family had hired David Nicholls, and Nicholls immediately questioned the validity of the DNA evidence. It was a common ploy for defense attorneys in those days, because while DNA analysis had been confirmed as a viable science, such attorneys hoped to win back some ground by questioning laboratory procedures and poor handling of evidence. Nicholls suggested possible problems with the technicians, exposure of the samples, questionable internal procedures, and the reliability of the test itself.

Supervisory Special Agent Harold Deadman, with the FBI lab, put the specimens through testing, along with specimens from other men in the area with a history of sex crimes, but only Robinson was a match for the samples retrieved from the victims. The state-police lab confirmed this with its own tests.

The first case to be decided involved Denise Sam-Cali. D.A. Steinberg told her that Robinson would plead guilty in return for a reduced sentence and no trial. She initially declined this offer, but, on April 13, accepted the terms. Semen samples removed from the victim shortly after she was attacked were matched via DNA analysis to Robinson, and she identified him as her attacker. In addition, he had a gun in his possession that he'd stolen from her house, and Officer Lewis identified him as the man with whom he'd had a shoot-out there.

Robinson said nothing during the hearing and his

attorney called no one to speak on his behalf, although Robinson's mother and half sister were present. Nicholls made it clear that the defendant had long been a troubled young man who'd had a difficult life. He offered no motive, but he did set forth the young man's good qualities: a high IQ that allowed him to obtain his high school equivalency diploma when he was sixteen (and in juvenile detention) and a good relationship with a loving mother.

Steinberg told reporters afterward, "He is everything that is evil in society, all rolled up in one person." But Nicholls asked for leniency and suggested that Robinson could be rehabilitated. Steinberg countered this with Robinson's lengthy juvenile record and the threats he had made against other prisoners at the facility where he was currently detained. In fact, since the first grade (which he repeated) Robinson had been resistant to rules and aggressive toward others, and he'd committed his first juvenile offense, a theft, at the age of nine. Each time he was released from juvenile detention, he committed more antisocial acts and refused to take advantage of prosocial opportunities. Given this history and set of behavior patterns, his chances for rehabilitation seemed slim to nonexistent.

Despite Nicholls's argument, Robinson was sentenced to forty to eighty years in state prison for the rape and assault of Denise Sam-Cali, and for burglarizing her home and shooting at a police officer. Nicholls then relinquished his duties, leaving it to a public defender to take on the murder cases. In the meantime, reporters were busy learning more about who this young offender was.

Robinson was biracial, although he normally passed for white, and his black-Hispanic father, who was dead, had been convicted of manslaughter. For that, he'd served a seven-year prison term. The man had frequently gotten drunk and quarreled with Barbara Brown, Robinson's mother, sometimes hitting her. (Robinson denied having been physically abused himself.) His parents divorced when he was three years old and he remained with his mother, although one source indicates that he idealized his father and occasionally saw him. Robinson's older stepbrother had also spent time in prison.

Robinson had been an impulsive child with little ability to focus, a great deal of moodiness, and a hair-trigger temper. He was nine years old when he was first arrested, and over the next eight years, he piled up a dozen more arrests, mostly for theft and property crimes. He fought with authority figures, had a history of substance abuse, and had been diagnosed with conduct disorders that were precursors to an adult antisocial personality disorder.

The family frequently changed its residence, but Robinson spent many years on and off in different juvenile facilities. He once assaulted a male middle school teacher who was assigned to watch emotionally disturbed youths in the classroom, and female teachers reportedly felt threatened by him. He was fifteen when he committed his first known burglary, and two years later, he'd become a rapist and murderer.

Yet he did have his good points. At Dieruff High School, he wrestled, participated in cross-country sports, and played soccer and football, receiving trophies for his skill and ability. He was also a good student, excelling academically and earning awards for his essay writing. But awards and trophies, and even recommendations, are difficult to reconcile with a rash of rapes and brutally violent murders.

The Trial

Robinson was assigned a public defender, Carmen Marinelli, who, on July 24, requested three separate trials and a change of venue, because of the amount of publicity the case had garnered in the Lehigh Valley. Yet Steinberg hoped for a single trial, and he demonstrated the strong similarities of the three cases, all containing DNA links to Robinson. He called FBI analyst Stephen Etter to explain the indicators known to experts that the murders were the work of a sexually motivated serial killer. The judge considered both arguments and decided to hold one trial, in Allentown. James Burke was appointed to join the defense.

The prosecution lined up fifty witnesses to prove Robinson's participation in all three murders. Along with blood and semen evidence against him, there had also been a sneaker impression on the face of one victim that was similar to sneakers that he'd worn. In addition, the strands of pubic and head hair found on Charlotte Schmoyer had been linked, microscopically, to Robinson. Denise Sam-Cali testified again, letting the jury know in a determined voice that Robinson was the man who had raped and assaulted her. He did not speak on his own behalf, despite his attorneys' request that he do so.

The proceeding lasted three weeks, and on November 8, 1994, Harvey Miguel Robinson was convicted of the rapes and murders of Burghardt, Schmoyer, and Fortney. The jury was then sequestered in order to avoid outside pressure as they listened to evidence about how the defendant should be sentenced. His life was on the line.

During this phase, Robinson once again rejected his attorneys' plea to testify on his own behalf, so the jury heard from other witnesses about his difficult life and multiple juvenile arrests. One side used these incidents to demonstrate his incorrigibility, while the other said Robinson had not yet had the chance to do better.

"If there ever was a case where the death penalty was warranted," Steinberg was quoted as saying, "this is such a case." He offered four aggravating circumstances: multiple victims, murder committed during other felonies, torture of the victims, and a history of violent aggression and threats.

Dr. Robert Sadoff, a forensic psychiatrist, testified for the defense. He indicated that Robinson suffered from a dependency on drugs and alcohol and had an antisocial personality disorder. He had also experienced visual and auditory hallucinations. It was not unusual to find petty juvenile crimes and aggression among children who later developed such problems, Sadoff stated, and he then suggested that Robinson may have turned to rape and murder to relieve stress. However, the psychiatrist added, if young

offenders like Robinson received help in a controlled setting at an early age, they could improve.

On November 10, the jury sentenced Robinson to die
by lethal injection. He showed no reaction, retaining the
same blank expression he had worn throughout the trial.
Six months later, when he was convicted of rape and the
attempted murder of a five-year-old girl, fifty-seven years
were added to his sentences, and forty more for his July
31 shoot-out with the police.

Legal Issues

Robinson decided that his trial attorneys had failed to tell
him the importance of testifying on his own behalf, hurt-
ing his chance for a fair trial, so he wanted an opportunity
to undo the error. He requested a hearing to challenge
his convictions and sentences. However, Marinelli stated
to reporters that during the trial, Robinson had refused
to testify.

In November 1998, Robinson's new attorney, Philip
Lauer, challenged Robinson's convictions at a postsen-
tencing hearing, on the grounds that there were funda-
mental flaws in the trial procedures. Other issues involved
racially biased jury selection, an error in allowing the
three murders to be tried jointly, and an error in not
changing the venue. On November 24, to the surprise of
many, Robinson got his day in court.

Now twenty-three, Robinson testified in front of about
thirty people, denying that he had committed the slayings
and indicating that he regretted not proclaiming his

innocence to the jury members who had convicted him. He testified for three hours, with five deputies in close proximity, casting blame on his former lawyers. At the time of his trial, he said, he'd given Marinelli and Burke the names of several people who could testify to his whereabouts when the three women were killed, as well as friends, coaches, teachers, and relatives who could attest to his character and accomplishments. Yet they called no alibi witnesses and presented few character witnesses. In addition, he continued, they did not inform him of the best strategy for defending himself and they did not use information about his childhood that might have helped him.

Robinson said he had declined to testify during his trial because he'd worried that prosecutors could have questioned him about his guilty plea to raping Denise Sam-Cali. "I was under the impression," he stated, "that if I did testify then my past record was admissible." He said he had not been informed otherwise.

Burke, one of Robinson's former defense attorneys, also testified, disputing his claim about the defense strategy. He insisted that he and Marinelli had repeatedly encouraged Robinson to testify, both at his trial and at his sentencing. "I begged him," Burke stated. While he could not dispute the fact that only a few witnesses from Robinson's list had testified, he claimed that his and Marinelli's choices at the time had been made in their client's best interest. Many potential witnesses were contacted, he stated, but it was deemed that the testimony of some of them would be damaging to Robinson, while others refused to testify or could not be located because Robinson had given insufficient information about their whereabouts. Robinson mistrusted lawyers, even those working on his behalf, so he had been less than cooperative.

Robinson agreed, but said in his defense that he'd developed that mistrust during the Sam-Cali rape case, in which, he contended, his lawyer coerced him to plead guilty. He now regretted that decision.

The court deliberated over these revelations and decided that Robinson's attorneys had acted in his best interests and had not been ineffective in their counsel, so he did not receive a new trial.

Two Down, One to Go

In June 2001, Judge Edward Reibman vacated Robinson's death sentences in the murders of Burghardt and Schmoyer. In that trial, Reibman said, the instructions to the jury had not properly defined the aggravated circumstances of multiple murder. He allowed the defendant to have a new sentencing hearing.

More than four years later, in December 2005, the Pennsylvania Supreme Court affirmed the death sentence in the Fortney case and the first-degree murder convictions in the other two cases. The high court stated that although Robinson believed that his attorney had not presented mitigating circumstances on his behalf, the trial jury had indeed considered reasons against imposing the death penalty and had given him death anyway. The court similarly rejected Robinson's claims that the prosecutor had improperly labeled him a predator (as well as his claim that the jury-pool selection system had been racially biased). Steinberg's remarks during Robinson's murder trial were found to be consistent with claims that Robinson had targeted a certain type of victim within a specific geographical area. So Robinson's situation remained the same as it had been four years earlier—that is, until a legal development occurred the following year.

On March 1, 2006, the U.S. Supreme Court ruled that juveniles age seventeen and under were ineligible for the death penalty. This ruling affected Robinson's conviction in the Burghardt murder, committed when he was seventeen. However, that death sentence had already been vacated. The Supreme Court's decision simply meant that Lehigh County district attorney James Martin would not reopen that case, but he was nevertheless determined to seek a new hearing in the Schmoyer case.

Robinson's death-penalty appeal to the U.S. Supreme Court had been denied in October 2005. In February 2006, Pennsylvania governor Ed Rendell signed his death warrant, with an execution date set for April 4, 2006. This, too, was stayed by a federal appeal.

From prison in Waynesburg, Pennsylvania, Robinson posted on prisoner Web sites, looking for correspondents. He indicated that he enjoyed exercise, writing, music, and reading self-help books. He particularly liked, he wrote, to help others. "Life is so truly precious," he wrote, "so anything I can do for another is something I'm interested in and like." In August 2007, he requested a brain scan to test for a possible impairment in cognitive function that might have influenced his actions during the murders. A judge allowed it, and as of this writing, the results are pending.

For Brian Lewis, now retired, this case was one of the significant experiences of his career. He believes that he and his fellow officer were chosen for the risky assignment because they had proven themselves up to the task. "We were hard workers," he said. "We were young, we were go-getters, and we loved the job." He received a well-earned commendation for valor. "Looking back, it turned out good for everybody. I didn't have to kill anyone and wrestle with that the rest of my life. I didn't get hurt, no one else was hurt, and we caught him."

Sources

"Allentown Man Guilty of Homicides." *Philadelphia Inquirer,* November 10, 1994.

"Allentown Murder Suspect Pleads Guilty in Separate Case." *Philadelphia Inquirer,* March 2, 1994.

Alu, Mary Ellen. "A Survivor's Story." *Morning Call,* April 17, 1994.

Bucsko, Mike. "Juvenile Executions Ruling Affects Three." *Pittsburgh Post-Gazette,* March 2, 2005.

Casler, Kristen. "Allentown Man Charged in Serial Murder, Rapes." *Morning Call,* December 7, 1993.

———. "Experts Link Robinson to Crime Scene Evidence." *Morning Call,* January 7, 1994.

———. "Allentown Crimes Fit Mold of Serial Killer." *Morning Call,* December 8, 1993.

Devlin, Ron. "Killer Says Trial Flawed." *Morning Call,* July 17, 1998.

Garlicki, Debbie. "Jurors' Quest: What Makes Harvey Robinson Tick?" *Morning Call,* October 22, 1994.

————. "Jurors Choose Death for Robinson." *Morning Call*, November 11, 1994.

————. "Trial Revealed Life of Robinson Victim." *Morning Call*, November 11, 1994.

————. "Witnesses and Science Finger Robinson." *Morning Call*, November 2, 1994.

————. "Robinson Gets 40 Years for Rape, Assault." *Morning Call*, April 15, 1993.

————. "Robinson's Lawyers Seek Three Murder Trials." *Morning Call*, July 26, 1993.

————. "Analyst Says Same Killer Took Three Lives." *Morning Call*, July 27, 1993.

————. "Robinson Trial Clues Go Under Microscope." *Morning Call*, October 29, 1994.

Grossman, Eliot. "Robinson Recalls Childhood, Insists He's No Murderer." *Morning Call*, November 25, 1998.

Petherick, Wayne. *Serial Crime: Theoretical and Practical Issues in Behavioral Profiling.* Oxford: Academic Press, 2006.

Rosen, Fred. "The Rapist Tried to Murder Her and She Knew He Would Try Again." *Cosmopolitan*, March 1, 1996.

Todd, Susan. "Allentown Teenager Held in June Attack on Woman." *Morning Call*, September 3, 1993.

Interview with Brian Lewis.

NINE

RICHARD ROGERS:
The Most Expensive Fingerprint

Peter Stickney Anderson walked into the Townhouse Bar at 206 Fifty-eighth Street, on Manhattan's East Side. He looked around at the burning candles on each table, which enhanced the intimate atmosphere. It was early May 1991. Anderson had driven to the city that day from Philadelphia, where he once worked as a Center City investment broker, to attend a political fund-raising dinner for a friend, Tony Brooks. They had arrived together at a Central Park West apartment, but while Brooks returned home that evening, Anderson elected to stay.

A member of several elite clubs and a former staff sergeant in the National Guard, Anderson could trace his ancestry back to a cavalry officer in the Revolutionary War. Acquaintances viewed him, with his sport coats and bow ties, as urbane and charming, an exceptional raconteur. Even his estranged wife said he was a gentleman. Yet there were things about him that many acquaintances did not know.

Despite his affiliation with the conservative Republican Party, Anderson lived a secret gay life, and when he chose to visit the Townhouse, he may have been looking for company. He had only recently separated from his second wife, and his acquaintances had noticed his mood becoming profoundly sad; one person even called him a "lost soul." They knew that while he was barely eating, he was nevertheless drinking a lot, and had squandered most of a recent inheritance. Some expected his body to give out, but he kept going, and in a city like New York, he could do as he pleased without anyone noticing. At five-foot-two and one hundred pounds, he was apparently no match for whomever he met that night.

Anderson was just one of several men who attracted an unusual killer, one whom it would take years to nail, in part because early investigators of the case lacked the

Richard Rogers, who murdered and dismembered at least five men—and made the mistake of leaving fingerprints behind.
Ocean County Prosecutor's Office

right tools used in the right ways at the right time. Once it all came together, though, there was no room from reasonable doubt.

Body Parts

On May 5, a maintenance worker sorting through trash cans along the Pennsylvania Turnpike in Lancaster County for recyclables, spotted several tightly wrapped plastic bags. They gave off a foul odor, and when he examined their shape and bulk, he decided to call the police.

Each package, unwrapped, proved to contain different parts of a middle-aged man's dismembered nude body. From the torso, it was clear that the victim had been stabbed numerous times in the abdomen, bound with a rope around the neck, and sexually mutilated. Oddly, it appeared that blood from the wounds had been washed off. Using the recovered head, a police artist was able to draw a portrait of the victim, and police taped posters of this image at booths and rest areas along the turnpike. Eventually people driving west from Philadelphia recognized him: the dead man was the missing Peter Anderson.

Yet while a number of people knew him, no one could offer information about whom he might have seen in New York, so it was difficult for detectives to run down leads. They learned that he had been at the Five Oaks Bar and the Waldorf-Astoria, where he had declined a room and was put, highly intoxicated, into a cab. Police also developed a suspect in the Philadelphia area who was about to start a psychiatric residency at a hospital. He had lied about his past record of mental illness and seemed a viable candidate on whom to pin this murder, but there was no solid evidence linking him. Police retained the bags that had held the body parts as potential evidence.

The ability to identify someone from fingerprints has been around since the late nineteenth century. The first successful case occurred in Argentina, where a killer's fingerprint was left in blood at the crime scene, and the ridge patterns matched her fingertips. This was a visible print. There are also "plastic" prints, left as indentations in pliable surfaces, such as wet paint. Yet fingerprints also leave impressions, via grease or perspiration, which are invisible, or latent. Since unique patterns on the fingertips distinguish an individual from all others, it's important to be able to lift and accurately preserve the impressions, visible or latent.

The typical procedure is to lightly brush a surface with fine powder, which sticks to the residual sweat and shows the pattern. Police can then photograph or lift the prints onto a transparent piece of adhesive tape and mount them onto a card. Smooth surfaces obviously provide the best results, but techniques have been developed for rougher or more porous surfaces. Amino acids in sweat react with ninhydrin and several other dyes, also producing an image of the pattern. In some cases, prints can be developed from human skin. In addition, latent prints exposed to cyanoacrylate fumes, or Super Glue, will turn up as whitish prints against darker backgrounds. These can then be dusted and photographed. Even before the Anderson murder, other methods were being developed or refined, including laser beams.

The Automated Fingerprint Identification System
(AFIS), a searchable computer database available via the
FBI to every state, assists in associating fingerprints to
known criminals. The program digitally encodes prints
scanned into it as a mathematical algorithm, based on the
characteristics of, and relationships among, their physical
features. Using a standard classification system, the digital
transmission of images from one AFIS system to another
was perfected, and the process of making a match from a
print to a suspect was consequently streamlined from
weeks to hours, even minutes. A key hurdle, however, was
that not all states were hooked up to this database, or all
systems were not in sync with one another. Thus a print
processed in Pennsylvania might not connect with a suspect in Oregon or Arkansas.

Investigators tried but failed to lift usable prints from
the bags containing Anderson's body parts. Even so, pre-
serving the bags proved to be wise, because new technologies were developing fast and there was no telling what
the future held. The 1990s, in fact, was the era of cold-
case investigations, when determined detectives reexamined cases and either repeated previously used techniques
more carefully or looked for a new approach. Anderson
would not be forgotten.

More Body Parts

The following year, two New Jersey state workers unload-
ing trash at a Burlington County Department of Transportation maintenance yard spotted several heavy parcels

wrapped in tan and white plastic bags. Since these bags did not resemble the typical garbage from the area, they wondered what was inside. One worker picked up a bag and thought it felt like a pumpkin, but it was July not October. In fact, some of the bags appeared to be bloody, the way butchered meat looks, so he peeked inside the one he was holding. He was startled to see a decomposed human head.

The police arrived to take over, and each parcel, unwrapped, contained the body part of a middle-aged male. A hunk of skin in one bag showed a bruise resembling a bite mark, and another bag contained the intestines, stomach, a plastic cup, and a latex glove. The dismembered upper and lower torso had been separated, and all the parts were present except the legs. One more bag included a pair of latex gloves, a bedsheet, a shower curtain, and a bloodstained compass saw. Packaging from latex gloves bore a tag from a CVS store on Staten Island. Near all of this was a briefcase with identification and a pair of shoes, a box of Acme plastic garbage bags, and a sewing needle. Two hours later, the legs were located in a trash can along the Garden State Parkway at the Stafford Forge rest area.

This victim was Thomas Mulcahy, fifty-seven, a business executive from Sudbury, Massachusetts. At first, he appeared to have been at low risk to encounter a killer. A sales executive for Bull H. N. Information Systems and an active church member, he'd been married for over three decades and had four children. He'd gone to New York on July 7 to make a sales presentation at the World Trade

Center and had met a friend for drinks at the Townhouse Bar, known for its gay clientele. The next day, he had drinks at a bar near the World Trade Center and withdrew two hundred dollars from an ATM on Forty-ninth Street and Sixth Avenue.

Family members who knew about Mulcahy's secret life informed police that he was bisexual. He might have picked up someone he didn't know at a bar. The autopsy revealed that he had suffered several stab wounds and a bite mark, and it appeared that his body parts had been washed clean of blood.

That same month, body parts that had turned up in a dump outside Schenectady, New Jersey, were traced to fifty-year-old Guillermo Mendez, a gay Cuban refugee. His arms, legs, and torso were found fifteen miles from his home, but he was not known to have been in New York or at any gay bars. His fingertips and genitals had been removed and most of the blood was drained from his body. Three weeks later, a couple of youths walking through a cemetery found his decomposing head in a bag. Despite the similarities, the New Jersey authorities believed that this crime was unrelated to the others. No more victims were found for almost year.

On May 10, 1993, Donald Giberson was driving on Crow Hill Road in Manchester, New Jersey, when he spotted a plastic bag on the side of the road. It was clear from rips in the plastic that animals had been at it, so he assumed it was a deer carcass. He rolled down his window to look. When he saw human fingers, he contacted the police.

By showing photographs of the victim to prostitutes, investigators soon identified the arms of forty-four-year-old Anthony Marrero, who was missing from New York. Five other bags scattered along the roadway contained more of his parts, wrapped first in shopping bags and then in larger plastic bags. The body had been cut into seven parts. Fingerprints confirmed the identification.

Unlike the other victims, Marrero was a crack addict and gay hustler, known around the Port Authority bus terminal at Forty-second Street and Eighth Avenue. With a failed marriage behind him, he had moved to New York in 1985, but kept only sporadic contact with his family. He'd earned his money for the next decade from custodian jobs and then from pickup dates willing to pay. Last seen at a gay bar, he'd encountered it seemed, a bad trick. His body parts, too, appeared to have been cleaned up after dismemberment. Then another gay man went missing from New York.

Michael Sakara, fifty-six, was openly gay. At six-foot-four and 250 pounds, he made an impression. He worked the afternoon shift as a typesetter at the *New York Law Journal* and was considered to be both bright and intense. His longtime lover had recently moved out of the studio apartment they had shared on Manhattan's West End Avenue, so he was often out in the evenings looking for company. He was easy to like.

For two decades, Sakara frequented the piano bar at the Five Oaks so often that the owners knew his favorite seat. He liked to talk and sing, and he greeted everyone freely with a firm handshake. He often remained at the bar until the early hours of the morning. Whoever he went off with on July 30, 1993, was also there, but no one could remember who it might have been. Someone did see Sakara enter a car.

At midmorning on July 31, a hotdog vendor in Haverstraw, New York, discovered Sakara's head and arms wrapped in two garbage bags and tossed into a fifty-five-gallon can. On top of these bags, before the refreshment stand had opened, a bottle collector had come across clothing, traced to Sakara. Nine days later, on August 8, the legs and torso turned up in bags at a second location along the same road, ten miles north, in Stony Point, New York.

An autopsy showed that Sakara had been killed by blows to the head but was also stabbed five times. In addition, like the other men, it appeared that his body parts had been cleaned up before being wrapped. Also like the two men in New Jersey, he had been cut into exactly seven pieces.

Bartender Lisa Hall said she recalled seeing Sakara with a man whom he introduced, but she did not know a name. She remembered only that he was a nurse at St. Vincent's Hospital. If authorities ever apprehended a suspect, they at least had a witness who could place him with the victim.

Several reporters wrote about a potential serial killer on the loose, a predator of middle-aged gay men. Investigators stated that they had no hard evidence for the assumption. Nevertheless, customers of gay bars in New

York began taking extra precautions. In the West Village, the New York City Gay and Lesbian Anti-Violence Project handed out flyers that offered a $10,000 reward for information. They wanted the killer caught.

Rockland County investigators on the Sakara case sent a teletype to other police agencies to inquire about similar murders. New Jersey state troopers responded, forming a task force with seven other New York and Pennsylvania law enforcement agencies, determined to stop this grisly killer. They based their headquarters in Rockland County, where the most recent victim had been dumped.

Found variously in Pennsylvania, New Jersey, and New York, the four key victims had been murdered, dismembered, and wrapped tightly in several layers of plastic bags. (Guillermo Mendez was left off the list.) From the method of cutting with both a saw and a knife, and the technique of wrapping and disposal, it seemed to be the work of a single perpetrator, soon dubbed the "Last Call Killer." There were also similarities in the way the victims were bound and in ligature marks on the wrists. That August, Lieutenant Matthew Kuehn, a New Jersey state trooper in charge of the Mulcahy investigation, collected photos of male nurses working in hospitals in the area and showed them to bartender Lisa Hall. She picked out Richard Rogers as having the same hairstyle as the man she had met, but she thought the name used was something more common, like John. She could not make a positive ID from the photo. Since this potential lead failed to go anywhere, this case, too, went cold.

Lieutenant Kuehn had promised Mulcahy's widow that he would stay on the case until he found the killer, and during the late 1990s, she inquired into their progress. Although Kuehn had nothing to offer, he decided to reexamine the bags. The cold-case squad used cyanoacrylate fuming once more, and while they were able to obtain prints that were scannable for AFIS, they had no hits on a suspect.

Then, in November 2000, Kuehn learned about a fingerprint-lifting technique called vacuum metal deposition (VMD), which involved an expensive high-tech machine and was supposedly superior to Super Glue fuming for obtaining prints from plastic bags. He contacted scientists in Toronto, where this process was available, and they agreed to subject the bags from the body parts to the VMD analysis. However, they had to work on their own time, so it would not be a quick turnaround.

With VMD, an exhibit is placed inside the chamber of a machine, and four to five milligrams of gold and several grams of zinc are loaded into evaporation containers beneath it. Pumps are activated that reduce pressure and a low-voltage current evaporates the gold, leaving a minute deposit over the exhibit. The gold apparently absorbs into the fingerprint residue. In a separate dish, the zinc is then subjected to a similar method, heated and vaporized, and then deposited onto the exhibit. It adheres to the gold (but does not penetrate) to produce an image of the fingerprint valleys that lie between the ridges. This makes the print visible in sharp relief for photography.

Although this method had only recently been applied

to latent-fingerprint analysis, it had been in use since 1976 for other purposes. It was most effectively used for prints on plastic and glass but had also worked on cloth and currency. Reportedly, VMD develops more fingerprints than any method of Super Glue fuming or other reagents. It can develop prints on more types of articles than other methods, including on leather surfaces, synthetic clothing, and polyethylene garbage bags. However, one issue that a defense attorney could raise is that, to get the best results, significant experience is required on the part of the examiner.

The New Jersey investigators sent the plastic gloves found with Mulcahy's body and more than three dozen bags from the body parts of all four victims for analysis. It took six months, but finally the scientists were able to lift thirty-five fingerprints and a few palm prints from four bags that were of sufficient quality for identification. This supported what the New Jersey investigators had found with their most recent go at Super Glue fuming.

Lieutenant Kuehn sent packets with the prints and case details to all fifty states and Puerto Rico, to be run through all state-based AFIS systems. This time, he received the call he was waiting for. The prints were a match to a man in the system in Maine, Richard Rogers. His name had not popped up before, although his prints had been on file for three decades, because Maine had not been online with AFIS until 2001.

But Kuehn had encountered this name before: Rogers was a fifty-year-old registered nurse from Staten Island who had worked for the past twenty years at Mount Sinai

Hospital in Manhattan. Kuehn had shown his photo, along with those of other male nurses, to Lisa Hall. He had certainly been in the area during the times of these crimes and it remained to be seen whether he had alibis. In addition, in 1988, he had been arrested for unlawfully imprisoning a man who had visited him, but was acquitted.

More interesting, Rogers had a checkered history. In 1973, he had used a hammer to bludgeon a housemate, Frederick Spencer, killing him. He then wrapped the body in a plastic tent and dumped it on the side of a road. When charged with manslaughter, he claimed he had attacked Spencer in self-defense and he was acquitted. While he had not dismembered this man, he'd wrapped him in plastic and dumped him along the road. It's often the case that serial killers who have been linked to a victim but not convicted take pains to avoid future arrests. Cutting up a body to dump in the trash was less risky than dumping it whole.

It turned out, after checking records and talking with his colleagues, that Nurse Richard Rogers had no alibis for the times of the murders. In fact, he'd been seen with Michael Sakara just before he vanished. The D.A.'s office in New Jersey believed they had enough to bring him in, so on May 27, 2001, Rogers was arrested and charged with the 1992 murders of Thomas Mulcahy and Anthony Marrero. When confronted, he neither admitted nor denied his guilt, but instead nodded and passed gas.

Rogers resisted extradition to New Jersey. To get him

there, the authorities had to prove that the incident considered a crime in that state was likewise considered a crime in New York, that the man in the warrant was the man detained in New York, and that the suspect had been in New Jersey. The crime was murder and they had his fingerprints, so the legal issues were easily resolved. He was brought to Ocean County.

A dozen detectives from New Jersey, New York, and Pennsylvania searched Rogers's condominium for evidence that the murders had been committed there, but found no blood or cutting instruments. They did turn up a bottle of Versed, often used as a date-rape drug; rug fibers consistent with those found on Mulcahy's body; a Bible with earmarked pages in the Book of Kings, in which passages that mentioned decapitation and dismemberment had been highlighted; videotapes of horror films, including *The Texas Chainsaw Massacre;* and photos of shirtless men on which wounds had been drawn with red ink. They also found plastic bags similar to those in which body parts had been wrapped, as well as a New Jersey road map. The bags were an Acme brand, and there was an Acme store in the same mall on Staten Island where the gloves had been purchased. Despite failing to turn up the proverbial smoking gun, this was a lot of good circumstantial evidence.

The D.A.'s office announced what they had against Rogers: eighteen of his fingerprints on bags that wrapped the remains of Peter S. Anderson; sixteen on the bags wrapping Thomas Mulcahy; and two fingerprints and a palm print on a bag wrapping parts of Anthony Marrero. Rogers had been seen in the company of Michael Sakara, the *New York Law Journal* typesetter, and they had a witness for that. In addition, there was potentially a fifth victim linked to Rogers—or sixth, if one counted Spencer. Matthew Pierro, twenty-one, who was last seen in 1982 leaving a gay bar in Orlando, Florida, had been found murdered off Interstate 4 in Lake Mary. While he was not dismembered, he'd been stabbed multiple times, a nipple bitten off, and an odontologist indicated that another bite mark on his body could be a match to Rogers's teeth. Rogers had been in Florida at the time for a class reunion.

On January 21, 2003, a New Jersey grand jury indicted Rogers on two counts of murder and two counts of hindering apprehension. He denied involvement and said he was innocent. Prosecutors hoped to bring all five cases into evidence against him, believing that the patterns from one case to the next would be convincing. Failing that, they still had his fingerprints associated with both victims found in New Jersey.

The Same Case, but Different

At a hearing in September 2005, Detective Steven Colantonio, from Rockland County, testified before Judge James N. Citta in Toms River, New Jersey, about the similarities between the Sakara murder and the other three. "It was the opinion of the investigators [and] the opinion of the medical examiners," he said, "that there were such similarities that if you found the person who did one of them, you would find the person who did all three of them . . . It was as if you were looking at the same case, but they were different."

Dr. Fred Zugibe, the chief medical examiner of Rockland County at the time, described how the victim had been expertly decapitated by someone familiar with the easiest places to saw through a body. Similar testimony was offered about the Anderson case. In addition, fingerprints from the bag holding Anderson's parts were a match to the defendant, as were prints on bags from Mulcahy and Marrero.

Deputy Chief Mark Whitfield, a member of the task force from Ocean County, New Jersey, discussed how the body parts had been cleaned up in each of the cases, "as if they were drained so they were not as messy to move." He also discussed the similarity of victim type, adding that Rogers had frequented both the Five Oaks Bar and the Townhouse, connected to three of the victims. All of the men had been drinking or high when they went missing, and all appeared to have been incapacitated before they disappeared.

Judge Citta found the testimony compelling. He ruled that, based on significant similarity, he would allow accounts about the Anderson and Sakara murders into the double murder trial, which considerably strengthened the collection of evidence against Rogers. However, he thought the fifth case, the murder of John Pierro in Florida, was too far removed in time and place, and too dissimilar. That one would not be allowed.

The trial of Richard W. Rogers got under way on October 26, 2005. During jury selection, Rogers was offered a deal: plead guilty to manslaughter in both cases and receive two thirty-year sentences with the possibility of parole in fifteen years. Also, if he pleaded to third-degree murder in the Anderson case from Pennsylvania, he would receive just ten to twenty years in prison. Rogers indicated that he'd take it under consideration. Trial watchers anxiously waited out the weekend, wondering if he might short-circuit the process and admit to guilt. It wasn't a bad deal, unless he believed the case against him was weak. No one knew what his attorney, David Ruhnke, told him.

On Monday, it was clear that jury selection would resume; Rogers was not accepting the deal. William Heisler, the assistant prosecutor and chief trial attorney for Ocean County, had teamed up with Hillary Bryce. They told the jury the state could prove its case against Rogers beyond a reasonable doubt. In an interview later, Heisler recalled the experience. "It's difficult when you have a defendant with no statement. You don't know what he's going to come up with. He's a meek, mild-looking guy, which struck me as kind of strange. But nothing about this case *wasn't* strange. He's a smart guy. I don't know what he would have said. Half the time, these guys make stuff up on the fly and then you have to check it out and disprove it. But what could he say about his fingerprints?"

In his opening address, defense attorney David Ruhnke indicated that Rogers was innocent, and that his

fingerprints on these bags indicated only that he had carried something in them at some point in time. In addition, a few prints on the bags were not linked to him,
indicating that others had handled them. "Maybe," he
said, "they don't have the right guy."

The prosecution opened with accounts from the various witnesses who had discovered the bodies. Then Deputy Chief Mark Whitfield, the lead investigator on the
Marrero case, described how he had looked at several
suspects just after the dismembered bodies were found,
and took their fingerprints, but was unable to make reliable comparisons until 2001. (Describing the situation
in Maine was disallowed because it would bring in suggestive details from a case in which Rogers had been
acquitted.)

Two fingerprint analysts, Detective Sergeant Jeffrey
Scozzafava of the New Jersey State Police and Detective
Eugene Thatcher of Ocean County's Criminalistics Investigation Unit, testified that the sixteen fingerprints on
the bags used to wrap victim Thomas Mulcahy and two
fingerprints and a palm print from the bags containing
the arms and head of Anthony Marrero matched former
surgical nurse Richard Rogers. One fingerprint from the
Mulcahy bags and a palm print from the Marrero bags
remained unidentified. Ruhnke attempted to attack the
examiners by noting mistakes made in fingerprint analysis,
including those committed by the FBI. He talked about
how the FBI had mistakenly identified a U.S. citizen as
the person who had planted a bomb on a train in Madrid.
Ruhnke also tried to discredit the unusual method of

VMD. While it was not the only method used, it had contributed sufficiently to the case to warrant an expert in the courtroom. (Allen Pollard from the Toronto Police Service testified about the process and results.) While the method was not widely used, because of its expense, this was no indication that it was not a viable scientific technique. When Judge Citta limited Ruhnke's questioning about fingerprint analysis, the lawyer retorted that the jury was "entitled to learn that it is not a perfect system."

Medical Examiner Lyla Perez then described the wounds she had noted during Mulcahy's autopsy. After he was stabbed to death, she said, his body had been eviscerated and cut into seven separate parts. She had photographs of the gory remains, but because of their disturbing nature, Ruhnke attempted to limit what the jury would actually view. They reviewed five photos. Mulcahy's blood alcohol level was high, Perez told them, and there were ligature marks on his wrists that indicated he'd been bound.

The next day, Lieutenant Kuehn described the murder of Michael Sakara. Its relevance lay not just in the way it resembled the two in New Jersey, but that it was the only case in which Rogers had been identified by a witness. This brought in Lisa Hall, the former bartender at the Five Oaks, who stated that on the night Sakara disappeared, July 30, 1993, he had introduced her to Rogers. While he had used a generic name, Hall had identified Rogers from a photo and was able to point him out in the courtroom. She said she had no doubt he was the man she had met.

But there was another issue. Lieutenant Kuehn stated that a rigorous search had produced no evidence that Rogers had killed either man on Staten Island, which would have transferred the case to New York's jurisdiction. Defense attorney David Ruhnke challenged this, saying that no crime scene had been established in New Jersey, only dump sites, and indicating that Rogers (if he did it) would more likely have committed murder on familiar turf. Lieutenant Kuehn responded that it would have been quite difficult for Rogers to have killed and dismembered the victims in his fifth-floor condo and then carried the bloody bags through the halls without anyone noticing.

Also testifying that day was Sergeant George Kegerreis, who indicated that eighteen fingerprints and a palm print lifted from the bags containing parts of victim Peter Anderson had been matched to eight of Rogers's fingers and his palm. With this testimony, the state rested its case.

John O'Brien, a reporter for the *Staten Island Advance*, described Rogers's demeanor during this final stretch. In contrast to his earlier calmness, he now "wrung his hands, bounced his legs and grimaced at his attorney."

On November 10, Rogers indicated he would not take the stand to testify on his own behalf. Ruhnke also stated he would call no witnesses on Rogers's behalf. This surprised many people. It seemed that Ruhnke's challenge of the fingerprint testimony had been his sole strategy. While he also asked for an acquittal based on the fact that no one knew where the men had been killed, the judge dismissed this concern.

Closing arguments from both sides were brief. Prosecutor William Heisler reiterated the circumstantial and physical evidence that linked Rogers to the crimes from all four cases.

- Mulcahy had disappeared after attending a business meeting in Manhattan, and he was seen in a gay bar that Rogers frequented. There were sixteen fingerprints on bags that wrapped his remains.

- Marrero, a known gay hustler from Manhattan, was cut up and wrapped in plastic before being dumped in New Jersey. A palm print and two fingerprints linked him to Rogers.

- Peter Anderson, found in Pennsylvania, was a gay man who went to a bar Rogers frequented in Manhattan. A palm print and eighteen fingerprints on the bags that wrapped his parts were matched to Rogers.

- Michael Sakara was seen with Rogers at a gay bar the evening before his body parts were found wrapped in several bags.

- Rogers's employment records indicated he'd taken a few days off during the time of each of the four murders.

• The murder MO and disposal of all four were strikingly
  similar, including the way the parts were cut, cleaned,
  and wrapped, as well as how they were dumped near
  roadways.

Defense attorney Ruhnke reiterated that with no crime
scene, New Jersey had no jurisdiction; he also disputed the
argument that his client's fingerprints on bags were proof
that he'd committed murder. They had the wrong man.

In the middle of the afternoon of November 11, the
jury retired. During their deliberations, they asked Judge
Citta about jurisdiction issues. He indicated that New
Jersey did have jurisdiction over the two cases, because
the law allowed them to infer that if the bodies were
found in the state, the men had been killed there. There
was no proof that they had been murdered anywhere else.

By six o'clock that evening, they had a verdict. People
filed back into the courtroom, despite the fact that it was
a Friday, until the place was packed. The forewoman wept
and held the hand of another woman as she rose to announce their findings. Clearly she was shaken—always a
bad sign for the defense. And it was. Richard Rogers, fifty-
five, was found guilty of the first-degree murder of Thomas
Mulcahy and Anthony Marrero. He was also found guilty
on two counts of hindering his apprehension by dismem-
bering the victims and disposing of them the way he had.
As the forewoman spoke, Rogers showed no reaction. He
simply stared at the front of the courtroom.

Since the D.A. had not requested the death penalty,

Rogers was remanded to Ocean County's jail to await his January 26, 2006, sentencing, which everyone knew would be life imprisonment. Ruhnke announced his plan to file an appeal over the jurisdiction issues. Heisler told reporters that he felt better knowing that the killer was no longer out on the streets. It was a victory for him and his team, as well as for the tristate task force that had worked so hard on making sure that a killer had been brought to justice.

"When you put everything in the mix," Heisler said in retrospect, "it's pretty tough to explain all these fingerprints and all these bodies dismembered in the same way, and try to lay it off on anyone else. I'd like to have had more information about what motivated the guy."

Judge Citta had no qualms about putting a label on these acts. At the sentencing, he said to Rogers, "You are an evil human being." He added that he would do everything in his power "to assure society that you never walk free again and that you die in some hole in some prison." He gave Rogers two consecutive life terms, plus ten years, ensuring that he must serve sixty-five years behind bars before he could be considered for parole. "If we had to measure a depraved murderer on a scale of one to ten," Judge Citta said, "I would have to conclude that Mr. Rogers' participation and actions in these murders would make him a ten."

Whether Rogers will be tried for the other murders remains to be seen. However, relevant technology will continue to be at the forefront of such investigations. The use of science is compelling to juries, who are swayed by its seemingly objective irrefutability. The next case in this chronicle, also a long-term investigation, involved computer technology.

Sources

Bean, Matt. "Gold-Dust Fingerprint Method Catching On." CourtTV.com, November 14, 2004.

"'Body Chop' Nurse Charged in Grisly Dismemberment Slayings." *New York Post,* January 22, 2003.

Cave, Damien. "As Killer Faces Sentencing, His Motive Remains Elusive." *New York Times,* January 27, 2006.

Cummings, Amanda. "Vacuum Metal Deposition: The Future of the Last Call Killer Saga." Associatedcontent.com, retrieved December 9, 2007.

Dimeo, Lisa. "Vacuum Metal Deposition: Its Value in Developing Archival Prints," SCAFO.org, October 3, 2002.

"Fingerprint Identification using Vacuum Metal Deposition," rcmp.ca/firs/bulletins/vacuummetal.

Fisher, Ian. "Do Threads of Five Lives Lead to One Serial Killer?" *New York Times,* August 8, 1993.

Holl, John. "Man Who Killed 2 He Met at Gay Bar Gets 2 Consecutive Life Sentences." *New York Times,* January 28, 2006.

Hopkins, Kathleen. "Chilling Warning Made by Suspect." *Asbury Park Press,* September 29, 2005.

———. "Ex-Bartender Says Rogers Was Last to See Her Friend." *Asbury Park Press,* November 3, 2005.

———. "Murder Trial to Start Sept. 20." *Asbury Park Press,* August 20, 2005.

———. "Prints Match, Detectives Testify." *Asbury Park Press,* September 23, 2005.

———. "Killer Gets Two Life Terms." *Asbury Park Press,* January 28, 2006.

———. "Ex-Nurse Guilty of Murder May Face More Charges." *Asbury Park Press,* November 24, 2005.

———. "New York Killing Identical to 2 in New Jersey, Detective Tells Judge." *Asbury Park Press,* September 22, 2005.

———. "Experts Connect Fingerprints to Killing Suspect." *Asbury Park Press,* November 2, 2005.

"Judge Rules Gay Prey Serial Killer Richard Rogers Jury Will Hear Similar Slayings." Queerday.com, retrieved September 29, 2005.

Osborn, Duncan. "An Accused Serial Killer on Trial." *Gay City News 3*, January 29–February 4, 2004.

Parry, Wayne. "Trial of Richard Rogers to Hear About Slayings, Dismemberment of Four Gay, Bisexual Men." Associated Press, October 15, 2005.

Rizzo, Nina, and Joseph Sapia. "Suspect Resisting Extradition, Home Searched for Evidence." *Asbury Park Press,* May 31, 2001.

TEN

DENNIS RADER:
Computer Forensics and a Clever Lie

A man crept into Joseph Otero's home in Wichita, Kansas. It was January 1974, the middle of winter. He took few pains to hide, yet no one saw him well enough to identify him later. Glancing around, he entered the backyard and cut the phone wire.

Joe and Julie Otero were in the kitchen, having taken three of their five children to school. Josie, eleven, and Joey, nine, were getting ready for the next run. The family had lived in this home for less than three months and had no idea that a man who had spotted Julie and Josie a month before had been stalking them. He had documented the family schedules and the number of children, calculating when he could move past his usual voyeurism and act out his fantasy of assault and murder. In the past, he had targeted others, but he'd always stopped short. He was seething for a chance to bind a woman, torture her, and then kill her.

Finally, the morning had arrived and he came equipped with rope, cord, tape, gags, and plastic bags. He also carried a .22 pistol and a knife. After severing the phone line, he spotted Joey outside and forced him back in. Ignoring the barking dog, purchased for protection, he prepared to tie up the boy and his sister and mother.

However, the intruder had miscalculated. Joe, usually gone by this time, was still at home, disabled by a recent car accident. The intruder drew his gun to show he meant business, quickly inventing a story that he was there to rob them. Joe thought it was a joke, but when he was forced to the floor, he realized it was not. The man tied the three family members up with rope, cord, and tape, Joe in the kitchen, Julie on her bed, and Joey in his room. He pulled two T-shirts and a plastic bag over the boy's head, wrapping a cord around his neck and letting him slowly suffocate. But the intruder had saved his full lust and rage for the little girl, Josie.

After the other three were dead, he put a rope around Josie's throat and a gag in her mouth, and then took her into the basement. He tied her feet together and her hands behind her back, lifting her up to hang her from a sewer pipe. As she struggled to free herself, he cut through her bra, pulled off her panties, and masturbated, finally ejaculating on her leg. She died by strangulation and he left her hanging.

Before he left the house and drove off in the family's Vista Cruiser, it seems likely that the killer thought about the other three Otero children, who would be coming home from school later that day only to find their murdered parents and siblings, and that this image added one more fiendish layer to his sadistic pleasure. He had finally carried out a fantasy he had devised with care and it made him feel powerful. This would hit the city papers and make him famous, albeit anonymously. That, too, gratified him. But then he realized he'd left the knife behind, so he went back for it, entering the home as if he belonged there. When he had the knife in his possession, he went to the woods to burn some notes and sketches he'd made, along with remnants of cord and rope. He finished in time to greet his wife as she came home from work. He also recorded what he'd done that day in a journal, naming himself "BTK"—for *bind, torture, kill*.

When the three surviving Otero children discovered their murdered family, they were horrified, and alerted neighbors and the police. Even the homicide detectives were stunned, especially when they found Josie. They set out asking around to try to solve the crime quickly, but conflicting witness reports made leads difficult to develop. They had a tall man, a short man; a white man, a dark-complected man. No one had seen his face. The abandoned car was found and processed, but that led nowhere. It made no sense that a stranger would just enter a home at random and kill a family, so they theorized a drug connection. However, that conjecture, too, had no support.

The detectives did learn that the killer liked knots; he had used a number of different ones to tie up his victims, as if he were having fun. They thought he might have a naval background. He also liked to hurt people. Julie's face showed bruises and she had several ligature marks, as if she had been choked more than once.

The *Wichita Eagle* and the *Beacon* both devoted priority space to the story, but no one was caught and leads dried up. The coverage stopped as well. Members of the homicide squad, having seen the family, were angry. They wanted this guy caught and punished. But they would be waiting for this for a long time.

BTK, otherwise known as Dennis Rader, was a church-going man with a job and family, who forbade people around him from telling offensive jokes in front of women. He was ordinary, polite, controlling, and sometimes nasty, but he was no one's idea of a serial killer. The cops didn't yet know they even *had* a serial killer on their hands. In the early 1970s, little was known about serial murder. Ted Bundy was not caught until 1978, and the Son of Sam would not terrorize New York for another two years. The decade before, Albert DeSalvo had been nailed as the Boston Strangler, while the Zodiac had terrorized San Francisco and Juan Corona had murdered twenty-five migrant workers in California, but such things were unheard of in Kansas. Even the FBI had barely begun to think about its Behavioral Sciences Unit, with its profilers. They would enter this case later, but for the time being, there was little that any investigator could do.

What made it worse was that Rader was a thinking man. He watched and waited, and made notes to improve upon his work and avoid mistakes. He was what the FBI would one day label "organized." Noting how much more difficult it had been to strangle a person than he'd realized, he started working out so he would be in top shape for dealing with victims who struggled. He wanted to kill more efficiently. In addition, he would find employment that allowed him to enter into people's homes legitimately so he could scope out the layout and calculate the best moment for attack. This was not going to be an easy man to catch. BTK would prove to be a slick and calculating killer who baited police and kept them guessing. An arrest in this case would boil down to a combination of wits and opportunity.

Factor X

A few months went by before Rader planned and enacted another "project" in April 1974. He had been out looking for women, following some and only dreaming about others. He often peeped into windows and finally settled on a small home on East Thirteenth Street. A twenty-one-year-old college girl, Kathryn Bright, lived there by herself, and she did not have a dog. That was a plus. However, she did have a brother, and after Rader broke in, he found himself unprepared for dealing with a strong young man determined to fight. He shot Kevin Bright twice in the head and left him to die. He then bound Kathryn and stabbed her eleven times, using what he'd read in detective magazines to disable her, but she still fought harder than he'd expected.

Despite his terrible wounds, Kevin managed to get up

and flee, alerting neighbors, and Rader quickly left. The police arrived, but they were unable to save Kathryn. She died at the hospital. Kevin described their attacker as being nearly six feet tall, around 180 pounds, in his late twenties, with dark hair and a mustache. While there was some discussion among detectives about the two deadly home invasions that year being related, they ultimately dismissed it. The MO had been too different.

While many men were questioned, no one was identified as the killer. Rader could hardly believe he'd escaped arrest. The entire episode had scared him and he was not sure he would risk it again. Twice he had made mistakes and, despite all his planning, had badly miscalculated. If he kept this up, he would be caught, and that was the last thing he wanted. Rader burned his clothing and wrote a detailed report in his BTK journal. When no one came for him, he began to feel bolder, even invincible. But one thing got his goat, and this personality flaw would ultimately betray him: someone else was taking credit for the Otero murders. He called a reporter at the *Wichita Eagle* and instructed him to go to the public library and look inside *Applied Engineering Mechanics.* There would be a letter detailing the Otero murders that would prove that the person currently bragging about it was not the killer.

The reporter called the police and they learned from the disjointed note, which described the exact positions of the Otero family members, that the offender, who named himself BTK, had studied the habits of other sexual criminals. He said he had a "monster" in his brain that compelled him to kill: "The pressure is great and somt-times he run the game to his liking." The letter writer indicated that this monster had "already chosen his next victim." It was a terrifying threat.

The unsolved murders inspired many Wichita residents to purchase security alarms and Dennis Rader got a job installing them. He watched for his next opportunity, certain that this time he would not make the same mistakes he had made in the Bright home. He also became a father and took classes at Wichita State University.

The Monster Acts Again

In 1977, more than three years after the Otero incident, Shirley Vian was murdered. She was not Rader's first choice, but his intended victim had not been home, so he had walked down the street to another place. He entered Shirley's home despite the presence of three children, all of whom could have identified him, and he locked them in a bathroom. He told Shirley she just needed to submit to what he wanted sexually and she would be all right. But then he bound her, put a plastic bag over her head, and strangled her. The children screamed at him the entire time, and after he left, they escaped to notify neighbors. However, they proved to be useless as witnesses.

Then Nancy Fox, a single woman living alone, drew BTK's notice. He watched her for a while and was pleased to see that she had no dog and did not entertain men. This house, he decided, would be a safe hit and he designated December 8 as the day on which she would die. Rader arrived to an empty house, cut the phone line, and greeted Nancy when she came in. He handcuffed her and told her he was BTK and she was going to die. When she expired from asphyxiation, he relieved himself in her clothing and walked away with her driver's license and other items. The next day, he called the police to report the homicide and send them to her address. He wanted to see this in the newspaper, because he felt elated. It was his way of "sharing" the feeling with others.

He then sent a poem to the press referring to Shirley Vian, but they failed to publish anything about it. Only in retrospect did they even understand what it was.

Suggestions for how best to handle this case were contradictory. Some investigators believed that downplaying it would prevent another murder, while others were sure the killer sought attention, and when he didn't get it, he would be angry enough to kill again. At this time, the profiling unit at the FBI was in its infancy and a couple of agents got involved. They agreed that coverage was the offender's goal, but wanted to see what he would do if he did not get what he wanted.

He soon sent another poorly written letter to a local television station, KAKE-TV, angry that he was being ignored and explaining that he was among the "elite" serial killers. He included a list of other such offenders he considered his equals—H. H. Holmes, Jack the Ripper, "Ted of the West Coast"—and described how serial killers were motivated by "Factor X." There was no cure for their illness and they could not stop. He whined that he had not gotten the amount of media attention that others had, and warned that he was already stalking victim number eight. "How many do I have to Kill," he asked, "before I get my name in the paper or some national attention? Do the cop think that all those deaths are not related?" He was not amused, he said, that the paper was failing to provide details. He included a drawing of the Nancy Fox crime scene.

He claimed seven victims, naming the Oteros, Vian, and Fox, but not the fifth victim. There were several possible candidates, but detectives decided it was probably Kathryn Bright, despite the initial decision to exclude her from the circle.

Soon BTK got what he wanted. The story was publicized: Wichita had a local serial killer who had murdered seven people and threatened to kill more. The police wanted residents to lock their doors. This guy was a stalker; he was careful, crafty, and he passed as ordinary. He watched and entered homes. No one knew where he would strike next and the police did not know how to stop him.

Rader liked to send cryptic notes, puzzles, and leads that proved to be false. No one was quite sure which of the things BTK said were truthful and which were lies. He continued to communicate until 1979, offering a sexually graphic signature by which to authenticate his communications, but there were no new murders that anyone could link to him. Detectives who noticed that most of the communications had been photocopied tracked down all the area copying machines to try to identify the signature of the one the killer used. The Xerox Corporation assisted, helping to pinpoint a library and a machine at WSU.

At one point, a panel of psychiatrists evaluated the communications and decided that BTK viewed himself rather grandiosely as part of a larger scheme. With his references to "the monster," he was possibly setting up an insanity defense, should he ever need it. A child psychologist thought he had an emotional problem or a learning disability.

The residents of Wichita felt terrorized, wondering who might become this man's next victim. Profilers suggested planting a subliminal message into a news program, as well as placing a classified ad to "BTK," but neither strategy hooked a response or goaded him to act out and make the hoped-for mistake. Rader was looking to his personal responsibilities, having become a father again. Now he had a son and a daughter.

Investigators had spent a lot of time and devoted a lot of resources to catching the BTK killer, but failed in their mission. Each and every officer directly involved was disappointed. As they marked the tenth anniversary of the Otero murders, they could only wonder if BTK had been arrested for something else, left the area, or died. The received wisdom on serial killers, especially given the way BTK had described himself, was that they did not just stop. In 1984, a new task force started going systematically through all the files to see if there was something they had missed.

People were asked for blood samples and suspects were summarily eliminated, one by one. The FBI profiler Roy Hazelwood offered a detailed portrait, albeit full of information that already seemed apparent: the killer was sadistic, controlling, and superficial. He read detective magazines and pornography, enjoyed S&M practices with a partner, and liked to drive around. Nothing Hazelwood said moved authorities closer to an identification.

A Change in the Wind

Rader had indeed stopped for a while. It was almost ten years from the last murder to the next, but in 1985, he attacked an elderly women, Marine Hedge, who lived on his own street. This time he dumped the body in a ditch in a wooded area, where it lay for nine days before it was found. No one on the task force could anticipate that Rader was trying to outsmart the FBI, with its stereotypical profiles. He had purposely stopped for a while, killed outside his victim type, and left a victim outside. He offered no communication and simply enjoyed in private the excitement of the hunt. In fact, he flouted his religion by taking the body to his church and abusing it there.

Soon thereafter, in 1986, he targeted Vicki Wegerle, who was married. Pretending to be a telephone repairman, he persuaded her to let him in. Once he dropped the disguise, she fought valiantly, but she was no match for him. He strangled her, took photographs for his collection, stole her driver's license, and left. He sent no communications and was not publicly linked to the crime, so Wegerle's husband became the chief suspect. He was never charged, but the police continued to believe he was a wife killer. Vicki's murder went unsolved.

With the development of DNA analysis for crime

investigation in the United States in 1987, investigators had a viable way to match semen samples with a suspect, if they ever developed one. It was much more precise than the blood tests they'd been using. However, the task force was disbanded and only one detective, Ken Landwehr, remained on the case.

But Rader stopped again, for five years. He was nearing fifty, but was still interested in trolling around to look for "projects." He found Dolores Davis, who lived alone in Park City. Again, this was close to home, but so far neither the cops nor his wife suspected him of anything. It seemed to him he could do whatever he liked, without consequence. He broke into Dolores's home, strangled her, took photos, and dumped her beneath a bridge. All the while he was assisting with a Boy Scout outing involving his son. Soon he became a compliance officer, helping to enforce Park City's ordinances, and lived by the letter of the law. He also became president of the congregation at his church. Some people liked him, others did not.

Remember Me

Nearly two decades passed before BTK was heard from again. In March 2004, a reporter for the *Wichita Eagle* decided to write a thirty-year retrospective of the Otero slaughter and other murders associated with BTK. The story mentioned that few people were even aware of the old BTK cases and said that a local author was writing a book about the unsolved murders. Rader did not like being forgotten or having his story in someone else's hands, and he went through his private files.

The newsroom received a letter on March 19 from "Bill Thomas Killman" that contained three photographs of a woman who was clearly dead. She had been posed in a variety of ways and a photocopy of her driver's license was included: it was Vicki Wegerle. Now her husband was finally off the hook. Clearly, BTK had killed her and taken trophies that he'd kept all these years.

The police had run a DNA test the year before on skin under Vicki's fingernails, and they used it to compare to thousands of suspects via an offender database, as well as to people who volunteered samples, but they'd failed to link it to anyone. A geographical profile indicated that BTK probably lived or worked not far from the crime scenes, which were only four miles apart, and that he had some association with Wichita State University. The Kansas Bureau of Identification's cold-case unit got busy on the old file—more than three dozen boxes of papers and items. Despite this renewed flurry of activity, it amounted to nothing.

In May 2004, a package was found that contained a partial manuscript with thirteen chapters entitled *The BTK Story* (which actually plagiarized an online site). Later, another package surfaced that detailed the Otero slaughter, and another that took credit for a murder that was more likely a suicide. The cops tried to bait this person, but he didn't respond until he was good and ready, which was late in October.

Dennis Rader was now fifty-nine. He went looking for another victim, but was thwarted in his effort. In December, he called KAKE-TV but could not get through, so he left another package in a park. It contained the driver's license of one of the 1977 victims, Nancy Fox, along with a doll, bound with string. BTK had reported this murder to police dispatchers. He also used the right signature, which had never been publicized. Although they could not necessarily trust his "autobiography," the task force believed they knew his age and some of his interests. They thought he was familiar in some capacity with law enforcement and soon had a blurred photo of someone they believed was him driving a dark vehicle and dropping off a package at Home Depot. They began to consider that BTK was linked to the two murders in Park City. Yet despite more than 5,600 tips, they still could not identify him.

While many profiles were offered, one was actually generated via a computer program. A Virginia-based company called EagleForce Associates gathered the evidence and weighted it for significance. The data analysts then cross-correlated all the data, showing that BTK was likely a white male around sixty, with military experience and a connection to the local university. EagleForce saw from the video that he drove a black Jeep Cherokee. Now the pool of suspects was further narrowed, but not by much.

Then the police got a break. BTK had left a message in an empty box of Special K cereal, and the note opened an interesting door. He asked if he could communicate with police via a computer disk without being traced, urging them to "be honest" and to run an ad in the *Eagle* to assure him. The detectives wondered if he could really be so stupid, but they had nothing to lose by telling him he could send them a floppy disk, so they ran the ad. Then they tested X-rays on floppy disks to make sure they would not ruin one by checking for a bomb, just in case.

Bait

Rader thought using a computer would save him a lot of time, because he would not have to photocopy anything. He asked his minister at the Christ Lutheran Church how to use it. He then prepared the disk with a "test" in rich text format that directed police to read the three-by-five card included for details on how to communicate with him in the newspaper. It said that all future communications would be assigned a number and he instructed officers to leave another ad.

They hardly cared about his orders. They had him. While they struggled with reporters who wanted to publish this development, the department's computer expert got to work on the disk. They did not want any "TV experts" letting BTK know that the disk could be traced. He might burn all evidence and run for the hills.

Computer forensics has become an important addition to investigations. It helps to organize evidence, link one piece of evidence to other crimes, identify offenders, and reveal offender communications. Officials can remove three types of data: archival, active, and latent. Active information is stored in files and programs, detectable on the hard drive. Archival data has been backed up and placed in storage. Latent data is the kind that computer users believe has been deleted but a trace remains that can be recovered.

On BTK's floppy disk, the police found the name Dennis, and by re-creating data on it that had been over-written were able to trace it back to a computer at Christ Lutheran Church. (Some reports indicated that there was a hidden electronic code on it that tied it to the church computer.) They learned on a Google search that the president of the congregation was Dennis Rader, and it was easy enough to use another program to get his ad-dress. Officers went to the church to question the pastor, who admitted that he had shown Rader how to use the computer to print out notes from a meeting. Digital foot-prints were found on the hard drive that indicated that this computer had been used to write one of the BTK messages to a local television station. But there was more: Rader had graduated from Wichita State University and in his driveway was a black Jeep Cherokee. A DNA sample subpoenaed from Rader's daughter's medical files clinched it. Rader, a family man, security specialist, and seemingly stable citizen, had bound, tortured, and killed from six to eight people.

Landwehr instructed the task force on how to approach the suspect. At this point, they had kept him under sur-veillance and knew his every move. Landwehr also called retired members of the force to be present. On February 25, everyone got into place, staving off calls from report-ers who had heard rumors. Then they waited for the designated lunch hour. Two detectives pulled Rader over as if they were making a traffic stop, and detectives and FBI agents swarmed in to subdue and cuff him. On his face, they saw panic. They forced him to the ground, under the threat of shotguns, Glocks, and submachine guns. He didn't have a chance. A hint of his guilt was clear when he failed to ask why they were treating him like this; clearly he knew. He merely asked them to call his wife to tell her he would not be home for lunch.

During the postarrest interview, Rader danced around the point, but they told him they could match his DNA to the crimes and that they had him dead to rights with the computer disk. This seemed to finish him. He finally told them he was BTK. He seemed disappointed that the cops had lied to him, tricking him and trapping him, acting as if he'd deserved more respect. This amused them, but they were quickly unsettled when Rader began mimicking what some of his victims had cried out as they were tortured. He went on to confess for many hours.

The police persuaded him to give up his hiding place, so he drew a map. The search produced photos of some of the victims, as well as photos of Rader himself in bondage. It was no surprise that he kept newspaper clippings about the incidents and copies of all his communications, but his gruesome drawings of torture turned stomachs. Detectives were alarmed to see the number of victims that Rader had stalked over the years, many of whom could easily have ended up dead. They wondered if there might be more victims in other places that he wasn't mentioning.

He was about to be charged with the known eight murders, but BTK had news for the police: he confessed to ten and said he'd already targeted his next victim. Had they not caught him, there would have been one more. In retrospect, it was clear when police reexamined his communications that in one of his enigmatic puzzles he'd actually provided his name and home address.

When Rader went to court to confess to his crimes as part of his plea deal, he obviously relished the attention. In a monotone voice, he went meticulously over the details of his "projects," describing them as if each murder had just been business. He appeared to revel in the national limelight, although many reporters were disappointed that a killer once deemed so cunning was such an ordinary, even boring man. He said he had killed to satisfy his sexual fantasies, but tried to minimize his actions by claiming that a demon had possessed and driven him to perform torture and murder.

In several interviews, Rader was adamant in asserting that his decision to resurface in 2004 had not been a way of trying to get caught. He'd made a mistake, which embarrassed him, but he certainly did not wish to spend the rest of his life in prison or embarrass his wife and children. He claimed to feel bad for them. As punishment, Rader received ten consecutive life sentences, to be served at the El Dorado Correctional Facility, for a minimum of 175 years before there was any possibility of parole. His wife divorced him.

The investigators realized that capturing BTK had relied on a carefully controlled media strategy, knowing that the person they sought paid attention to the newspapers. In fact, what had lured him back out in the open was the mention of someone else daring to undertake to write his story. His personality was such that he needed to control the way others viewed him. The police had also had to resist media pressure to provide more details, and stick to their plan. The whole investigation had been a difficult balancing act, and it was the cyber-forensics personnel who had made the difference. Knowing how to trace a disk, do an Internet search, and find files on a hard drive had all played a role, adding an extra layer of expertise to what many teams of detectives had accomplished over the years.

Other types of technology are also growing in prominence in criminal investigations, especially methods and protocols that appear to read minds. What could be better than discovering what offenders *really* know, whether they like it or not?

Sources

"BTK Killer: Demon Got Me Early in Life." Associated Press, July 8, 2005.

Chu, Jeff. "Who Was the Killer Next Door?" *Time,* March 7, 2005.

Cohen, Sharon. "Computer Fisk and DNA Led to BTK Suspect." Associated Press, March 3, 2005.

———. "Experts: BTK Lived Double Life." Associated Press, March 1, 2005.

Gibson, Dirk C. *Clues from Killers: Serial Murder and Crime Scene Messages.* Westport, CT: Praeger, 2004.

Grinberg, Emanuella. "Prosecutors Reveal Nightmarish Details of BTK Serial Killer Methods," CourtTV.com, August 20, 2005.

Jones, K. C. "Surveillance Technology Helps Catch Serial Killer." *Information Week,* January 5, 2007.

"Magazine Highlights BTK Search," kbsd6.com, retrieved January 6, 2007.

Nixon, Ron, and Dan Browning. "Computers Leave a High-Tech Trail of Crime Clues." *Minneapolis Star Tribune,* March 31, 2005.

Rosen, Fred. *There but for the Grace of God: Survivors of the Twentieth Century's Infamous Serial Killers.* New York: HarperCollins, 2007.

Shiflett, Dave. "BTK Killer: A Monster Tripped up by His Ego." *Newsday,* November 18, 2007.

Simons, Erica B. "Forensic Computer Investigation Brings Notorious Serial Killer BTK to Justice." *Forensic Examiner,* Winter 2005, 55–57.

Singular, Stephen. *Unholy Messenger: The Life and Times of the BTK Serial Killer.* New York: Simon & Schuster, 2006.

Wenzl, Roy, Tim Potter, L. Kelly, and Hurst Laviana. *Bind, Torture, Kill.* New York: HarperCollins, 2007.

ELEVEN

JAMES B. GRINDER:
The Brain Never Lies

Around 2:45 A.M. on a Friday morning in 1984, the Missouri Highway State Patrol discovered Julianne Helton's red-and-cream Citation abandoned at the Marceline junction in Macon County, Missouri. It was January 8, a cold day for a woman to have just walked away. Officers learned who owned the vehicle and made some calls. They found Julie's parents, also living in Marceline, who told the officers their daughter had failed to return home from a party in New Cambria the evening before, and they had filed a report that she was missing. Calls to her acquaintances and people from the party turned up nothing. She had simply vanished.

Julie, a lifelong resident of Marceline and an employee of the Walsworth Publishing Company, was only twenty-five. Her parents could think of no reason that someone might want to hurt her. She was reliable, gregarious, and well liked at her job, and having grown up in the area, she had a large network of relatives. Every indication supported the frightening possibility that she'd met with foul play.

Damage to a water hose had caused her car to stall, but closer inspection showed a deliberate cut. This discovery threw a spotlight on men at the party who might have seen her and decided to be her "rescuer" when the car inevitably failed. Investigators sensed a setup. It seemed unlikely to have been a random incident, where a predator just happens along when a young woman needs help, but no known associate of Julie's seemed a likely culprit. Since it was clear that the breakdown had been planned, it was also clear that someone had been watching her.

Investigators intensified their efforts to find her. She was last seen wearing a navy blazer, blue jeans, and a rose-colored sweater. The search party, armed with this

Dr. Lawrence Farwell, a neuropsychiatrist on the cutting edge of brain research.
Brain Fingerprinting Laboratories Inc.

knowledge, spread out around the area, covering more than a hundred square miles, in both Macon and Linn counties. They drove along roads that connected to where the car had stalled, and into wooded areas and farmland.

Three days later, on January 11, two volunteer searchers from the railroad company came across Julie's fully clothed body. It lay in a snow-covered field near the Santa Fe railroad tracks, about eight miles northwest of where her car had stalled. The area was quickly sealed off and the body examined. Julie's hands had been bound in front of her with baling twine and she'd been stabbed to death. There were two sets of footprints in the snow, the victim's and prints of a size that implicated an adult male. This set led to and away from her body. A pool of blood had settled in the snow more than ten feet from the body, where weeds were smashed down, but no blood was found beneath the body. It appeared that Julie had died on the morning she disappeared. Her purse and the implement used to stab her were both missing.

An impromptu coroner's jury was held at the site and these six people requested an autopsy. The frozen body was moved to the morgue, where the postmortem showed bruises and scrapes, as well as blunt-force trauma and deep stab wounds to the neck. Julie had also been raped. Her right hand showed defensive wounds, affirmed by broken fingernails, which suggested she had fought to save herself.

Julie's family held a funeral service and the police continued to investigate. However, all they had were the footprints, which had probably changed from the time

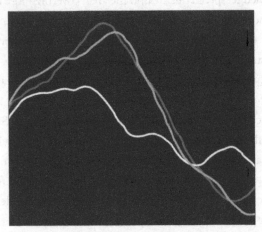

The result of Grinder's examination.
Brain Fingerprinting Laboratories Inc.

Farwell administering his brain scan test to suspected killer
James Grinder.   *Brain Fingerprinting Laboratories Inc.*

when they were left in the snow to the time when the body was found. A reward of $5,000 was offered for information. It would be the killer himself who would eventually supply this information.

Foreshadow

Two years after this incident, a deer hunter walking down a remote, dead-end road came across skeletal remains near Brock Cemetery, thirty miles north of Russellville, Arkansas. He also found shreds of clothing and jewelry. The police called in a forensic anthropologist who said the bones appeared to belong to young adolescents. The likely candidates were Teresa Williams, Crystal Parton, and Cynthia Mabry, who had disappeared on December 2, 1976, a decade earlier, and were never heard from or found. Two were thirteen and one was fourteen.

The anthropological examination indicated with about 80 percent certainty that some of the bones matched Teresa and Crystal. There appeared to be only two sets of remains in this area. A thorough search around the cemetery and in the woods yielded nothing more, leaving Cynthia's mother desperate to know what had happened to her daughter. She'd held out hope that the girl would one day come back.

At the time of the girls' disappearance, the police had a key suspect. Teresa's fourteen-year-old cousin told police he'd seen James B. Grinder, a local woodcutter, with Teresa that day. Grinder admitted he'd seen the girls hitchhiking and picked them up, but he'd dropped them off at the interstate exit for Pottsville. He gave them twenty dollars but claimed that was the last he saw of them. He returned home to his girlfriend. Since there was no evidence against him, he appeared to have an alibi, and since the girls were still missing, he was not charged. In fact, no one was charged, since two of the bodies were not found for over a decade and the third girl was still considered missing. Investigators had surmised that they were runaways.

Predator

More years passed and Grinder was arrested with two other men for burglary. The police questioned him about Julie Helton, offering him a deal for life in prison, so he confessed. He said he had planned the murder for about two months, watching and waiting. One night, he spotted her car parked at a business and punctured the radiator. Later that night, he saw her with her disabled car, the hood up, standing on an overpass—just what he'd been waiting for. He stopped to "assist," and then two other men stopped as well—the men involved with him in the burglary. He said that Julie agreed to get into one man's car, but they all ended up at a mobile home, three men and Julie. They used cocaine and then the men all raped her. Finally, they had to kill her to keep her from talking, so they took her to the railroad track, where Grinder stabbed her in the neck and in the mouth.

One of the problems with this confession was the testimony of the other two men, who claimed they had nothing to do with the rape or murder of Julie Helton. In fact, the physical evidence from the scene indicated that only one man had been with her when she died. Grinder then changed his story somewhat, adding the participation of a local police chief, and then recanted his confession altogether, saying that while he was present at the crime scene, he had not participated in either the rape or the murder. In addition, Grinder's nephew confessed to the rape and, in exchange for immunity, corroborated one of Grinder's statements.

The police chief, too, denied involvement, but he was subsequently suspended. The other two men remained in prison to await trial, although everyone knew that all the police had was Grinder's confession, which was a mess. It would be a tough case to win, but they had to do something to get justice for the victim and her family.

When the Russellville police learned that James Grinder had confessed to a Missouri homicide, they decided to try to get more out of him about their missing-person case. Lieutenant Ray Caldwell and State Trooper Dwayne Lueter traveled to Macon County in 1998 to inform Grinder that two of the girls' remains had been found. Grinder admitted to killing all three, providing details about physical evidence that had never been publicized, and clearing up the mystery.

He had picked up the three girls on December 2, 1976, he said, outside Russellville. They went with him to Morrilton, where he purchased alcohol. He then drove them to Brock Cemetery and raped Teresa and Crystal. Afterward, he strangled them and stabbed them in the neck.

He hid their bodies under some brush. Cynthia was still alive, and he took her to another location in the woods and raped her. She, too, had to die, so he used a soda bottle to hit her over the head. When this failed to work, he picked up a tire iron and bludgeoned her several times. The place was so forlorn that he figured he did not have to hide her body, so he just left it there. A week later, he returned to the cemetery to pile more brush on the other two, still undiscovered.

Grinder's former live-in girlfriend also admitted that he'd come in around midnight on that December 2 and told her that if anyone asked, she was to say he'd been with her all evening. He told her about the missing girls and gave her $200 to cover for him.

In 1998, David Gibbons, the Pope County prosecutor, filed one charge of capital murder against Grinder, which signified the premeditated killing of two or more people. However, the whereabouts of the remains of Cynthia Mabry plagued both the girl's family and the investigators who had long been on the case. Even after twenty-three years, they wanted to find whatever they could and give the girl a proper burial. They hoped to bring Grinder to Arkansas so he could point out the exact location, but before they could do so, his situation in Missouri took some interesting new turns.

Try Something New

In early June 1999, Missouri attorney general Jay Nixon asked that first-degree murder charges be dropped against two of the men implicated in Grinder's confession. Although it was initially believed that the semen samples removed from Julie had been used up in earlier testing, some turned up in a Colorado lab. DNA testing cleared the men and indicated that Grinder had lied when he described their involvement. Since Grinder had manipulated the evidence, Nixon stated that he would revoke the deal and reconsider the death penalty. Days later, after more testing, charges were also dropped against the police chief.

Sheriff Robert Dawson now faced a difficult situation. He had no physical evidence against Grinder, so the confession had been crucial. In 1993, court-ordered blood samples were taken, but the results were insufficient to support an indictment, especially for murder. Grinder had now changed his story so many times, even contradicting himself, that no one would have been surprised if he recanted altogether, which would have left Dawson with nothing. Given Grinder's unreliability, they might have nothing even if he didn't recant. After over ten thousand man-hours spent investigating the case and hoping for its resolution, the possibility that it could collapse alarmed everyone involved.

Dawson recalled recent news coverage of a neurological assessment technique called brain fingerprinting, a discovery of Dr. Lawrence Farwell, a neuropsychiatrist. With degrees from Harvard University and the University of Illinois, Farwell had been president and chief scientist of the Human Brain Research Laboratory since 1991. Along with brain fingerprinting, he had invented the Farwell Brain Communicator, a device that allowed a subject's brain to communicate directly to a computer and speech synthesizer.

Farwell claimed that brain fingerprinting was 99.9 percent accurate. What Dawson had learned from the media coverage was that since the brain is central to all human activities, it records all experiences. This finding had many applications, including use in the criminal justice system. The act of committing a crime, as well as details from a crime scene, would be stored in the offender's brain, which meant that the memory would have a measurable pattern.

Brain fingerprinting records distinct patterns, called event-related potentials, which are measures of the brain's electrical activity as it corresponds to events in the environment. By averaging the distinct patterns of electrical activity, a singular waveform arises that can be dissected into components related to cognitive functions. Those related to brain fingerprinting are the P300 and the MERMER. The P300 is a positive charge that peaks between 300 and 800 milliseconds in response to meaningful or noteworthy stimuli. Dr. Farwell found that the P300 was one aspect of a larger brain-wave response that peaks at 800 to 1,200 milliseconds after a response, which he called a MERMER (memory and encoding related multifaceted electroencephalographic response). If a suspect like Grinder was involved in a murder, for example, his brain activity when shown crime-relevant stimuli would produce a distinct spike on a graph. "Your brain says, 'Aha! I recognize this,'" Farwell explained. Innocent people, he claimed, or people who had never been to the specific crime scene, would display no such neurological response.

Farwell utilizes three types of stimuli for testing a subject: target, probe, and irrelevant. Target stimuli are made "noteworthy" by exposing the subject to a list of words and phrases before any testing is done. When flashed on the screen, they should all elicit a recordable MERMER. Probes also contain noteworthy information, and this set is derived from details that investigators know about the crime and crime scene. This information is meaningful only to the actual perpetrator, and includes things done to the victim, where she was taken, how she was killed, items removed from her, and items left at the scene. The subject does not see this list until the test itself is performed. Irrelevant stimuli, to which no MERMER should occur, might include a different type of weapon, landscape, MO, or acts that were probably not done during the commission of the crime.

To strengthen the results, Farwell might test another angle. If the suspect offers an alibi for the time of the crime, a scenario can be devised from it and tested with the scanning device to see if the brain has a record of it. Thus the technology is useful in more ways than one. Like a fingerprint at a scene, it does not necessarily prove murder, but it adds an indicator of guilt. If a suspect had no good reason to be present at the scene, the MERMER becomes strongly suggestive evidence.

Other researchers have studied violence and the brain, testing reactions, impulsivity, and areas of neural processing, but Farwell had developed a patented headband equipped with EEG sensors to detect the brain's response and chart it on a graph. Brain fingerprinting is an improvement over the polygraph machine, Farwell claims, in that it relies on neurological processes over which no one has control. Some people have managed to manipulate a polygraph, but they cannot fool his machine.

Farwell uses a specific protocol. First, details about the crime must be gathered by someone familiar with brain fingerprinting, just as fingerprints can only be properly lifted by a trained investigator. Then the subject responds to the material and the sets of responses are analyzed and compared; this is followed by what is called a statistical confidence reading, an evaluation of the reliability of the responses.

Dawson contacted Farwell to request that Grinder undergo the test, and the suspect agreed to participate. Farwell was happy to be involved. This would be a first for him. While he'd conducted field tests and lab experiments, including accurately distinguishing between a group of FBI agents and nonagents, he had not yet participated in an active criminal case. It was a good chance to prove his methods and device. Many who had heard of it assumed it was little more than a glorified lie-detector test, which would make the results potentially inadmissible in court. However, in the court of last resort, investigators on the Helton case were willing to try it.

Farwell brought his equipment to the Macon County Sheriff's Office and prepared to test Grinder's memory in the matter of the fifteen-year-old murder. Sheriff Dawson, Chief Deputy Charles Muldoon, and Randy King from the Missouri Highway Patrol, all of whom were involved in the investigation, provided the needed details for developing a case-specific test. Former FBI Supervisory Special Agent Drew Richardson assisted. He had been involved in earlier brain-fingerprinting experiments and had left the FBI to become a vice president of Farwell's company. From all this information, Farwell created a series of phrases and images to be flashed at Grinder at timed intervals on a computer screen.

The following facts were noted in Farwell's report. He followed the standard procedures, preparing to record the results for law enforcement. Before the test, Grinder was given a pretest in which details of the crime that he had already described were flashed on the computer. He was instructed to press a button when a certain type of "target" stimulus appeared, and to press a different button when something else appeared, which would include both probe stimuli and irrelevant information. If he was guilty, the probe stimuli should show the same response as the target stimuli.

The test itself was divided into blocks of twenty-four stimuli, each of which was presented three separate times. Grinder's response to all of them was graphed and calculated in such a way that responses to "relevant" stimuli could be mathematically compared to his responses to "irrelevant" stimuli. Grinder participated in seven separate tests with five different sets of probes. He sat in a chair in front of the screen, wearing his orange prison jumpsuit and the sensor-equipped helmet that measured areas in the parietal, frontal, and central areas of his brain.

If the test proved that Grinder was the perpetrator, and the testing was allowed into court (something that was not yet known), he faced a capital conviction, with a death sentence.

After forty-five minutes, the results seemed clear: the computer analysis showed "information present" for probe stimuli. The computed statistical confidence level was 99.9 percent accurate. There was no question about Grinder's guilt: he had quite specific concealed knowledge about the crime. "What his brain said," Farwell told reporters of the *Fairfield Ledger,* "was that he was guilty. He had critical detailed information only the killer would have. The murder of Julie Helton was stored fifteen years ago when he committed the murder." As far as Farwell was concerned, he had proven his theory: the record of a crime can be stored indefinitely in the brain of the perpetrator, and technology can detect it, thus excluding other suspects. "We can use this technology to put serial killers in prison where they belong."

Six days after submitting to brain fingerprinting, Grinder was in court to plead guilty. He was then taken to Arkansas to face a hearing. Sheriff Dawson acknowledged in a letter that the evidence provided by the test had been instrumental in obtaining the confession and guilty plea.

Arkansas authorities accompanied Grinder from Missouri so he could point out where he had murdered Cynthia. He showed them an area in the Ozark National Forest, but it was difficult to find anything so many years after the crime. For his guilty plea in Arkansas, he was sentenced to life in prison.

Brain Science

Clearly, brain fingerprinting is potentially revolutionary, although critics insist it needs more testing. Farwell has since been involved in other criminal cases, one with positive results for the future of the procedure, one without. In both cases, however, the procedure was not used in a jury trial but only during an appeal. At this writing, brain fingerprinting has yet to be allowed into court.

The issue of admissibility of new technologies purporting to be science is complex, dating back to 1923, when the District of Columbia Court of Appeals issued the first guidelines. In *Frye v. United States,* the defense counsel wanted to enter evidence about a device that measured the blood pressure of a person who was lying. The court had to scramble to figure out what to do, as there were no guidelines yet in place, and increasingly more attorneys were looking for scientific evidence to help convict or exonerate a defendant. The judge decided that the "thing" from which such testimony is deduced must be "sufficiently established to have gained general acceptance in the particular field in which it belongs." In addition, the information offered had to be beyond the general knowledge of the jury.

This *Frye* standard became general practice in most courts for many years, vague though it was. Over the decades, critics claimed that it excluded theories that were unusual but nevertheless well supported. Each attempt to revise the *Frye* standard had its own problems.

In some jurisdictions now, including the federal courts, the *Frye* standard has been replaced by a standard cited in the Supreme Court's 1993 decision in *Daubert v. Merrell Dow Pharmaceuticals, Inc.,* which emphasizes the trial judge's responsibility as a gatekeeper. The court decided that *scientific* means grounded in the methods and procedures of science and *knowledge* is more reliable than gut instinct or subjective belief. The judge's evaluation should focus on the methodology, not the conclusion, and on whether the evidence so deduced applies to the case. In other words, when scientific testimony is presented, judges have to determine whether the theory can be tested, the potential error rate is known, it was reviewed by peers, it had attracted widespread acceptance within a relevant scientific community, and the opinion was relevant to the issue in dispute.

Many attorneys look to these guidelines to distinguish between "junk science" and work performed with controls, scientific methodology, and appropriate precautions. But some guidelines are slippery, particularly when it comes to examining a suspect's state of mind at the time of the crime. Subjective interpretations are the norm: a clinical practitioner uses a battery of objective assessments to examine the defendant's background and activities just before the crime. The problem is that equally qualified practitioners can derive opposing conclusions from the same tests and observations, so state of mind at the time of the crime often comes down to whom the jury believes.

There are certainly records of cases in which a defendant ably duped a practitioner about his ability to commit the crime in question. If Farwell's invention can deliver on its promise, it could reduce reliance on subjective evaluation and perhaps increase the accuracy of assessments, at least as far as guilt is concerned.

"I have every reason to believe it will be viewed the same as DNA," Farwell states. "We're not reading minds, just detecting the presence or absence of specific information about a specific crime." He believes that in the future, his device will dramatically alter the way suspects are interrogated. He views it as a way to reduce the number of false confessions and convictions that postconviction DNA testing has revealed over the past decade.

In November 2000, in an appeal for postconviction relief, an Iowa district court held an eight-hour hearing on the admissibility of this technology. The accused, imprisoned for twenty-two years, submitted to brain fingerprinting to try to prove he was innocent of committing a murder, and he passed. The MERMERs supported his alibi but not his participation in the crime. He then sought to have his conviction overturned, but the court said that the results of the test would not have affected the verdict. Yet, in the process, District Judge Timothy O'Grady ruled that the P300 theory met the Daubert Standard as admissible scientific evidence. But when the key witness heard about the test results, he admitted he'd lied in the original trial, so the convicted man appealed to the Iowa Supreme Court and was freed, based on a legal technicality and lack of evidence. While brain fingerprinting received a legal stamp of approval in this case, it has not yet been truly tested in the legal system.

As of early 2008, with more than 170 tests performed (80 of which were real-life situations as opposed to laboratory assessments), brain fingerprinting has proven reliable and accurate. There was not a single error with either information present or information absent. The CIA has given a generous grant for the work to continue. "I have high statistical confidence in it," Farwell said.

One flaw, also relevant to the use of fingerprints, has been the inability of the test to distinguish between a person who was at a crime scene but did not commit the crime and one who was in the same place and is guilty.

Also, Farwell does not deal with memory research that demonstrates that memory is not a "storage tank" but an actively constructed process that can even result in false memories that are qualitatively as vivid as actual memories. More research must be done to accommodate issues such as age, substance abuse, stress, and memory disorders, all of which can affect the memory of a criminal. In addition, the subjective nature of the way investigators put together a case for test development—the basis for the probe stimuli—makes some scientists question its reliability.

In reports, Farwell says, "It is inevitable that the brain will take its rightful place as a central facet of criminal investigations." While he's probably correct in this prediction, there is still cause for concern. Brain fingerprinting might help to convict the guilty and exonerate the innocent, but its use might reinforce the use of other types of neurological testing that may appear to mitigate guilt. It could also force a reexamination of so many cases that this revolution could shake up the entire justice system. Whether we're ready or not, scientific measurements, even ambiguous ones, will be proposed in future criminal cases.

My Brain Made Me Do It

Philosophers and many proponents of cognitive psychology hold that moral judgments are within our control, and thus people who choose to commit crimes, barring delusions, know what they are doing and that it is wrong. The legal system depends on this notion. However, recent research suggests that damage to an area of the brain just behind the eyes can transform the way people make moral decisions. The results indicate that the ventromedial prefrontal cortex, implicated in the feeling of compassion, may be the foundation for moral regulations, assisting us in inhibiting (or not) harmful treatment of others. Failure in its development, or damage to it, might alter the way a person perceives the moral landscape, which will thus affect his or her actions. If juries include information of this kind in their deliberations, it could mitigate the harshness of the sentences they impose on convicted criminals. While more research must be done, other types of brain scans are being entered as evidence in the trials of some heinous crimes to show that the perpetrator could not help what he did.

Stephen Stanko kidnapped a young woman and served

nearly a decade in prison for his crime. While he was incarcerated, he collaborated with two professors on a book
about his experience. After his release, he got involved
with a librarian, whom he later murdered before raping
her teenage daughter. He also killed a seventy-four-year-
old man, and went on the run, stopping here and there
to socialize in bars. He was soon captured, already court-
ing his next victim. Despite his vow to be a good citizen,
he had proven only that he was a dangerous psychopath.
That meant he lacked empathy for others, had a strong
tendency toward self-interest, was able to charm and con
others, and felt no remorse for his actions. He used people
up for his own purposes and committed more crimes
without inhibition.

During his trial, the prosecutor said Stanko was a man
who lacked all remorse for his actions. He was a psychopath who knew what he was doing when he did it but felt
no remorse afterward. The defense attorney, William
Diggs, wanted to prove that Stanko had no control over
his actions, the result of a brain defect, and was therefore
insane. He hired Dr. Thomas H. Sachy, founder of Georgia Pain and Behavioral Medicine, to test Stanko. Sachy
scanned Stanko's brain with a PET-scan machine, and
testified that it "showed decreased function in the medial
orbital frontal lobes." He explained to the jury that one
region of the brain directly above the eyes and behind the
eyebrows did not function normally, and "this [is the]
area of the brain that essentially makes us human."

Although the jury rejected Dr. Sachy's notion and
convicted Stanko, the age of neuro-imaging had arrived,

and eventually defense experts will improve both their testing and their testimony until someone, somewhere, will convince a jury that psychopaths cannot help what they do any more than psychotic people can; both groups are mentally ill and both groups would be accorded equal freedom from criminal culpability.

Another effort to employ brain scans for deception detection comes out of Germany, from the Berlin Bernstein Center for Computational Neuroscience. As reported in 2007, people tested with MRI machines performed simple skills while scientists attempted to "read" their intentions before these intentions became actions. Because these machines can identify different types of brain activity and link them to certain brain states or behaviors, the scientists believed they could distinguish and accurately predict what a person would decide to do. Thus far, the accuracy rate on a small sample of subjects has been just over 70 percent—greater than chance. As the tests get more refined, that accuracy level is expected to improve.

Researchers at the Max Planck Institute for Human Cognitive and Brain Sciences in Leipzig, Germany, are also involved in making such predictions. Subjects were asked to make decisions about adding or subtracting numbers before the numbers were shown on a computer screen. Brain patterns indicated that these processes were different. Bursts of activity in the prefrontal cortex— "thought signatures"—helped researchers predict results. While the decision making was made on a simple level, which means the claims for this science must be limited, more disturbing possibilities are on the horizon. Scientists might one day be able to tell, without his or her consent, what a person is thinking or feeling. This may assist in criminal investigations, but it might also have unpleasant repercussion on other levels of society.

Our final case involves many areas of forensic science and psychology. Such coordinated teamwork is certainly the wave of the future. While a collective effort may take longer to find the truth than the use of a brain scan, especially when evidence and testimony are tenuous, such work can pay off.

Sources

Akin, David. "Brain Wave: A Test That Can Detect Whether Someone Has Seen Something Before Is Being Promoted as a Tool to Screen for Terrorists." *Globe and Mail,* November 3, 2001.

Bell, Bill. "Brothers Charged in Murder are Released." *St. Louis Post-Dispatch,* June 8, 1999.

Carey, Benedict. "Brain Injury Said to Affect Moral Choices." *New York Times,* March 22, 2007.

"Charges Dropped Against Third Man in Macon Murder Case." Associated Press, September 4, 1999.

Dalby, Beth. "Brain Fingerprinting Testing Traps Serial Killer in Missouri." *Fairfield Ledger,* brainwavescience.com, retrieved January 5, 2007.

"DNA Evidence Doesn't Support Case Against Two Men in 1984 Macon County Murder and Rape; Charges Dropped." Attorney General's News Release, June 7, 1999.

Farwell, Lawrence A. "Farwell Fingerprinting Testing." Forensic Report prepared for Sheriff Robert Dawson, August 5, 1999.

Feder, Barnaby. "Truth and Justice, by the Blip of a Brain Wave." *New York Times,* October 9, 2001.

"Federal Agency Views on the Potential Application of Brain Fingerprinting." *Investigative Techniques,* October 2001.

"German Scientists Reading Minds Using Brain-Scan Machines."
Associated Press, March 6, 2007.

Gross, Thom. "Rural Town Suspends Police Chief." *St. Louis Post-Dispatch,* January 27, 1993.

"Helton Case Still Open." *Chronicle Herald,* January 10, 1984.

Krushelnycky, Askold. "Brain Fingerprinting Proves Death Row Convict's Innocence." London *Independent,* July 18, 2004.

"Man Gets Life Without Parole After Guilty Plea in 1976 Slaying." Associated Press, September 8, 1999.

McKie, Robin. "It's the Thought that Counts for the Guilty." *The Observer,* April 25, 2004.

Meisel, Jay. "Killer's Confession to Let Mom Bury Daughter at Last." *Arkansas Democrat-Gazette,* September 8, 1999.

———. "Man Points to Location of Girl Killed 23 Years Ago." *Arkansas Democrat-Gazette,* August 17, 1999.

———. "Man, 55, is Charged in '76 Deaths of Three Girls." *Arkansas Democrat-Gazette,* October 6, 1998.

"Murder on His Mind." CBS *48 Hours,* January 13, 2007.

Obituary for Julianne Helton. *Chronicle Herald,* January 13, 1984.

Paulson, Tom. "Brain Fingerprinting Touted as Truth Meter." *Seattle Post-Intelligencer,* March 1, 2004.

Sloca, Paul. "Nixon Asks That Charges be Dropped against Murder Suspects in Macon Case." Associated Press, June 7, 1999.

TWELVE

ROBERT PICKTON:
Mass Fatality ID

Women were vanishing from the streets of Vancouver, British Columbia, but since most were prostitutes or drug addicts, little attention was paid. As early as 1991, community activists insisted the police must do something, but across the decade, as many as thirty women went missing and the numbers continued to rise. A Missing Women Task Force formed, but it was only after the Royal Canadian Mounted Police got involved that the effort became organized.

Then, early in 2002, when over sixty women were unaccounted for, Constable Nathan Wells, a rookie, learned something from a man named Scott Chubb that inspired him to get a court order to search a nearby pig farm in Port Coquitlam. Chubb had allegedly seen unlicensed firearms and ammunition on the property, owned by Robert Pickton, so Wells went to check. He was unaware of Pickton's alleged association with some of the missing women, but accompanying him were two members of the task force. In fact, this farm had been searched twice before, without results.

However, this time they found several asthma inhalers labeled with the name of Sereena Abotsway, one of the missing, so more members of the task force went in to look around. They did not realize then that they would find much more than just Sereena's inhalers.

Four people were arrested on various charges: fifty-three-year-old Robert Pickton, his friends Paul Casanova and Dinah Taylor, and a woman who had briefly lived on the farm, Lynn Ellingsen. All but Pickton were released after questioning. Pickton remained in jail, on two charges of first-degree murder filed on February 22, 2002. By October of that year, murder charges rose to fifteen, then twenty, and finally twenty-seven. However, some investigators thought Pickton might be linked to as many as sixty-nine missing women.

Details of the "Pig Man" case unfolded to the press and public through the trial, but the preceding investigation is the most fascinating part of the story. It would be the longest, most expensive, and most complex criminal investigation in Canadian history—for that matter, in the world. Even the United States had never undertaken an investigation of this magnitude, despite its worldwide reputation as the capital of serial murder. Pathologists, anthropologists, osteologists, entomologists, geologists, trace-evidence experts, latent-fingerprint examiners, DNA analysts, blood-spatter-pattern analysts, civil engineers, profilers, mass-fatality consultants, and other specialists were all coordinated to process and interpret the evidence. The trial itself lasted nearly a year, but even with all this impressive effort, it was felt that the jury's verdict could go either way.

Early Warning

Detective Dave Dickson launched an inquiry about the many women who'd been reported missing from Vancouver's Downtown Eastside since the early 1970s. A community group had made a list of names for the police, but since some women turned up alive and others were dead, the list seemed unreliable. Dickson wrote up a new one, finding sufficient reason to wonder what had happened to them all. In 1998, the official task force was formed to look into the disappearance of forty women. When sixteen prostitutes appeared to have vanished under suspicious circumstances, investigators wondered if there might be a serial killer in the area.

Vancouver detective inspector Kim Rossmo had devised a computerized method he called geographical profiling, which highlighted killing patterns specific to geographical areas. He'd devised the first such profile in 1990, and by the end of the decade his work had been utilized extensively in Canada and Britain, with limited application in the United States. In 1999, he analyzed the Vancouver area, concluding that there was indeed a serial killer at work, but his superiors dismissed his concerns.

They were not keen to go public with such an alarming notion unless solid evidence supported it. Rossmo thought the results of his analysis were proof enough. He had found an abnormally high concentration of missing women between 1995 and 1998, with no indication that any had filed a change of address for assistance checks.

A geographical-profile analysis highlights crime location, physical boundaries, and types of roads and highways that influence body dump sites. An analysis of known crime scenes or last places victims were seen provides clues about where an offender may live or work. Like behavioral profilers, those who concentrate on geographical analysis try to determine how sophisticated and organized an offender is, whether a crime was planned or opportune, and whether the offender approached a high- or low-risk victim. However, they take it a step further, using objective measurements to pinpoint as precisely as possible the locus of criminal activity.

Rossmo's program, Criminal Geographic Targeting (CGT), assessed the spatial characteristics of a crime. (Environmental Criminology Research, Inc. developed a prototype called Rigel.) Using specific measurements, it generates numerous calculations to produce a topographic map based on key locations. Via color arrangements and graphs, the resulting map reveals the "jeopardy surface," or likelihood that some area is the location of the killer's home or base of operation. This map is then superimposed on a street map on which the crimes are highlighted— "fingerprints" of the offender's cognitive map.

Rossmo had tested the accuracy of his program on

solved cases. For example, Robert Clifford Olson was arrested in 1981 in Vancouver, BC, for picking up two hitchhikers. He subsequently confessed to eleven murders, mostly young girls and boys. Rossmo generated a map of Olson's crimes and was able to pinpoint within a four-square-block area where Olson had actually lived.

The program's predictive power depends on the number of crime sites, the more the better (Rossmo preferred at least five). CGT takes into account an unknown offender's movement patterns, comfort zones, and hunting patterns, as well as what is already known about the way offenders in general behave. Right-handed criminals escaping in a hurry, for example, will tend to flee to the left and discard weapons to the right. When lost, males tend to go downhill while females go up. The profiler enters information about the crime scene, suspect lists, police reports, and motor vehicles and builds from there, modifying the parameters as needed.

The principal elements are distance, what are called mental maps, mobility, and locality demographics. Central to the approach is the idea that there is a difference between perceived distance and actual distance, which varies among individuals; certain factors influence how this disparity affects the commission of a crime. The availability of transportation, number of barriers (bridges, state boundaries), type of roads, and familiarity with a specific region all influence perceived distance.

Within this context, one of the most significant factors in geographical profiling is the concept of a mental map: a cognitive image of one's surroundings developed through experiences, travel routes, reference points, and centers of activity. The places where an offender feels comfortable is part of his or her mental map. As they grow bolder, offenders' maps may expand, with an increase in the range of criminal activity.

Some criminals are geographically stable and some travel around; this depends on their experience with travel, means for getting places, sense of personal security, and predatory motivations. The mental map may also depend on whether the killer is a hunter, stalker, or has some other mode of attack. In the Vancouver case, assuming the offender was a male, geographical profiling focused on the following issues:

- Why he picked his victims from a particular neighborhood

- What route he might have used

- When he utilized this route

- How the route was generally employed by others

- What the geographic patterns of the possible abductions were

- Whether the victims were high risk

- How victims might have been lured to go with the offender

Rossmo believed that plotting the travel routes of serial offenders makes the offender's mobility more predictable.

The more he offends and gets away with it, the more confidence he gains and the more his crime area tends to expand or the number of crimes escalates. That meant that the initial acts occurred closest to where the offender lived or worked—or both. Whoever was picking up these prostitutes was quite familiar with Vancouver's Downtown Eastside, the most disadvantaged ten-block area in the province. "Low Track" was where thousands of junkies shot up, low-class prostitutes turned the cheapest tricks, and dealers exchanged drugs for money or sex. Drug overdose and HIV infections were rampant.

Despite the results of Rossmo's analysis, his bosses dismissed his conclusion about a serial killer. Without an actual crime, body, or crime scene, just knowing that someone was picking up and doing away with a lot of women offered no leads. Getting information from pimps, prostitutes, and drug addicts was difficult, even if they feared for their lives. Yet authorities did make some effort: a substantial reward was posted for information and investigators sought DNA samples from relatives of the missing so they would have something for comparison in the event that human remains turned up. *America's Most Wanted* even ran a feature about the women.

By 2001, after reporters published sharp criticisms of police handling of the situation, officials turned over the files to the Royal Canadian Mounted Police (RCMP) and admitted that they probably had a serial killer taking prostitutes off the streets on their hands. The list now held thirty-one names, going back as far as 1983. That December, with forty-five women on the official list, sixteen investigators and five support personnel formed a task force; more investigators were added just in time for the first break in the case, in February 2002.

Searching the Farm

The seven-hectare farm, about seventeen acres, was where Pickton and his younger brother, Dave, ran a business butchering pigs. They also had an unofficial nightclub dubbed "Piggy's Palace," which hosted large parties. (Over 1,700 showed up at one, which forced authorities to close it down.) After the initial discovery of the inhalers, investigators divided the property into 216 grids, of twenty by twenty meters each, for an organized search. Dirt, excavated in layers from each section, was placed onto one of two conveyor belts for archaeologists and anthropologists to sift for bone fragments. Odontologists stood ready to examine suspicious items for teeth, as well as to assist with identifications in the event a jaw was found that could provide a bite-mark impression. Technicians could also extract DNA from the pulpy area, or freeze the tooth and smash it into a fine powder for a different kind of analysis. Pickton's mobile home and slaughterhouse were designated as top priorities, and a painstaking search began, but the task of looking through several buildings full of pig manure and offal was not pleasant. Even the Pig Man's residence was filthy, with blood spatters in many areas and a bloodstained mattress. Items belonging to some of the missing turned up in the place.

Several weeks passed without evidence of murder, but then a stinking freezer in a back room intended for storing meat drew the attention of a cop. Heavy items sat on top, so two officers removed them to lift the lid. An even more disgusting stench issued forth when they did this. When they were able, they looked inside. They spotted two buckets lying on their sides, one inserted into the other. One officer reached down to set the top bucket upright. What he saw appeared to be a human head, sliced into two pieces. When the bucket was removed, they found two hands and two feet shoved inside the area where the head was split. Inside the second bucket was another woman's head, hands, and feet. All items were carefully bagged for the morgue.

These remains would eventually be identified as what was left of Sereena Abotsway and Andrea Joesbury. A pathologist confirmed that the skulls had been partially sawed and then torn apart at the top, as well as shot with a .22-caliber weapon. The saw marks were similar to the treatment noted on a "Jane Doe" skull found in 1995 in a marshy area at a location off the property. This discovery sent a team of searchers to the area.

It was just the beginning. Two months later, a garbage pail near the pigpen yielded the skeletal remains of two hands and two feet, placed inside a severed skull. This was all that was left of Mona Wilson. Like the other two victims, she had been shot in the head. The sifting teams were also productive. With a backhoe and another machine, they had examined many piles of dirt, recovering three teeth and a fragile jawbone, the size of a woman's.

Another human jawbone was in a cistern, linked to Marnie Frey, and from inside a wood chipper were remains that suggested someone had ground up body parts to feed to the pigs or hide in fertilizer. Analysts eventually identified Brenda Wolfe through teeth on the jawbone, and a rib and heel bone matched Jane Doe's DNA. After dismantling part of the building around the pigpen, searchers looked through rats' nests and turned up fourteen hand bones, cut with a knife, one of which was linked to Georgina Papin.

With this evidence, the entire farm became a crime scene and more experts from various areas of forensic science arrived to assist. Teams ranged over the entire farm property to look for the most minute pieces of physical evidence—a bone, spots of blood, semen, teeth, hair shafts—for DNA analysis. They had to dig deep for evidence that might have been buried years before.

Over the course of some twenty months, more than 130 anthropologists and anthropology grad students worked with numerous biologists and crime-lab personnel to look for bones, distinguish between human and animal bones, and try to identify the victims. The painstaking effort produced over 600,000 exhibits. Investigators demolished all the farm buildings on the property, sifted 378,000 cubic meters of dirt and mud, and took over 200,000 DNA samples. So far, analysis had identified DNA from thirty women, twenty-seven of whom were on the list of missing women. All the evidence useful for trial was found within a hundred meters of Pickton's residence and several items identified as victim property had

Pickton's DNA on them. During this time, other investigators questioned witnesses to amass evidence for a trial. Finding human remains was one thing; nailing a killer quite another. The main problem was that the people who could offer significant accounts had drug-hazed memories or questionable characters. Their credibility would be an issue for a jury.

The search was finally concluded in November 2003, and by this time, Pickton was already in preliminary hearings. There was also good evidence related to him, much of which was presented in this closed session. In 1997, he'd been arrested for the attempted murder of a prostitute, but charges were dropped. He was known to entice prostitutes to his farm and had been seen with some of the missing and dead. An associate of his had also told the police what he knew, and the prosecution had a secret tape of Pickton's conversation with an undercover officer from the RCMP in which he implicated himself. He told his cell mate that the authorities were trying to "bury" him, and he considered it tantamount to a crucifixion. He also stated that his goal had been to kill fifty women, but he'd reached only forty-nine. He bragged that he'd used a rendering plant where he took pig offal to dispose of the bodies, but he'd gotten sloppy with cleanup, which was why he'd been arrested. He mentioned having planned to take a break after fifty and then kill another twenty-five. He said he was "bigger than the Green River [Killer]." He seemed to know he was being videotaped—he even looked at the camera—and not to care.

During the official police interview, however, when

asked if he had killed as many as thirty women, Pickton protested, "You're making me more of a mass murderer than I am!" He admitted, though, that he'd been sloppy in cleaning up after the murders, and he thought that perhaps three women had died in the trailer. He told police that what they had surmised about the death of Mona Wilson, whose blood was found on the mattress, was "close."

Charged with twenty-seven murders (one of which was later dropped), Pickton pleaded not guilty. Enigmatically, he had hinted that others might be involved.

A confession alone is worth little, especially once a defense attorney gets involved to challenge either how it was gained or the suspect's competence for giving it. Pickton's attorney would do both. Thus the prosecution team needed as much direct and circumstantial evidence as possible. Everyone in law enforcement could foresee that getting a conviction in the case was going to be a tough battle.

Because it was too much to ask one jury to consider twenty-six cases, the judge split the indictment between two trials, selecting six cases that appeared to be "materially different" from the others. Yet even laying out these six was expected to take a year, with over two hundred participants. Finally, the stage was set for Robert "Willie" Pickton to be tried for the murders of Sereena Abotsway, Mona Wilson, Andrea Joesbury, Marnie Frey, Georgina Papin, and Brenda Wolfe. All were clearly dead and had been identified via DNA from bones or body parts found on the pig farm.

Down to Business

After a six-month preliminary hearing to determine the admissibility of several key items, the trial got under way in December 2006. With British Columbia Supreme Court judge James Williams presiding, it took only two days to seat the jury and its members were warned that it was going to be a long and sometimes gruesome experience. The press was not allowed to take photos, so artists prepared sketches of Pickton watching the proceedings from inside a specially built box surrounded by bulletproof glass.

In its opening statement, the Crown, represented by Derrill Prevett, Mike Petrie, and five others, presented its case in graphic detail, emphasizing Pickton's own admissions in two different circumstances. Defense attorney Peter Ritchie, working with Adrian Brooks and Marilyn Sandford, asked the jurors to remain open-minded, assuring them they would see that the case against his client was anything but tight.

The first exhibit was a videotape of Pickton's eleven-hour interview. He claimed he was just a "plain farm boy" who had nothing to do with the deaths of the women whose remains had been found on his farm. However, the videotape from Pickton's conversation in the jail cell told a different story. Here, he looked grandiose and eager to take credit for all the murders, going so far as to double the number of victims.

Then experts and investigators took the stand, one after another, to detail their part in the investigation and analysis of evidence. RCMP officer Jack Mellis described the blood evidence from a mattress in Pickton's mobile home, matched to Mona Wilson, whose head and hands were recovered from the farm grounds six months after she'd gone missing. Two more officers described the grisly remains found in the buckets—Sereena Abotsway and Andrea Joesbury. Yet after sixty witnesses had testified, attorneys for both sides met to try to shorten the proceedings. Since the RCMP forensic lab had processed some 235,000 exhibits, it could take many months to prove chain of custody for each. The defense agreed to stipulate that the remains had been properly handled.

Day in and day out, Pickton's expression rarely wavered as he stared into space or glanced at a witness. Each day, he put on one of four shirts in his possession and carried a binder for his notes and doodles. His boredom seemed to mirror that of the media as the recounting of scientific evidence droned on. A law professor suggested that the drop in attendance at the trial was due to the lack of a "gripping narrative," because the victims were drug addicts and prostitutes, and the accused was a bald, aging, uneducated pig farmer.

Yet grisly descriptions still commanded attention. Pickton showed interest—and even appeared to smile—during the analysis of a handheld reciprocating saw allegedly used to bisect three skulls and cut through other human bones. There were cut marks on Brenda Wolfe's jawbone, as well as several ribs, two heel bones, and several vertebrae that had been collected. Ten of the saw's forty-five blades came into evidence, only because they could not be eliminated as the blades that had caused the cuts in the bones (but also not definitely tied to them). On a plastic skull, Brian McConaghy, a firearms-and-tool-mark expert, used color-coded dots and lines to demonstrate where the saw had bisected the heads. With Mona Wilson, a cut had split her head from the back, and then bisected her jaw. Three other victims had been treated in the same manner. And while holes indicated a .22-caliber weapon, Pickton had no weapons that matched. He did own a .22, with a dildo pulled over the barrel, but it had not been fired while the dildo was on it. Biological evidence did link it to both Pickton and Mona Wilson.

A forensic entomologist, Dr. Gail Anderson, also testified that the remains of Abotsway and Joesbury had been exposed to the elements from several weeks to several months before being stashed in the freezer where they were found. Insects apparently infiltrated the buckets when the remains were picked up for storage, and their type and stage of development helped to scientifically establish a time frame.

Forensic chemist Tony Fung testified that a substance found in a syringe that came from Pickton's office was methanol, commonly used in windshield-wiper fluid. An acquaintance of Pickton's had mentioned his statement about using this type of fluid to kill drug addicts. However, no methanol had shown up in tests on the remains of the victims. Traces of cocaine were found in all the tissue samples, along with methadone and diazepam (Valium), but toxicologist Heather Dinn declined to state for the defense whether the concentration of drugs had been fatal.

Several anthropologists took the stand to describe the examination of tens of thousands of bone fragments from a dirt pile, most of which proved to be from animals, but a few of which were human. Specifically, they found several human toes, a heel, and some rib bones. Another investigator described clumps of human hair, pieces of clothing belonging to the victims, and a condom.

After seventy-eight witnesses, the forensic stage of the proceedings briefly gave way to the "human face," with no challenge from the defense. A twenty-four-page booklet, made for the court, described all six victims, but testimony was notably spare, as their relatives had not been called.

The Victims

Elaine Allen, employed at Women's Information Safe House (WISH) drop-in center, had known five of the six victims and told the jury about them: how Andrea spoke softly, and Georgina was charming and outspoken; how the opinionated Sereena was often beat up and showed numerous tracks on her body from drug use, while Mona had a demanding boyfriend who sent her out to make money. Andrea, she said, had been the best-behaved client she'd ever dealt with, both polite and aware of the needs of others. She often spoke quietly about her difficult life.

Others who had known these women before they

disappeared also testified. One had run a focus group attended by women from the streets, and the jury learned that in some cases, the women worked as prostitutes to feed their children, because welfare payments were insufficient. Another witness was a friend of Georgina Papin, and she described how they had spent time baking and playing cards together, but Georgina fell back into drug use and was soon gone. Then a former prostitute and drug dealer told about her friend Brenda Wolfe, who vanished in the spring of 2000. This mother of two had requested government assistance for food because she'd spent what little money she had to make Christmas good for her kids. Brenda had deteriorated to the point of not bathing or washing her clothes, and had lost fifty pounds.

The next stage involved what Pickton might have done with the women after they died. Jim Cress, a driver for a Vancouver rendering company, described how he had picked up between two and five forty-five-gallon barrels of pork offal and burnt meat chunks from the Pickton farm to take to West Coast Reduction. Before 2002, customers could dump stuff at the plant themselves, unsupervised, and Cress had seen Pickton there. While this testimony was suggestive, given the statement Pickton made about victim disposal, it was proof of nothing—just one more circumstance.

The following day, Yolanda Dyck took the stand to say she had seen Pickton in Vancouver talking with victim Sereena Abotsway. She remembered the event because he was wearing rubber boots on a summer day. However, her memory proved inconsistent: she'd been unable to ID either the victim or the accused from photos.

More interesting was Gina Houston, a friend of Pickton's for over ten years (and a woman he'd wanted to marry), who said he'd admitted to her he knew about several bodies on the farm grounds and was pondering suicide. This conversation occurred two days before he was arrested, while police were searching the farm. Pickton estimated that there were six bodies in the "piggery," behind the barn, and he seemed to think that Houston should kill herself with him. She believed he was trying to implicate her, although she was unsure why. Still, he stated that he was to blame "for everything." Yet when she asked him if he had killed any of the woman, he denied it and suggested that a woman named Dinah Taylor was responsible for "three or four." (DNA performed on items taken from Pickton's trailer did link Taylor with several victims.)

Houston, thirty-nine and dying from cancer, admitted that of forty-eight photos of missing women on a poster, she recognized eight. Specifically, she had seen Sereena Abotsway and Dinah Taylor in Pickton's trailer, sitting on his bed, "doing drugs." She also described an incident in November 2001 in which she'd been on the phone with Pickton and heard people in the background in what sounded like a "scuffle" and a woman screaming. Pickton had ordered them to stop. Pickton later told her that the woman she'd heard—"Mona"—was one of the victims and that "she didn't make it."

To prove Pickton's association with Eastside prostitutes, prosecutors had Giselle Ireson, a prostitute and drug addict, testify. She told the court that in 1998 Pickton had invited her to the farm. He said he'd "dated" a number of women from the Eastside who would vouch for him and kept urging her to come because he did not want to do a "car date." She had declined. Pickton also invited Monique Wood, introduced to him by Dinah Taylor, and she went to his trailer. Once inside, she shot up heroin and spent the night without incident. Taylor's association was a telling point, although the defense would use it as well.

Drama entered the courtroom during the first half of June with a controversial witness offering potentially explosive testimony. Pat Casanova, arrested early in the investigation, used to regularly butcher pigs on the Pickton farm. He claimed he could not recall using the freezer where remains from two of the victims were found, although he had seen Pickton using it. However, this testimony contradicted statements from the preliminary hearing in which he admitted he'd used it up until a month before Pickton's arrest. Married and suffering from throat cancer, Casanova admitted he'd received oral sex from one of the victims, Andrea Joesbury, while in Pickton's trailer. Dinah Taylor had brought her and he'd paid Taylor. He had noticed clothing and some purses that belonged to women who were not present at the time, but admitted that Pickton had never spoken with him about missing women. Regarding certain pieces of evidence, he explained the presence of his DNA on a slaughterhouse door as being the result of mucus spewed after his throat treatments.

Scott Chubb, the original informant, was another key witness, having visited the farm a great deal and been privy to certain comments Pickton had reportedly made. Chubb had met Pickton in 1993, becoming an employee, and one day Pickton had mentioned that a woman named Lynn Ellingsen was costing him a lot of money; he wanted Chubb to "talk" to her. Chubb understood that Pickton wanted her killed. (The police had suspected that she was blackmailing Pickton over something she had witnessed.) Chubb said Pickton had offered him $1,000. Then the conversation grew even darker. Pickton commented that it was easy to kill drug addicts because they had needle marks and tracks already; if a person injected windshield-washer fluid into them, they'd die and police would dismiss it as the result of a drug overdose. Since the jury had already learned that investigators had found a syringe with windshield-washer fluid in Pickton's trailer, this was damning testimony.

Under cross-examination, defense attorney Ritchie tried to show that Chubb was an easily exploitable witness who would state whatever facts the prosecutor required, even contradicting things he'd already said. He wanted Chubb to admit he'd tried to get money in exchange for his testimony—to the tune of several thousand dollars. However, Chubb countered that the payment was for protection for himself and his family, in case Pickton's brother, who'd threatened him, came after him. Other contradictions Chubb excused on the grounds of a poor memory resulting from a head injury. He denied and then admitted to certain facts, such as his claim that he did not know much about guns when, in reality, he had a conviction for possession of an unregistered weapon. Chubb retorted that Ritchie was free to attack his character, perhaps, but he was not the one on trial for murder.

Stunning Testimony

After introducing several witnesses acquainted with Pickton, all of whom had issues with drugs, memory, or deception, the Crown brought in its star witness, whose testimony was the most shocking to date. Lynn Ellingsen, thirty-seven, cried softly at times as she described her association with the notorious pig farmer. The woman whom Pickton had wanted Chubb to "talk to," she had lived for a while on the farm, offering cleaning services for a place to stay. Ellingsen had been called to the trial to describe an incident she witnessed one night on the farm. It began when she went with Pickton to pick up a prostitute in Vancouver, after which they purchased drugs and returned to the farm. Pickton then asked, "Who's first?" and the other woman volunteered. Elingsen went to her own room on the other side of the trailer.

Later, she woke up, heard a noise in the slaughterhouse, and saw a light, so she went to investigate. Before she saw anything, she smelled a powerful odor of offal, as if Pickton were gutting pigs. He was busy cutting something and she saw a woman's body hanging from a chain. Pickton, covered in blood, noticed her, pulled her inside to take a look, and allegedly said if that she didn't keep her mouth shut she'd be "right beside her." She saw dark fluid on a table that looked like blood, near a mass of black hair. She promised not to tell in exchange for money for drugs. He got her a taxi and sent her away.

Unfortunately, Elingsen had kept this information from the police, so her statements were vulnerable. In fact, she admitted that on the night she had seen these things, she was using both drugs and alcohol. But she stated, "You can only get so high. I was high enough that I heard a sound that drew me out of my room. It was not a matter of hallucinating." In fact, she said, the scene had shocked her into sobering up. She added that while cocaine "numbs you" and makes you sense things more acutely, it does not make you "see things that are not there." She could not recall a date for this incident or the woman's name. She only remembered feet with red toenail polish that hung at the level of her eyes.

The defense attorney raised the fact that Ellingsen had also been arrested in connection with the disappearance of the women, suggesting that she had a motive to lie. However, she had not been charged with anything and thus had little reason to protect herself. There was also a money angle: the RCMP had reportedly paid over $16,000 toward her living expenses over the past few years. She did not deny it.

Andrew Bellwood also gave disturbing testimony, and he took the most heat from the defense team. He was the ninety-seventh witness to date. He seemed nonchalant about sitting down to a pork dinner with Pickton in 1999, the day after Pickton had described how he had killed prostitutes before feeding their remains to the pigs. Allegedly, Pickton had sex with the women first and then murdered them there on the grounds. Hacked-off body parts were tossed to the pigs and others were mingled in barrels with pig entrails and dumped at a disposal plant. It was an easy operation, Pickton supposedly implied, after he lured them to the farm with their drug of choice.

Pickton's murder method, Bellwood said, involved gagging the victims, handcuffing them, and using a wire with looped ends. He even acted it out. "He motioned to me he would put them doggy-style on the bed and have intercourse with them," Bellwood told the jury. "As he was telling me the story, it was almost like there was a woman on the bed. It was like a play."

Defense attorney Adrian Brooks found it hard to believe that after Pickton described such disgusting events, Bellwood then ate a meal with him—especially a meal whose main course was pork. Bellwood's reply was that Pickton was a "nice fellow" who had loaned him money and he'd decided the story was probably fabricated. He wasn't about to go to the police, since he himself was using drugs. Brooks then pointed to a serious inconsistency in the testimony: Bellwood claimed to have been alone with Pickton during the gruesome conversation, but earlier he had said that Lynn Ellingsen was with them. In response, Bellwood blustered that he would not have gone through all that he had over the past five years only to sit there now and lie. He had simply confused two events, he explained, and Ellingsen must have been present for something else.

With this, the prosecutors wrapped up their case. They had called fewer than half the number of witnesses they anticipated, but they were confident they had fully supported their position.

The Defense

In September, Justice James Williams threw out several days' worth of evidence and instructed jurors to disregard any mention of the Jane Doe skull found off the grounds. He said it was not directly related to the charges, though other bone fragments matching the skull's DNA had been found on the farm and the skull had the same saw-mark patterns as those from the farm.

The defense team used thirty witnesses, many of whom described Pickton as a helpful man and good person. Ritchie and Brooks had experts as well, and one point of contention was the bloodstained mattress found in the trailer. A blood expert from the RCMP had testified early in the trial that the mattress had been in place for a significant bloodletting event. The blood was a match for Mona Wilson, whose DNA was found on the sex toy attached to the revolver. Two defense experts questioned this interpretation of the bloodstains. Jon Nordby, a death investigator who was given only poor-quality crime-scene photographs, stated that from what he could see, there was not enough blood in Pickton's mobile home to indicate a fatal event involving bloodletting (although he could not conclude that no murder had occurred there). The other expert, chemist Gordon Ashby, thought that some of the stains on the mattress came from glue.

Also at issue was the fact that DNA from someone else, unidentified, had been found on some of the items and on one victim's teeth—raising the possibility that someone else had killed the women. In addition, Pickton's IQ was quite low—about eighty-six, low average. Ritchie insisted he could not have masterminded such a massive number of murders. As to his confession, he merely parroted back information the police fed him or responded out of fear to the lies they told. "He did not have the knowledge of the murderer," Ritchie stated. Still, his own expert admitted that a low IQ did not preclude the ability to plan a murder or to kill and that a score of eighty-six did not indicate a mental handicap.

Closing

In review, Prosecutor Mike Petrie went over the significant testimony methodically. Among the items of physical evidence were items with DNA from several dead women, buckets of body parts, a dildo with a revolver attached, and remains of three deceased females in a freezer and a pail. Five of the sixty-one items linked by DNA to the missing women had a confirmed or possible link to Pickton, and an eyewitness had seen Pickton with a saw where a woman's body was hung. Then there were the incriminating statements that Pickton made to the police during his interrogation and to an undercover plant in his cell. Another witness said Pickton told him about strangling and gutting women, whom he fed to pigs, and had discussed the best way to kill a prostitute.

"Let's have a reality check," Petrie had said. "This case is about the police finding the remains of six dead human beings essentially in the accused's back yard."

Adrian Brooks insisted that the victims had not been clearly linked to Pickton. He argued that the investigation was clumsy, neglectful, and contaminated. The defendant was an amiable, subservient guy with a low IQ who had allowed plenty of questionable characters onto his property, which, along with the unidentified DNA samples and an eyewitness who was a drug addict, should be sufficient to establish reasonable doubt. In addition, there was no smoking gun, Pickton could not be tied to the buckets holding the heads, the dismemberment method was unlike Pickton's method for butchering pigs, and some of the evidence pointed to other suspects. He named Pat Casanova and Dinah Taylor as prime possibilities and said the police had failed to conduct a thorough investigation of Pickton's associates. For example, a fingerprint on the freezer where body parts were found had never been identified.

The Crown countered that Pickton's IQ did not matter. He had experience as a butcher and was inured to death. He had an easy means for the disposal of remains. Common sense should dictate the verdict, not the "straw man" issue of an unknown perpetrator.

Then it was Justice Williams's turn. He instructed

jurors on the fine points of the law as he read for hours from a thick binder of notes. He cautioned them to ignore their knowledge that Pickton faced a future trial for other murders. He then recounted the results of the extensive search on Pickton's property and the points on which experts had disagreed. Finally, he explained the concept of reasonable doubt, adding that they did not need to find that Pickton had acted alone in order to decide he was guilty. But to be guilty, he had to *act,* not just be present or in the vicinity. Finally, in order to deliver a verdict, it was not necessary that all their questions be answered. "You have only to decide those matters that are essential for you to say whether the offenses charged have been proven beyond a reasonable doubt."

The jury had a lot of evidence to get through: more than 40,000 photos had been taken of the crime scene, 235,000 items were seized, and there were some 600,000 exhibits from the lab. Ninety-eight witnesses testified for the prosecution and thirty for the defense, both lay and expert, and there were half a million pages of documents, as well as nearly twenty hours of videotape. To complicate matters, during deliberations, the judge rephrased his instructions, as he decided he'd made an error.

The jurors took nine days, all of them nerve-racking for the families of the victims, but they did reach a verdict: Pickton was guilty of six counts of second-degree murder, but not guilty of six counts of first-degree murder. The accused listened and then looked at the floor, while many in the courtroom were stunned and disappointed. While he would receive a life sentence, he would be eligible for parole, possibly in a decade. The verdict meant that the jury did not believe either that Pickton had planned the murders or that he had acted on his own. They believed only that he was somehow involved. During Pickton's sentencing, the judge gave him the maximum—no parole for twenty-five years.

At this writing, Pickton faces trial for another twenty counts of murder, and there are still more than a dozen women on the list of the missing from Vancouver's Downtown Eastside. The estimated cost of the investigation thus far is over $100 million.

Aftermath

After some deliberation, the Crown decided to appeal the verdict. Since there were irregularities about the trial—the judge's change of mind during deliberations and some of his decisions about evidence admissibility—there was reason to argue for a new trial. However, the defense attorneys, who also filed an appeal, insisted that since Pickton's trial for the twenty remaining murder charges would involve entirely different personnel all around, it should begin as soon as possible. The prosecution said that a second trial should involve all twenty-six counts, since a considerable amount of evidence had been left out of the trial for the six murders. It remains for the legal system to sort it all out. The most likely outcome is that if Pickton's appeal fails, the second trial will be considered unnecessary, since he is already serving the maximum penalty.

In December 2007, the *Sun* published copies of two letters that Pickton had written the year before to a pen pal. He said he'd been put on earth to rid people of their evil ways and it bothered him when others failed to live by the Ten Commandments, stating that "the terrible anger of God comes upon all those who disobey him." He indicated that he was writing a book about his life. "I myself is not from this world," he wrote, and showed himself to be amused about all the attention paid to him. He was impressed with how much the investigation and trial had cost.

One of the lessons of this case, we could say, is that despite the intensity and complexity of the Pickton investigation, a conviction for first-degree murders had not been a sure thing. Indeed, there are some important lessons that law enforcement can take from each of the twelve cases we have presented. The next chapter offers a summary.

Sources

"A Look at the Final Summation from Pickton's Defence Lawyer." *Canadian Press,* November 21, 2007.

Baron, Ethan. "Crown Details Horrific Evidence in Pig Farmer's Murder Trial." *Vancouver Province,* January 22, 2007.

_____. "Pickton Sent Barrels of Meat to Rendering Plant." *CanWest News,* May 16, 2007.

_____. "Prostitute Said She Was Invited to Pickton Farm." *CanWest News,* May 31, 2007.

_____. "Pal Ate with Pickton After Story About Feeding Victims to Pigs." *Vancouver Province,* July 19, 2007.

Cameron, Stevie. *The Pickton Files.* Canada: Knopf, 2007.

Culbert, Lori. "Pickton's Lawyer's File Appeal, Allege Errors in Six Areas." *National Post,* January 9, 2008.

———. "Exclusive Pickton Letters." *Vancouver Sun,* December 11, 2007.

———. "Jury Hears Autopsy Results." *CanWest News,* May 3, 2007.

———. "Pickton's Friend's DNA Found in Slaughterhouse." *CanWest News,* September 12, 2007.

DiManno, Rosie. "IQ Tests Can't Gauge Capacity to Kill." *Star,* October 22, 2007.

Glaister, Dan. "Pig Farmer and Pillar of Community: Alleged Serial Killer Faces Trial." *The Guardian,* January 20, 2007.

Hibbitts, Bernard. "Canada Serial Killer Given Maximum Sentence for BC Pig Farm Murders." *Jurist,* December 12, 2007.

Jones, Deborah. "The Case of the Serial Killer." *Time,* January 26, 2007.

Joyce, Greg, and Terri Theodore. "RCMP Interrogator Says He Concluded Pickton Was a Serial Killer in Interview." *Canadian Press,* January 31, 2007.

———. "Eleven-hour Interrogation Gives Some Indication of Accused Serial Killer's Personality." *Ottawa Sun,* January 27, 2007.

———. "Judge in Pickton Murder Trial Calls for Short Recess." *Canadian Press,* May 1, 2007.

"Judge in Pickton Trial Explains Law and Evidence in Lengthy Jury Charge." *Canadian Press,* November 28, 2007.

Matas, Robert. "Exclusion of Evidence Sparks Debate." *Globe and Mail,* December 18, 2007.

———. "Rookie Officer Responsible for Raid on Pig Farm." *Globe and Mail,* December 3, 2007.

———. "Trial Pathologist Describes Dismemberment." *Globe and Mail,* May 3, 2007.

"RCMP Blood Expert at Pickton Trial Testifies About Bloodletting at Farm." *International Herald Tribune,* February 12, 2007.

Rolfsen, Catherine. "Crown to Appeal Pickton's Second-Degree Convictions." *Vancouver Sun,* January 6, 2008.

THIRTEEN

LESSONS FOR LAW ENFORCEMENT

Common to all the cases presented in this book are persistence, flexibility, the importance of innovative thinking, and the ability to initiate dialogues across disciplines. In many cases, an investigator became aware of a scientific advance as yet untested in the criminal arena. Over and over, we see someone at a dead end in a frustrating investigation looking around for a technique, approach, or technology that no one had yet considered, and boldly trying it out. Often this not only led to the arrest of a serial killer but also added or confirmed a tool that future investigators would use—sometimes with dramatic results. The discovery of DNA as a crime-fighting technique is a case in point, but in the future we're likely to see more involvement with bioinformatics and computer technology.

Following is a list of guidelines that emerged from the successful resolution of these cases of serial murder. While not exhaustive, it's a start. Hopefully it will inspire both dedication and invention in current and future investigations.

1. Read widely in fields that might seem relevant but have not yet been used in law enforcement. It was a police officer not a scientist who introduced the discrimination of animal and human blood, DNA analysis, and brain fingerprinting into an investigation. This requires creative thinking and awareness of what's available. Seminars, trade journals, college courses, and even popular books or documentaries about science and technology can provoke new ideas.

   We've already seen examples from serial murder cases, but here's another. When Denise Johnson was found on May 2, 1992, strangled and left nude near a cluster of palo verde trees in Maricopa County, police developed a lead and arrested Mark Bogan. Inside his truck were seedpods from a palo verde tree. Bogan denied being near the crime scene, so investigators wondered if it was possible to extract plant DNA that would prove Bogan was at that specific tree. They contacted a professor of molecular genetics. He did not know the answer either, but agreed to test the pods from the truck. He compared trees in the area against one another and then matched the crime-related pods to a specific tree. This finding tied Bogan's truck to the scene. When other evidence confirmed his presence, he was convicted of first-degree murder.

2. Be proactive. Detective William King kept planting items in newspapers, even years after the crime was committed, in order to bait the offender who'd kidnapped Grace Budd. Finally, his effort paid off. The Allentown police set up a sting operation, and Viktor Burakov read up on the FBI's profiling methods, despite rebuke, to try to stop Chikatilo. In the case of the dismembered gay men, running the fingerprint evidence again and again, as well as seeking out another technique, finally solved the case and got a killer off the streets. So take the extra step.

3. Become educated about psychological angles on criminal behavior, which get updated with research on a regular basis. This arena is not reserved for profilers or psychologists. Most good detectives already have a sense of criminal psychology, but psychopathic serial killers require greater savvy. No officer should believe he already knows enough from what he's picked up on the streets. Too many innocent people have been harmed by detectives who are certain they can always spot a liar or who jump to conclusions based on simplistic formulas. People will often surprise you; Staniak's admission that he started killing blondes as stand-ins for a reckless driver who killed his parents is a case in point. No one had suspected such a motive.

The earliest murders committed by a serial killer tend to reveal most about their comfort zone—what kind of weapon they prefer, the MO they adopt, and the area with which they're most familiar. Unless they're very clever or careful, they usually start killing somewhere near where they live. They might change their weapon preference or MO along the way, but their first attempts reveal a lot about them. It's important to know the details and to bone up on the latest research. All databases are limited to what's already known and we learn new things about killers all the time.

4. Be flexible and, in particular, prepare to be wrong. In the Village Path murders in Britain, the interrogators were certain they'd nailed the man who'd killed two young girls, but they were wrong. It's possible that their misplaced confidence influenced this suspect's false confession. DNA analysis exonerated him and pointed to another man, but had this case happened only two years earlier, an innocent man would have gone to prison.

5. Be persistent. With cold cases, go over old ground and get a fresh perspective from others not familiar with the crime. Blind spots can trip up investigators who won't let go. No investigation belongs to a single cop; it's always a coordinated effort and others might contribute in surprising ways. Detective Geyer enlisted the help of local officers as he traveled from one city to another in search of the Pitezel children, as well as getting constant feedback from his team back in Philadelphia. He also refused to give up. He could have decided he'd done enough and would never find the

missing boy, but he returned to an area he'd already explored to reexamine his approach. More recently, Pierce Brooks pushed for a national database for over two decades, which finally resulted in the FBI's VI-CAP. Thanks to this, a solid case was made a decade later against international serial killer Jack Unterweger using mathematical linkage analysis.

6. Be meticulous. Perhaps no case was more painstaking than the Pickton investigation, with all the forensic personnel sifting through piles of dirt and manure and underneath every building to locate fragments of human remains that would yield DNA. The Canadian government approved the expense, of course, which is certainly a factor, but the tiniest details were examined and recorded, both for the sake of the families who awaited word about their missing daughter or sister, and the attorneys waiting to prosecute.

7. Anticipate the future. Future investigations will involve cooperation among seemingly unrelated fields, especially the fields of technology and informatics. Fortunately, scientists have grown more interested in helping the police and have begun to suggest some innovations themselves. Police officers must have at least some basic technical knowledge about computers and the World Wide Web. There are courses that teach officers how criminals keep and erase records, communicate with their networks or cells, and engage in illicit acts such as child pornography. Officers who were savvy about

how computers work knew how to trap Dennis Rader and then extract evidence from his hard drive.

In addition, your "Lie-Q," or awareness of new methods in brain scans for deception detection, can assist with recalcitrant offenders. The brain-fingerprinting work on the James Grinder case is a good example, and these methods are only going to improve. More research might be needed, but rest assured that innovators are moving fast. Eventually, the courts will take notice.

The bottom line is this: officers eager to become detectives, and detectives hoping to excel at their jobs, will seek out knowledge in areas that offer the promise of new developments and will persist in implementing such knowledge. Dogged, educated, and flexible detectives will spot opportunities and step forth to utilize new approaches. These are the investigators who could end up being part of the kind of success stories that are described in this book. These stories are better than fiction, so let's hope for some real-life sequels.

The story of one of the most bizarre mass murders ever recorded—and the girl who escaped with her life.

From national bestselling author

ROBERT SCOTT

with Sarah Maynard and Larry Maynard

The GIRL *in the* LEAVES

In the fall of 2010, in the all-American town of Apple Valley, Ohio, four people disappeared without a trace: Stephanie Sprang; her friend Tina Maynard; and Tina's two children, thirteen-year-old Sarah and eleven-year-old Kody. Investigators began scouring the area, yet despite an extensive search, no signs of the missing people were discovered.

On the fourth day of the search, evidence trickled in about neighborhood "weirdo" Matthew Hoffman. A police SWAT team raided his home and found an extremely disturbing sight: every square inch of the place was filled with leaves, and a terrified Sarah Maynard was bound up in the middle of it like some sort of perverted autumn tableau. But there was no trace of the others…

INCLUDES PHOTOGRAPHS

Praise for Robert Scott and his books:

"Compelling and shocking…[A] ground-breaking book."
—Robert K. Tanenbaum

"Fascinating and fresh…[A] fast-paced informative read."
—Sue Russell

RobertScottTrueCrime.com | penguin.com

M1129T0613

The shocking continuation of the
national bestseller *Zodiac* by

ROBERT GRAYSMITH

ZODIAC
UNMASKED

The Identiy of America's Most Elusive
Serial Killer Revealed

"[GRAYSMITH'S] ACCESS IS AS GOOD AS IT GETS.
A meticulous reconstruction of the way the case
evolved. By far the best book on the subject of the
Zodiac murders." —*New York Press*

After painstaking investigation, and more than 30 years of
research, Robert Graysmith finally exposes the infamous
Zodiac killer's true identity. With overwhelming evidence he
reveals the twisted private life that led to the crimes, and
provides startling theories as to why they stopped. America's
greatest unsolved mystery has finally been solved.

**INCLUDES PHOTOS AND A COMPLETE
REPRODUCTION OF THE ZODIAC'S LETTERS.**

penguin.com